Date Due

KARSTEN JUNIUS

The Economic Geography of Production, Trade, and Development

KIELER STUDIEN 300

Herausgegeben von Horst Siebert

Institut für Weltwirtschaft an der Universität Kiel

Mohr Siebeck

Die Deutsche Bibliothek – CIP-Einheitsaufnahme

Junius, Karsten:
The economic geography of production, trade, and development /
Karsten Junius. - Tübingen : Mohr Siebeck, 1999
  (Kieler Studien ; 300)
  ISBN 3–16–147251–9

© Institut für Weltwirtschaft an der Universität Kiel; J. C. B. Mohr (Paul Siebeck) Tübingen
1999

Printed in Germany

ISSN 0340-6989

Preface

For long, economists and geographers have studied the fundamental determinants of the spatial distribution of industries. They analyzed why industries locate where they do, why some concentrate regionally while others do not, and how the spatial concentration of industries is affected by the economic integration between two regions. Several reasons can be found for why either a peripheral or a core region should be the main winner. Political implications of the answer are enormous. Motivated by the possible effects of the Common European Market, Paul Krugman and Anthony Venables have developed a new field to model rigorously under what conditions core or peripheral regions may lose or win through economic integration.

My study extends their so-called economic geography models. I concentrate on and structure my analysis along the narrow view of these new economic geography models only, despite being aware of the wide range of other spatial approaches of economists in Kiel and elsewhere. My special focus is on how economic development may influence the location of industries. The theoretical part is complemented by an analysis of the empirical support for my development model in particular and the empirical relevance of economies of scale and trade costs, the two main building blocks of economic geography models, in general.

This study has greatly benefited from the continuous guidance of Erich Gundlach, who provided numerous comments on all parts of the study. Additionally, I would like to thank Professor Horst Siebert, Professor Rolf J. Langhammer, and Professor Karin Peschel for their support and helpful comments on an earlier draft. I would like to thank the former two for making the Kiel Institute of World Economics and especially its Development Economics and Global Integration Department such a hospitable, efficient, and stimulating research environment. This has led to many helpful discussions for which I thank all my colleagues. I would like to especially mention Elga Bartsch, Andreas Gröhn, Andreas Kopp, and Rainer Thiele.

I am also grateful to Michaela Rank and Angela Husfeld for excellent research assistance and the provision of the figures in this study, and Tanja Götzke for the editorial advice. Ute Heinecke deserves acknowledgment for her final layout work. Finally, I would like to thank Ingrid Gleibs, who not only typed the numerous versions of this study, but also brought the study into a professional form. Of course, none of the foregoing are implied by any remaining errors in this study.

Kiel, October 1999   Karsten Junius

Contents

List of Tables

List of Figures

List of Abbreviations

AC	average costs
ASEAN	Association of South-East Asian Nations
CBD	central business district
CES	constant elasticity of substitution
CHELEM	Comptes harmonisés sur les échanges et l'économie mondiale
c.i.f.	cost-insurance freight
DC	developing country
EC	European Community
EFTA	European Free Trade Association
EOS	economies of scale
EU	European Union
ExEOS	external economies of scale
f.o.b.	free on board
FTA	free trade area
GATS	General Agreement on Trade in Services
GATT	General Agreement on Tariffs and Trade
GDP	gross domestic product
GDPC	gross domestic product per capita
GNP	gross national product
IMF	International Monetary Fund
InEOS	internal economies of scale
ISIC	International Standard Industry Classification
ITU	International Telecommunication Union
JaEOS	Jacobs economies of scale
LDC	less developed country
LocEOS	localization economies of scale
MAREOS	Marshall–Arrow–Romer economies of scale
MC	marginal costs
Mercosur	Mercado commun del sur

MES	Minimum Efficient Plant Size
NACE	Nomenclature général des activités économiques dans les Communautés Européennes
NAFTA	North-American Free Trade Agreement
NTB	nontariff trade barriers
OECD	Organisation for Economic Co-operation and Development
OLS	ordinary least squares
PPP	purchasing power parity
RESET	Regression Specification Error Test
SEE	standard error of estimates
TFP	total factor productivity
UN	United Nations
UNCTAD	United Nations Conference for Trade and Development
UR	Uruguay Round
UrbEOS	urbanization economies of scale
VER	voluntary export restraints
WEPZA	World Export Processing Zone Association

List of Variables and Parameters Used in Chapter B

Indices:

c	core
j	index for industrial goods and firms (1, ..., N)
p	periphery

Parameters and variables:

α	fixed cost parameter (> 0)
β	variable cost parameter (> 0)
δ	parameter
γ	speed of the adjustment process (inverse index of moving costs)
ϕ	marginal propensity of income to spend on industrial goods
ε	share of actual income spent on industrial goods
θ	indicator of external scale economies ($\theta > 0$)
λ	Lagrange multiplier
μ	share of intermediate goods in the inputs of a good
ξ	congestion elasticities
π	share of workers in overall population
ρ	decrease in input requirements per time period
σ	elasticity of substitution (inverse index of internal scale economies) ($\sigma > 1$)
τ	amount of goods that have to be shipped so that one good arrives ("iceberg-type" trade costs) ($\tau > 0$)
ω	real wage
A	agricultural goods
AC	average costs
B	parameter
c	single product variety
C	commodity group

d	elasticity of demand
e	Euler's number
H	present value of life time wages
k	parameter (> 0)
K	total costs of production
L	industrial workers
m	single industrial good
$\overline{m}$	parameter
M	industrial goods
MC	marginal costs
$\overline{n}$	parameter
N	number of potential firms and product varieties
p	price of an industrial good expressed in input terms
q	value of having a job in region c rather than in region p
Q	output
r	interest rate
$RGDPC$	real GDP per capita
S	sales of all firms of a region
SE	stable equilibrium
t	level of economic development
t_0	initial point of time
T	price level
U	utility
UE	unstable equilibrium
v	percentage of industries that are located in the core
V	parameter
w	nominal wage
W	wage sum in the industrial sector
X	expenditure on industrial goods
Y	income
Z	inputs

List of Variables and Parameters Used in Chapter C

Indices:

1	product 1
2	product 2
i	firm (1, ..., N)
j	industry (1, ..., M)
k	city (1, ..., s)
m	importing country
t	time
x	exporting country

Parameters and Variables:

α	elasticities of inputs in production
α_c	elasticity of unit costs with respect to cumulative output
β	elasticity of productivity growth toward own industry output
γ	elasticity of productivity level toward output of all industries
δ	parameter
ε	constant
λ	Lagrangian parameter
μ	error term
ρ	elasticity of productivity level toward own industry output
σ	elasticity of productivity growth toward output of all industries
ϕ	Pareto coefficient
A	general productivity parameter
A'	general productivity parameter net of learning effects
b	parameter
c	real unit costs
c_ρ	production costs of the first unit

d	slope of the learning curve
EX	exports
k	composite term in cost function
k'	composite term in cost function net of learning effects
K	parameter
L	parameter
M	number of different industries and industrial sectors
n	cumulative output
N	number of firms in an industry
p	prices of inputs
P	population size of a city
r	returns to scale
R	rank of a city
s	city size categories
x	inputs
X	parameter
Y	firm output
z	primacy function

Names of the Variables in the Regressions

ADJ	dummy for (adjacency) common land border
COLONY1815	dummy for colonies in 1815
COLONY1950	dummy for colonies in 1950
DENSE	population density
DENSE1919	population density in 1919
ENGLISH	dummy for English as common language
FRENCH	dummy for French as common language
GDP	gross domestic product
GDPC	GDP per capita
GDPC1913	GDP per capita in 1913
HISTO1800	urban concentration in 1800

HISTO1850	urban concentration in 1850
INDUSTRY1900	employment share of industry in 1900
JEFFRATIO	urban concentration in 1935
LAN	dummy for country pairs with a common language
LAND	size of the land area
NLAND	normalized land
NRGDPC	normalized real GDP per capita
NRGDPC2	squared NRGDPC value
NTEL1919	normalized telegraph mileage per square mile
OPEN	openness
P_k	population in city k
POLITICS	political freedom
POPTOT	total population
POPURB	urban population
PR	primacy
PRIMA1–4	primacy 1–4
RAIL1919	railroad mileage per square mile in 1919
RGDPC	real GDP per capita (PPP-adjusted)
ROADLAND	density of the transportation system
SPANISH	dummy for Spanish as common language
TEL1919	telegraph mileage per square mile
X	vector of conditional variables

A.   Aim and Scope of the Study

Since the beginning of the decade, there has been a strong revival of interest in questions where industries locate, why it comes to industrial concentration and agglomeration, and how economic integration of regions may influence the distribution of industries between them. This interest was strengthened by a strong trend to form institutional regional trading blocs such as the EU single market, NAFTA, Mercosur, Andean, or ASEAN. This trend was welcomed but also feared by both core and peripheral regions, since it was unclear whether increased economic integration would mainly benefit core or peripheral regions. While peripheral regions feared that the concentration of production and demand would give core regions strong competitive advantages, which would be reinforced by further integration, core regions feared that their higher factor costs, higher environmental standards, and other congestion externalities would pull industries out of core into peripheral regions (Commission of the European Communities 1992: 46–47).

To answer the question which region might attract industries from the other, a theory was needed that explains in one model the tension between centrifugal and centripetal forces to attract mobile industries and their relation to the degree of economic integration. Therefore, a new field in economic theory has evolved, building on the work of Krugman (1991a, 1991b, 1993), Krugman and Venables (1990, 1995, 1996), Venables (1996), and Fujita and Krugman (1995). The papers combine the tools of modern trade theory and the ideas of traditional location theory to formulate so-called economic geography or new location theory models. My study is based on these papers. It tries to answer the question how we can explain the spatial distribution of economic activities between trading regions in the course of economic development — hence, the economic geography of production, trade, and development. It extends the existing models in order to make them applicable for analyzing real world phenomena. The study tests the underlying assumptions of economic geography models in order to check whether they provide an adequate framework for analyzing spatial phenomena. Furthermore, it tests the ability of my extended model to describe existing patterns of spatial concentration adequately.

There are three stages in the life cycle of economic fields. The first is the development of a theory; the second is testing the theoretical models empirically; the third is deriving policy conclusions. Economic geography is a relatively young field, which is still somewhere in between the first and second stage of its life cycle. This means empirical work is increasingly done, but not enough so to find a consensus on which profound policy conclusions can be given. Therefore, this study focuses on the theoretical and empirical analysis of economic geography models. Only in the conclusion, I point out to some policy implications of the models.

Economic geography models intend to explain the location of economic activities. Their object of study is one of the most striking and undisputed facts in economics; i.e., that industrial production is not evenly dispersed, but often is spatially concentrated, such that some industries are clustered while others are not, and some regions are heavily industrialized while others are not. Several examples for economic agglomerations have been discussed in the literature. Among the most prominent are those provided by Porter (1990) and Enright (1990). Porter analyzes the concentration of the printing machine industry in Southern Germany, the ceramic tiles industry around Sassuolo in Italy, the American patient monitoring equipment industry, and the Japanese robotics industry. Enright (1990) adds to these the pharmaceuticals industry in Basle, packaging and filling machinery in Bologna, cutlery in Solingen, motion pictures in Hollywood, and musical instruments in Hamamatsu. Porter and Enright give explanations for the success stories of particular sites and particular agglomerations. Their analyses are useful as illustrations, but are unsatisfactory for ex ante predictions because they lack a theoretical concept. This means a model is needed to explain why some industries in some regions do stick together while others disperse. To answer this question, geographers and urban economists have long devoted considerable efforts.

Geographical models like those of central place theory by Christaller (1933) and Lösch (1940) have tried to explain the emergence of a lattice of production sites across the landscape. Central to their models was the trade-off between trade costs and economies of scale. Different degrees of economies of scale in production and trade costs lead to a hierarchical structure of economic activities across space. The main weakness of these models is that they have no explicit microeconomic foundation and disregard the market structure that leads to their spatial results. Thus, this strand of literature focuses too much on the geometry of the market area, the optimal city size, and the location of facilities, instead of modeling the market itself. This might be due to the difficulties in modeling other market structures than perfect competition.[1] Advances in industrial organization, notably by Spence (1976) and Dixit and Stiglitz (1977), have now made new approaches possible.[2]

---

[1]   Modeling the market structure requires abandoning standard neoclassical assumptions, as Starret's spatial impossibility theorem proves (Starret 1978). He argues that in a neoclassical economy with a homogeneous landscape and positive trade costs, no spatial division of labor can exist.

[2]   The Dixit–Stiglitz approach is now widely used in modeling imperfect competition. It allows modeling economies of scale (EOS) that are internal to the firm while pre-

Another strand of the literature that explains the spatial concentration of economic activities is regional and urban economics, descending from models like that of von Thünen (1826). Important modern contributions to this literature are Henderson (1974, 1988), Fujita (1988), Rivera-Batiz (1988), Abdel-Rahman (1988), and Abdel-Rahman and Fujita (1990). Henderson (1988) contrasts local external economies of scale in production with higher land rents in a competitive market setup. In his model, trade between countries is entirely driven by comparative advantage. Fujita (1988) and Rivera-Batiz (1988) use an imperfectly competitive market setup, where nontraded inputs lead to economic agglomeration. These models do not consider that final-goods trade is costly. The major drawback of this strand of the literature is that in these models, the central market place (or in later models, the central business district (CBD)) is exogenously given, and not explained by the models. They cannot determine the relative location of production in space, since they do not rigorously introduce the costs of economic space in their models. As long as models do not consider the costs of overcoming economic distance, they have little to say about where production is located.[3]

Thus, traditional models either lack a microeconomic foundation of the market structure and of the interaction of market participants, or they lack an explicit consideration of economic space and of the costs of overcoming economic distance. As early as 1969, Siebert (1969: 1) wrote, "...the classical models and the reasoning behind them were based on the assumption of one-point economies without any spatial dimension. The core questions of economic analysis — what to produce, how to produce, for whom to produce — were analyzed for a world in which no distance, no transportation costs, and no other friction of space ex-

---

venting strategic interactions between firms. This facilitates modeling EOS enormously, but, of course, also neglects one of their important implications. With an increasing demand for models with a more rigorous microeconomic foundation and an increasing interest in different market structures, internal EOS and Dixit–Stiglitz approaches to monopolistic competition have become a standard ingredient in several fields of economic theory. See Matsuyama (1995) for a survey, where monopolistic competition models are applied to explain cumulative phenomena in macroeconomics and for further references to discussions of monopolistic competition from a purely theoretical or industrial organization point of view.

[3] Some further theoretical approaches to the explanation of agglomeration economies should be mentioned. See also Fujita and Thisse (1996) for a survey of the literature. For instance, Helsley and Strange (1990) present a model where agglomeration economies arise from a better match between jobs and workers' skills. On the advantages of a pooled labor market, see also Krugman (1991a). Kopp (1994) uses demand side externalities to explain agglomeration. In his model, consumers' search costs and imperfect information about the availability and quality of goods lead to advantages of the agglomeration's final-good suppliers. Arthur (1990: 241) points out that industrial agglomeration could also reflect preferences for the same type of resource endowment, like the film industry which initially has clustered near Los Angeles due to dry weather and good outdoor lighting.

isted." More than 20 years later, Krugman (1991a) picks up this point and won-
ders why traditional economics does not care where production takes place. In
order to analyze where a good is produced, the models need a spatial dimension.
Therefore, one major ingredient of economic geography models is the explicit
consideration of the costs of overcoming economic space and distance — hence-
forth called trade costs.

The other major ingredient in economic geography models is economies of
scale (EOS). They are the reason why economic concentration might arise at all.
Without economies of scale, one could build a factory for each product in each
local market, with no additional costs. EOS are a necessary (though not sufficient) condition for the advantages of industrial concentration. Internal economies of scale can explain why production is divided between equally endowed
and skilled economic agents. External economies of scale can explain why economic agents may want to produce close to each other. Hence, internal EOS explain the division of labor between firms, and external EOS explain the division
of labor between regions and industries. Therefore, the explanation of agglomeration economies by EOS has been called the Folk Theorem of spatial economics (Scotchmer and Thisse 1992: 272).[4]

The distinct features of economic geography models can be summarized as
the explicit treatment of trade costs and economies of scale, the microeconomic
foundation of centrifugal and centripetal forces in an imperfect competition
model, and the modeling of externalities as an endogenous outcome of market
forces instead of assuming the more elusive exogenous technological externalities. This leads to endogenous spatial structures.

The consideration of EOS determines the further properties of economic geography models: The models are *nonergodic*, which means that they are self-
perpetuating. They do not necessarily return to their initial state when the initial
conditions are replicated after some interim events. Nonergodic systems can
underlie irreversible evolutionary processes as a reaction to small changes in initial conditions because they mean increasing returns to colocation of economic
agents.[5] Hence, the models inhibit path dependencies, which mean that any ran-

---

4   Besides location theory, economies of scale have been at the heart of many other developments in economic theory in the past two decades. Departing from industrial
organization, EOS have been used for the explanation of intraindustry trade, endogenous growth, economic development, real business cycles, strategic trade policy, and industrial or regional policy. See Junius (1997a) for an overview of the theoretical impact of EOS in these fields and an extensive discussion of the empirical literature.

5   Early examples of such nonergodic models in location theory are Engländer (1926),
Palander (1935), and Hoover (1937). In contrast to these models, in ergodic models
like those of von Thünen (1826), Predöhl (1925), Lösch (1941), and Isard (1956), the
spatial pattern of industry location is predetermined by natural or geographic en-

dom disturbance from an equilibrium would be amplified by the existence of external EOS. These have a self-reinforcing mechanism. Myrdal (1957) calls this *circular causation*, Arthur (1987, 1990) uses the term *positive feedback*, and Hirschman (1958) refers to *forward and backward linkages*. All these expressions mean that if one region starts with an initial cost advantage, EOS put it on a path that reinforces this advantage. Such a path leads away from the initial configuration. Thus, nonergodicity means that "...small events are not averaged away or forgotten by the dynamics — they may decide the outcome..." (Arthur 1989: 117).

Therefore, economic geography models may have *multiple equilibria*. This means that out of several equally endowed regions that compete as locations of industrial production, each could end up with the bulk of industries if firms are free to set up production in any region. If EOS are unbound, circular causation leads to the dominance of one region and, consequently, to a new equilibrium in which a randomly enlarged region specializes in the production of industrial goods. But any other region could have been in its place as well. This means that EOS also lead to *unpredictable* and *indeterminate* solutions. Furthermore, it implies nonlinearities that may introduce *analytical difficulties* in the calculation of explicit solutions.

Multiple equilibria mean that there may be *lock-in effects*. The self-reinforcing mechanism that favors a region that experienced an initial head start can exclude other regions from successful competition. An equilibrium that is once reached may be locked in and may be irreversible by the market process. This means that EOS may lead to *inflexible* solutions out of which exit is difficult.

If multiple equilibria are possible, then it is equally well possible that an inferior equilibrium could become dominant merely because it had an initial head start. EOS can create barriers to entry, thereby protecting early entrants from effective market competition. Therefore, EOS may lead to monopolistic and inefficient solutions. This, together with the failure to internalize positive external effects of production and output levels that are too low, is why EOS may lead to *market failures*. Under certain conditions, in turn, these may justify government intervention.[6]

---

dowments, relative prices, and trade costs. After any accidental perturbation of the system that led it away from its initial pattern, it will always revert to a unique and predetermined final pattern. In ergodic models, regional policies have no long-run effect in shaping spatial patterns, since they cannot induce cumulative and self-reinforcing processes.

[6] For long, the above properties of EOS did not appear very appealing. About multiple equilibria, Schumpeter wrote:

Multiple equilibria are not necessarily useless, but from the standpoint of any exact science the existence of a uniquely determined equilibrium is, of course, of the utmost importance, even if proof has to be purchased at the price of very restrictive assumptions;

These properties give historical accidents and conditions a very important role as they can set in motion a cumulative process that reinforces the agglomeration of industries in one region. The market forces that drive this process are backward and forward linkages.[7] They lead to home market effects, as first modeled by Krugman (1980) in an intraindustry trade model and later used in all economic geography models. Home market effects imply that the larger region has the advantage of a larger market for its own products, so that home firms face a relatively higher demand. A further advantage of being in the larger market is the presence of a larger number of firms in that region. This implies a better access to a larger number of intermediate suppliers so that a larger percentage of intermediate inputs can be purchased without paying additional trade costs. Thus, input-output linkages between firms lead to external economies of scale, which favor industrial concentration.

Cost and demand linkages between industries create forces that favor agglomeration, but any immobile factors of production and the location of consumer demand are working in the opposite direction. A firm's location decision depends on the interaction between production costs and the ease of access to markets. If trade costs — the costs of supplying different locations — are low, then firms are highly sensitive to differences in production costs. With high trade costs, firms become tied to markets, and their location decisions are much less sensitive to differences in production costs.

Economic geography models consider centrifugal forces in the form of market access to the demand of the dispersed part of the population. Firms may have an incentive to locate in the periphery because of the competition for the demand from the immobile sectors of production. The competition for local consumers' demand is less severe in the periphery than in the core region.[8] Hence, economic

---

without any possibility of proving the existence of [a] uniquely determined equilibrium ... a field of phenomena is really a chaos that is not under analytical control.

(quoted from Arthur 1990: 95). In 1939, Hicks even warned that admitting increasing returns would lead to "...the wreckage of the greater part of economic theory..." (quoted from Arthur (1996: 102). This did not happen, mainly due to improvements in the theory of industrial organization. Progress in computer technologies has made it easier to handle even very complex models and to work with models exhibiting analytically awkward properties like path dependencies and multiple equilibria. Consequently, numeric solutions and simulation methods become increasingly accepted as methodological approaches in economics.

[7]   As suggested by Hirschman (1958), backward linkages affect the demand for the output of a firm. They result from good access to consumer markets. A greater number of consumers supports a greater number of firms. Forward linkages affect the cost side of a firm. They result from good access to suppliers of intermediate inputs. The availability of a greater number of goods increases the input choice of firms such that inputs can be used that fit best the specific needs of firms.

[8]   Imperfect competition is important since the price in a location depends on the number of firms.

geography models provide an intuitive explanation for the existence of economic agglomeration or dispersion by contrasting centrifugal and centripetal forces in one model.

In the present study, I try to confront these models with economic reality. This is done in two parts — one theoretical, the other empirical. The theoretical part augments the existing models in order to better describe existing patterns of industry location. My development model will be able to explain different patterns of industry location across regions and time. The empirical part answers two questions. The first is whether the crucial assumptions of economic geography models are empirically justified. That is, are economies of scale and trade costs empirically important phenomena? The second question is whether the models are right in the sense that they can explain differences in the spatial concentration of economic activities in a cross-section of countries.

In detail, I proceed as follows. In Chapter B, I start with a verbal description of two basic economic geography models, which have been developed by Krugman (1991b) and Krugman and Venables (1996). I proceed with a technical description of what I call a "prototype" economic geography model. The model combines elements of the two above-mentioned approaches. The model has two regions, two sectors, and two factors of production. It includes a core and a peripheral region, a mobile increasing-returns sector and an immobile constant-returns sector, and industrial workers and farmers. The model allows for consumer preferences for variety, as in Krugman (1991b), and producer preferences for the availability of a large number of specialized inputs, as in Venables (1996) and Krugman and Venables (1996). Both forces favor a cumulative process toward industrial agglomeration. Market access to the demand of a peripheral and immobile part of the population constitutes a centrifugal force that works in favor of industry dispersion.

I solve this prototype model for different parameter values and show how economic integration influences the regional distribution of industries. The distribution of industries results from the interplay of the realization of economies of scale in the core region and trade costs to the peripheral regions. For high trade costs, production in a single location does not pay, because any cost saving from concentrated production is outweighed by the high costs of transporting goods to the peripheral market. A spatial structure emerges, in which both regions produce industrial goods in proportion to their population. For intermediate trade costs, cost savings from joint production outweigh the costs of transporting goods to the other market. An industrial structure emerges, in which all production takes place in the core region. For zero trade costs, distance and hence space does not matter. Economies of scale are not restricted locally, so that production costs are the same in the core and the periphery. Thus, any spatial structure can emerge.

In the third section of Chapter B, I augment this prototype model in order to explain the existence of subcenters. Therefore, I discuss several possible centrifugal forces that may explain why complete concentration of economic activities can rarely be observed. I find that congestion effects are the most likely to matter. Including them in the model increases the spatial structures that the economic geography model theoretically can explain.

The concentration of spatial structures can be measured by different indicators. Two of the most popular are the population in the largest city in percent of the total population or in percent of the urban population. The latter is also called the primacy ratio. For individual countries, the primacy ratio is, for instance, 6 percent for India, 38 percent for Argentina, 33 percent for Korea, and 8 percent for the Netherlands. Table 1 shows ratios of spatial concentration for several country groups.

Table 1 and the above examples show that spatial concentration does not change linearly with income levels and does not converge to a common spatial structure. Nor are spatial structures within economies fixed over time such that stable spatial equilibria may shift over time. The concentration of economic activities varies considerably in the course of economic development and across countries. They are often highest for middle-income countries. Therefore, one long-discussed hypothesis in development economics and regional economics suggests that the relationship between economic development and spatial concentration takes the form of an inverted U-curve (Williamson 1965, Alonso 1980). That is, spatial concentration first increases and then decreases with the level of per capita GDP (GDPC).

Table 1 — Concentration and Urbanization

Country group	Average ratio of the population of the largest city of each country to its urban/total population		Urban population in percent of total population		Population in agglomerations of 1 million or more in 1990 in percent of urban population	
	Urban 1990	Total 1990	1980	1994	1980	1994
World	15	6	39	45	34	35
Low-income economies	12	3	22	28	32	34
Middle-income economies	26	14	52	61	32	33
Lower middle-income	n.a.	n.a.	47	56	28	30
Upper middle-income	22	15	64	74	40	40
High-income economies	11	9	76	77	40	43

Source: World Bank (1994; 1996b).

However, a rigorous theoretical model to explain this hypothesis is missing so far. Therefore, I further extend the economic geography model in the fourth section of Chapter B. I show that the observed differences in the concentration of economic activities can be explained by extending the model by two features relevant to economic development. These are the assumptions of nonhomothetic demand and technological change. The resulting model displays an inverted U-curve between economic development and spatial concentration.

In Chapter C, I review the empirical support for economic geography models. In the first section, I present the empirical evidence for the importance of the first main assumption of the economic geography model — the relevance of economies of scale. Despite their important impact on economic theory, empirical evidence on EOS so far remains elusive. There is no consensus among economists whether they matter or not. Part of the reason for the lack of consensus is that the different levels of aggregation and the different approaches to estimate EOS are not clearly distinguished. As a consequence, empirical results seemingly contradict each other. Therefore, I propose a classification of different scale effects to structure the literature. I give an overview of the vast range of approaches to explore the topic. Instead of discussing each contribution in detail, the reader gets an overall assessment of the importance of economies of scale rather than a specific result for a specific subgroup of scale economies.

In the second section of Chapter C, I review the empirical evidence for the importance of the second main assumption of the economic geography model — the relevance of the costs of overcoming economic distance. These so-called trade costs go far beyond tariffs and transport costs and also include search costs, for instance. The current debate on the increasingly "globalized" world gives the impression that trade costs are becoming less important and are ceasing to matter much for trade flows and the decision of firms about where to locate their production. I analyze whether there is a trend toward the marginalization of trade costs in two ways. As an illustration, I first present some data to show the evolution of the absolute magnitude of several types of trade costs. Second, I test whether the marginal impact of distance on the spatial division of production and trade has declined in the last three decades. A gravity model is the suitable and natural framework for assessing the importance of the declining trend of trade costs for the economic geography of international trade. I estimate such a model for a cross-section of 45 countries and test whether the coefficient of geographic distance on the volume of trade has declined between 1967 and 1995. Sectoral regressions show in which sectors transport costs as compared to search costs matter most.

In the third section of Chapter C, I test the predictions of my development model of economic geography concerning the spatial structure of economies. Thereby, I focus on my hypothesis that the relationship of economic development and spatial concentration can be described by an inverted U-curve. Furthermore, the prototype and the augmented model predict that several other variables influence the pattern of spatial concentration. Using a cross-country setting with up to 70 countries, I test whether trade costs, congestion effects, and different geographic and demographic conditions have the supposed impact on the spatial distribution of economic activities.

In Chapter D, I summarize the analysis, mention some policy implications of the models and my analysis, and make some suggestions for future research.

B.   Economic Geography: Theory

This chapter presents the theoretical analysis of new economic geography models. It shows how the spatial distribution of industries can be explained using a clear and consistent microeconomic foundation. At first glance, this structure and the spatial solutions derived from the models seem very restrictive. Therefore, I thoroughly discuss the underlying assumptions and the implications of economic geography models in this chapter.

I begin with a description of the original contributions of Krugman and Venables explaining the linkages between economic geography, international trade, and the costs of economic distance. This description introduces the developments of the field and the motivation behind the work of Krugman and Venables. It describes in a nontechnical way the two mechanisms to explain economic agglomeration and concentration. Technical aspects of modeling spatial economics in the new approaches are discussed in Section II. That section combines in a single model the two mechanisms described in the first part. I discuss in detail the structure of the model. Numerical simulations show the solutions of this model, as is common in this type of nonlinear models. The qualitative results are confirmed in the Appendix, which shows analytic corner solutions to this model. Further simulations show the (non)sensitivity of the model to specific values of parameters.

The framework of the model can be used to analyze various questions. The first and most important question is how the degree of economic integration affects the spatial distribution of industries between two regions. A bifurcation diagram shows that there may be multiple equilibria. This opens up the field for further topics that can be analyzed with help of the model of Section II, or with more specific variants of that model. These topics are, among others, the possibility of "big-push" industrialization, poverty traps, the case of regional policy, import-substitution versus export-promotion policies, Zipf's law or the rank-size rule of the distribution of the urban population, agglomeration, and endogenous growth, the spread of industry from one country to another, or the dynamics of urbanization.

Instead of covering all these questions in detail, I focus on the spatial implications of the models. In Section III of this chapter, I discuss several other economic forces that may explain why centrifugal forces are often much more pervasive in reality than they are in the model. These forces can easily be included in the model. But care should be taken when including further centrifugal forces. It is important that the forces be really relevant to the specific spatial level that the model intends to describe because spatial economics is a wide field that encompasses urban economics, regional economics, and international economics.

Another question that I will analyze with the model is the changing spatial structure of economies in the course of economic development. Here, the model has to be extended by several factors that are relevant to economic development. Out of these, the most important spatial effects result from the structural change that usually accompanies economic growth. A model that describes these spatial effects is presented in the fourth section of this chapter.

I.   Krugman and Venables' Approaches to Link Geography and Trade

Research in the field of new economic geography has started with the paper by Krugman and Venables (1990). Motivated by the Single European Market, Krugman and Venables analyze whether the different comparative market access of the Southern European countries and the original EU members may affect possible gains from economic integration. They state (p. 56):

Optimists believe that the mutual opening of markets, reinforced by 1992, will make manufacturing in Southern Europe highly attractive; they thus expect that manufacturing sectors in the entering countries will expand, and that manufacturing sectors in the Southern entrants will converge over time towards Northern European levels. Pessimists worry that in spite of lower wages, Southern industry will have difficulty competing with Northern, and that there will have to be both a shrinkage of manufacturing and a reduction in relative manufacturing wages.

In their paper, they set up first elements to model this ambiguity. They show that the existence of economies of scale and trade costs may lead to a situation in which peripheral regions suffer from the partial elimination of trade barriers. The central model that is the cornerstone of new economic geography has been provided later by Krugman (1991b). In this model and in his book *Geography and Trade* (1991a), Krugman sets up the main arguments for the consideration of space in international trade theory. The model is the base for several extensions and applications in the literature.

Krugman considers two regions with two sectors of production and sector-specific labor. The regions differ in the size of their manufacturing sector only. The larger number of manufacturing workers leads to a larger population and higher domestic demand for manufacturing products in the larger region. Therefore, it is called the core, while the other region is called the periphery. The manufacturing sector produces differentiated goods with increasing returns. These increasing returns can make it advantageous to concentrate the production in one location.

Krugman's main contribution is the explicit consideration of trade costs for the shipment of differentiated goods in this setup. He shows that the payment of trade costs for the shipment to the other region may outweigh the savings of concentrated production. If these costs are very high, concentrated production may not pay. Then, the manufacturing production will be distributed according to local demand in both regions. In turn, for low levels of trade costs, the gains from concentrated production outweigh the costs to ship goods to the other region. For zero trade costs, space and the distribution of the production between the regions do not matter.

Trade costs are paid on top of domestic prices. Hence, consumers have an advantage to be located in the region that has the largest manufacturing sector in order to save on these trade costs and to realize higher real wages. Krugman assumes that manufacturing workers are mobile. They move to the region in which they can realize higher real wages. This results in a process toward the complete agglomeration of the manufacturing sector in the larger region, if trade costs are low. It results in a convergence toward equal economic structures in the two regions, if trade costs are high and outweigh the increasing returns from concentrated production.

In order to realize scale economies while minimizing transport costs, manufacturing firms tend to locate in the region with larger demand but the location of demand itself depends on the distribution of manufacturing" (Krugman 1991b: 483).

The second main mechanism to explain economic agglomeration and concentration has been developed by Venables (1996) and Krugman and Venables (1996). Again, they consider two regions with two sectors. But now, both sectors produce differentiated goods with increasing returns. Their trade is subject to trade costs. The crucial difference of these models is that they consider that firms use intermediate inputs in the production of final goods, i.e., there are vertical linkages between them. Here, Krugman and Venables assume that the inputs of each sector are produced by each sector itself. Hence, the output of each sector can be used in final consumption and as intermediate inputs. This creates cost and demand linkages between firms. In these models, Krugman and Venables do not consider labor mobility and assume that both regions are of equal size. Nevertheless, economic integration of these regions may induce firms to move to the other region or to change the sector of production. Again, the realization of scale economies stands against the need to pay trade costs for goods shipped to the other region. For high trade costs, firms find it advantageous to locate close to final consumer demand. Then, production of each sector will be divided equally between the two regions. For low trade costs, firms care more about the availability of intermediate inputs that can be obtained in the own region without paying further trade costs. Then, these cost advantages outweigh the trade costs that have to be paid for the shipment of final goods to the other region. An adjustment process will result after which each region will be specialized in the production of one sector. As in the Krugman (1991b) model, the trade-off between trade costs and the realization of scale economies determines whether agglomeration and concentrated production results.

In the following section, I present a technical description of the mechanism described above. Thereby, I combine the models of Krugman (1991b) and Krugman and Venables (1996) by including cost and demand linkages of intermediate input usage in the original model of Krugman. Hence, the model is related to the existing approaches, but differs from Krugman (1991b) in that it considers the cost and demand linkages that result from the presence of other firms. It also differs from Krugman and Venables (1995), Venables (1996), and Krugman and Venables (1996) in that it allows for regional mobility of industrial workers, and it differs from the latter two models in that it also considers a constant returns to scale sector. In the second part of this chapter, I include one further element in my model, namely, congestion effects as first formalized by Brakman et al. (1996) in an economic geography framework. I solve the model for various exogenous parameters and show that the qualitative results derived in the existing literature can be replicated in this model variety. After a discussion of the results, I propose a new extension to the model in the third part of this chapter. The extension considers technological change and nonhomothetic demand in order to describe changing patterns of industry distribution in the course of economic development.

II.   The Prototype Model

1.   Description of the Prototype Model

The prototype economic geography model of industry agglomeration shows the working of centrifugal and centripetal forces. The framework of the model is adopted from Krugman (1991b) and Krugman and Venables (1996), who in turn draw on the Dixit–Stiglitz approach (1977) to model monopolistic competition, and on Ethier's (1982) formulation of an intermediate input sector. Specifically, equations [1], [2], [3], [5], [12], and [15] can be found in Krugman (1991b). Equations [4], [6], [7], [8], [9], [13], and [14] can be found in Krugman and Venables (1990). The latter are needed in order to include intermediate input usage in the economy. Although the equations look the same, they do not always have the same economic content, as the economic structure of the prototype model does not respond in all aspects to the existing models.[9]

---

[9]   The model has first been described in Junius (1996a).

I follow Krugman (1991b) and assume that there are two regions in the economy, which are called core (*c*) and periphery (*p*). I mainly refer to the core region and use the indices *c* and *p* only where necessary. With different indices, the same equations hold for the peripheral region. For expositional ease, I also refer to the core as the domestic region and to the periphery as the foreign region, without implying that a region equals necessarily a political unit that is distinct from the other region.

Each region has two sectors — an increasing-returns-to-scale sector, which is called industry, and a constant-returns-to-scale sector, which is called agriculture. The industrial sector consists of firms. The agricultural sector consists of farms. Labor is the only primary factor of production and consists of workers and farmers. Workers can only work in firms. Farmers can only work on farms. Thus, there is no mobility between sectors. However, workers are interregionally mobile, while farmers are interregionally immobile.[10]

Initially, the regions are symmetric in all possible aspects except for the size of the industrial sector. The region with the larger industrial sector, i.e., the region with the larger number of firms and workers, is called the core. The size of the arable land is equally distributed, so that the number of farmers living in each region is the same. This means that the core has a higher ratio of firms to farms. This economy is illustrated in Figure 1.

The total number of workers and farmers in both regions is normalized to one, so that π is the share of industrial workers (*L*) in total population:

[1] $\pi = L_c + L_p$.

The share of farmers in total population is $(1 - \pi)$. Since each region has the same number of farmers, $(1 - \pi)/2$ is the number of farmers per region. For simplicity, I follow Krugman and further normalize wages and marginal productivity of farming to one and assume that agricultural output can be transported costlessly within and between regions.

---

[10]   This shall take into account that a certain part of a population is immobile and barely responds to economic incentives. This part of the population lives dispersed over the economy, because of the former focus of an economy on the primary sector, which is dependent on natural resources like land for agriculture or deposits for mining. Both are dispersed over the economy and so are the people engaged in these activities. Thus, the initial distribution of the population in an agrarian economy is dispersed rather than concentrated. The demand from the immobile population provides a reason for firms not to be located in the core of an economy. A spatial model needs one immobile factor in order to rule out solutions in which one country is completely depopulated and all economic activities are concentrated in another country. The immobile sector does not necessarily have to be called the agricultural sector, but will so in order to be in line with other economic geography models.

Figure 1 — The Core-Periphery World

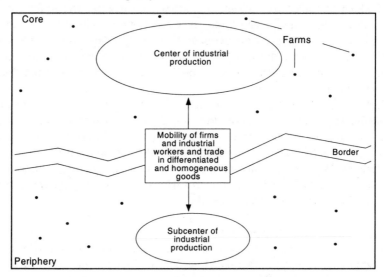

Preferences for the consumption of industrial and agricultural products are described by the standard Dixit–Stiglitz (1977) utility function U, consisting of a Cobb–Douglas and a CES part[11]:

[2] $U = M^{\varepsilon} A^{1-\varepsilon}$,   where $M = \left[\sum_{j=1}^{N} m_j^{(\sigma-1)/\sigma} \right]^{\sigma/(\sigma-1)}$.

$1 - \varepsilon$ is the share of income spent on the consumption of agricultural products (A). ε is the share of income spent on the consumption of industrial goods (M), m_j is a single product variety, σ is the elasticity of substitution between the product varieties, and N is a large number of potential products.

Production per firm (Q_{cj}) can be described by the input demand function:

[3] $Z_{cj} = \alpha + \beta Q_{cj}$,   with $\alpha, \beta > 0$,

where α are fixed costs and β are variable costs. Inputs are a composite of workers and industrial goods (M), the latter being used as intermediate inputs.

---

[11] CES means constant elasticity of substitution. In a CES-utility function, the elasticity of substitution is independent of consumer's income, the initial prices of the goods, and the number of goods in the economy that have already been consumed. A change in relative prices always leads to a proportional change in the quantities consumed.

Labor has a share of $1-\mu$ and intermediate inputs have a share of μ in total inputs:

[4] $\qquad Z_{cj} = L_{cj}^{1-\mu} M_j^{\mu}$.

Due to fixed costs, firms produce with internal economies of scale. Industrial goods are differentiated goods. Industrial goods may be close, but imperfect substitutes, with σ the elasticity of substitution between the different product varieties.[12] Only some of the infinitely possible product varieties can be produced. In order to save on additional fixed costs, each firm produces only one good. Because no firm wants to share the demand for its good with any other producer, and because goods can be differentiated costlessly, every firm produces a different variety of the industrial good. Consequently, the number of firms equals the number of industrial goods. Firms have some monopoly power, because they are the only supplier of a specific variety. Thus, they face a downward sloping demand curve and set their price with a markup over marginal costs. However, free market access guarantees that prices equal average costs — the so-called Amoroso–Robinson condition. This leads to the following two conditions for prices of industrial goods, expressed in input units:

[5] $\qquad \beta + \alpha/Q_{cj} = p_{cj} = (\sigma/\sigma-1)\beta, \quad \sigma > 1$.

The pricing conditions can be used to calculate the output per firm:

[6] $\qquad Q_{cj} = (\sigma-1)\alpha/\beta$.

---

[12] The elasticity of substitution in consumption is defined as the percentage change in the quantity ratio of two goods in consumption induced by a relative price change; i.e., $(p_c/p_p)^{\sigma} = c_p/c_c$. For $\sigma > 1$, the share of expenditure falls if the price rises. For $\sigma = > \infty$, goods are perfect substitutes. In the case of a large number of goods, Dixit and Stiglitz (1977) argue that firms neglect their product's marginal contribution to the price index and to the total amount of consumer expenditure. The elasticity of substitution then equals the elasticity of demand (d). See also Yang and Heijdra (1993), Dixit and Stiglitz (1993), and d'Aspremont et al. (1996) for a discussion of this assumption. Under monopolistic competition, firms set the price such that marginal revenue equals marginal costs. Consequently, marginal revenue is at a positive level. Because firms have some market power, prices are set such that marginal revenue equals $p(1 - 1/d)$. For a positive marginal revenue, it follows that $d > 1$ must hold. This means that under monopolistic competition firms produce on the elastic part of the marginal revenue curve, i.e., where the elasticity of demand exceeds 1. Since the elasticity of demand equals the elasticity of substitution in this framework, $\sigma > 1$ must hold as well. See also Helpman and Krugman (1985: 119).

It can be seen that output per firm is independent from the number of domestic customers and from domestically available inputs. It is always the same for all firms in both regions. This market structure prevents any strategic interaction between firms.

In the output equation, the elasticity of substitution also determines the level of scale economies (EOS). The degree of EOS can be measured by the ratio of average costs (AC) to marginal costs (MC). Using equations [5] and [6], this ratio can be expressed as $\sigma/(\sigma-1)$, the markup that monopolistic firms charge on top of MC. Prices additionally equal AC, since firms earn zero profits in monopolistic competition. The markup compensates firms for the fixed costs of production. The higher σ, the smaller is the markup. With a small markup, firms have to produce a larger output to break even. Thus, σ is positively correlated with output per firm. The higher the output, the lower is AC/MC. Consequently, a higher σ indicates lower EOS.

The assumption that industrial goods are differentiated instead of being homogeneous leads to the crucial point that makes agglomeration advantageous in economic geography models. Firms as well as households have preferences for variety. Firms prefer variety, because the availability of a large number of differentiated inputs makes it possible to use varieties that best fit the production process. This reduces the cost of production.[13] Consumers prefer variety, because they like to consume as many different industrial products as possible. Thus, diversified consumption increases both consumers' and firms' utility.

To simplify further, symmetry of consumption goods and intermediate goods is assumed. First, the elasticity of substitution in production and consumption is the same. Second, industrial output can be used for consumption or as an intermediate good. Thus, intermediate inputs can be expressed like consumption goods as:[14]

---

[13]   See Ethier (1982) and Markusen (1989), who introduced Dixit–Stiglitz-type preferences for variety on the producer side.

[14]   Equation [7] implies that each consumer always buys a small amount of each available product. This is a very unrealistic assumption and should be interpreted in the way that consumption follows a normal distribution over all goods, such that the condition is met on average or in the aggregate at least. See Helpman and Krugman (1985: 116). By symmetry, the same applies for producer preferences. It can easily be proved that this type of subutility function implies preferences for variety. Say B is the total quantity of intermediate inputs used. Since goods enter the utility function symmetrically, the same quantity of all goods is used. Then $m = m_j$ and $B = M \cdot m$. From equation [7], one gets $M/B = N^{1/\sigma-1}$, which is increasing in N, since $\sigma > 1$. This means that, holding the total quantity of intermediate inputs constant, the utility increases with the number of different goods used.

[7] $$M = \left[\sum_{j=1}^{N} m_j^{(\sigma-1)/\sigma} \right]^{\sigma/(\sigma-1)},$$

where both consumers and firms face increasing returns to variety. In this setup, where the number of firms is endogenous, this leads to aggregate increasing returns. The process of how increasing returns can lead to the agglomeration of industries is illustrated in Figure 2 and can be described verbally as follows.

Once there is an unequal regional industry distribution with more workers and firms in the core, demand for goods is higher in the core as well (see Figure 2). Due to fixed costs, no region ever produces all possible and sellable goods. A larger number of workers and thus a higher domestic demand means that a larger number of firms can be supported in the core. A larger number of firms means that a larger number of different goods are produced in the core, since all firms produce different varieties. With more goods being produced in the core, fewer goods have to be imported. Thus, for fewer goods trade costs have to be paid. This satisfies firms as well as consumers, because both have preferences for variety, such that they always want to use goods from both regions. Firms can produce more cheaply if they have a lot of different varieties of inputs, out of which they can use the most suitable for their specific needs. Following equation [7], this reduces total input demand and raises nominal wages of workers in the

Figure 2 — Circular Causation Leading to Industrial Agglomeration

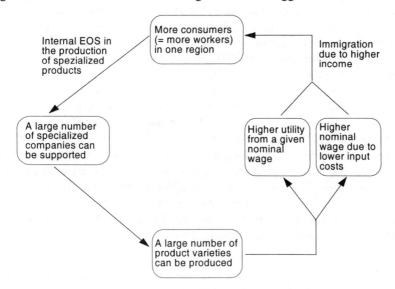

core. The outer circle in Figure 2 presents this argument. The inner circle shows the effect of consumer preferences for variety. A larger number of varieties yields a higher utility and higher real wages from a given nominal wage. Thus, with more varieties produced in the core, wages are rising and are making the core even more attractive. This leads to migration from the periphery to the core, which reinforces the process. As a result, such a cumulative process may eventually lead to complete concentration in the core. This completes the centripetal forces of the model.

The demand from the agricultural sector constitutes the centrifugal force in the model. Firms may wish to locate near peripheral farmers in order to be closer to final consumption and local demand for their products. A firm is facing higher local demand from farmers in the periphery, because the ratio of firms per farmers is lower in the periphery than in the core. Thus, firms might have an incentive to locate in the periphery instead of in the core. In order to evaluate when centripetal and when centrifugal forces dominate, further conditions concerning the market have to be specified.

Firms employ labor and intermediate inputs in such a proportion that the ratio of wages to the price index of intermediate inputs equals the marginal rate of technical substitution of industrial goods and labor:

[8] $$\frac{w_c}{T_c} = \frac{1-\mu}{\mu} \frac{M_j}{L_{cj}} \ .$$

T is the price index for industrial goods. A firm uses industrial goods from its own region and the other region. The relation with which industrial goods from the two regions are used depends on the price of the goods and the elasticity of substitution between the goods. The price for domestic varieties equals their marginal costs times the markup. For foreign varieties, trade costs have to be paid in addition. Prices for goods from one region are always the same, so that always the same amount of all goods from one region is used. Because the price of foreign goods includes trade costs, the amount of each foreign good used is the smaller, the higher trade costs are. As is common in this type of models, "iceberg-type" trade costs are assumed. This means that $\tau > 1$ goods have to be shipped for one good to arrive. Iceberg-type trade costs have the advantage that no further transportation sector has to be added to the model. The price of an imported good, therefore, is τ times the price that it is charged in its region of origin.[15] The regional price index for industrial goods results from the weighted prices of domestic and foreign industrial goods:

---

[15]   Iceberg-type trade costs have first been suggested by Samuelson (1954). However, the underlying idea of real trade costs goes back to von Thünen (1826). See Bottazzi

[9] $\quad T_c = \left[\dfrac{N_c}{N_c + N_p}\left(\dfrac{s}{s-1} MC_c \right)^{1-s} + \dfrac{N_p}{N_c + N_p}\left(t\,\dfrac{s}{s-1} MC_p \right)^{1-s} \right]^{1/(1-s)}.$

The price index in the core is the lower, the higher the percentage of domestic goods as a fraction of all goods produced in the economy $N_c/(N_c + N_p)$ is, since the price for foreign goods additionally includes trade costs. Thus, the price index for intermediate inputs is always lower in the core.

In the Appendix I.1, it is shown that marginal costs depend on the weighted average of wages and the price index for intermediate goods:

[10] $\quad MC_c = w_c^{1-\mu}\, T_c^{\mu}\, \beta(1-\mu)^{\mu-1}\, \mu^{-\mu}.$

It is also shown in the Appendix I.2 that in this setup, the number of firms and different goods produced in a region is endogenously determined as:

[11] $\quad N_c = \dfrac{L_c}{\alpha\sigma}\left[\dfrac{\mu}{1-\mu}\dfrac{w_c}{T_c} \right]^{\mu}.$

In order to solve for the static equilibrium of the economy, expressions for total income and sectoral wages have to be found. Wages in the agricultural sector equal their constant productivity, which was defined to be one. Income in the agricultural sector per region, therefore, equals the farmers' share in the total labor force, which is $(1 - \pi)/2$ per region. Total income consists of the wage sum in the industrial sector ($w_c L_c$) and income in the agricultural sector:

[12] $\quad Y_c = w_c L_c + (1-\pi)/2.$

Total expenditure on industrial goods by consumers and firms in the core (X_c) equals the share ε of the region's income plus the expenditure on industrial goods ($M_c T_c$). By the use of equation [8], expenditure on industrial goods can be expressed in terms of the sum of wages, such that :

[13] $\quad X_c = \varepsilon Y_c + \dfrac{\mu}{1-\mu} w_c L_c.$

In the Appendix I.3, it is shown that the nominal wage rate is:

[14] $\quad w_c = \dfrac{(1-\mu)N_c}{L_c(N_c + N_p)}\left(\dfrac{\sigma}{\sigma-1} \right)^{1-\sigma}\left[X_c\left(\dfrac{T_c}{MC_c} \right)^{\sigma-1} + X_p\left(\dfrac{T_p}{\tau MC_c} \right)^{\sigma-1} \right].$

and Ottaviano (1996) for a discussion of the usefulness of iceberg-type trade costs and alternative approaches to model trade costs in international trade models.

Real wages ω_c are calculated as:[16]

[15] $\omega_c = w_c / T_c^{\varepsilon}$.

In this prototype economic geography model, all possible profits of firms are distributed in form of wages. Hence, the real wage for workers in the periphery relative to the real wage in the core (ω_p / ω_c) determines whether the core or the periphery is a more attractive place to locate. Workers and firms have an incentive to locate in the core if the ratio is below one. In this case, centripetal forces dominate centrifugal forces. If the real wage ratio exceeds unity, workers and firms have an incentive to locate in the periphery. In this case, centrifugal forces dominate.[17]

2.   Mechanics of the Prototype Model

In order to evaluate whether centrifugal or centripetal forces dominate, I solve equations [9]–[15] simultaneously for both regions and various sets of exogenous parameters as well as for a given initial distribution of workers.[18] From that, I calculate the relative real wage of the periphery. This yields a static short-run equilibrium of the model for a specific set of parameters. In this equilibrium, the relative real wage indicates the direction of the dynamics in the economy. Workers move according to wage differentials and increase the size of the industrial sector of the region that pays higher wages.

Migration of workers sets in motion a process leading to further dispersion or further agglomeration of firms and workers. A ratio of peripheral to core wages below one in the static short-run equilibrium indicates that centripetal forces outweigh centrifugal forces. In this case, trade amplifies differences between re-

---

[16] Real wages are calculated by dividing nominal wages by the consumer price index. The consumer price index is distinct from the price index of industrial goods, because it additionally includes agricultural goods. For Cobb–Douglas preferences and a price of agricultural goods normalized to one, it can be expressed as $T_c^{\varepsilon} 1^{1-\varepsilon}$, which reduces to T_c^{ε} .

[17] In this monopolistic-competition-type economy, all possible profits are dissipated by the free entry of firms. The revenue net of the costs of intermediate inputs is distributed to workers through wages. Thus, it seems somewhat meaningless that firms might relocate to the other region when workers move due to regional differences in real wages. However, with zero moving costs and zero costs of setting up the production of goods, the assumption that firms always move in proportion to workers is no restriction for the model. If so, the calculated wage can be interpreted as the maximum wage that firms can pay without making losses.

[18] To solve the model, the Newton procedure of Mathematica for Windows Version 2.2.3 is used. Analytical corner solutions are derived in the Appendix II.

gions (and does not lead to factor price equalization). As a result, this model can explain where firms locate, independently of technological or taste differences and despite factor and goods mobility.

a.   *Centripetal and Centrifugal Forces*

I first analyze how the strength of different parameters influences the strength of centrifugal and centripetal forces. This is important in order to fully understand the working of the model, to see how sensible it is to variations of the parameters and how robust its results are. The strength of the model is that symmetry between the two regions is assumed for almost all parameters. The size of the industrial sector is the only parameter for which the symmetry between the two regions is broken. By knowing how the centripetal and centrifugal forces are influenced by varying the parameters, one can assess situations where the symmetry is broken at another point.[19]

In Figure 3a, I have solved the model for various levels of σ, the elasticity of substitution of the single product varieties. On the horizontal axis, the exogenously predetermined level of σ is shown. On the vertical axis, the endogenously determined level of the relative real wage of the periphery is shown for which the economy is in a static equilibrium. The curve in the figure is composed out of several single points for which the static equilibrium is calculated. A lower elasticity of substitution means higher economies of scale. With high economies of scale, firms benefit from being in the larger region, because in the larger region, economies of scale can be realized to a larger extent than in the smaller region. Moreover, in terms of the model, with low elasticities of substitution, workers and firms have high preferences for variety and do not react very sensitively toward price differences between goods.

In contrast, in the limit of an infinite elasticity of substitution, perfect competition results, and consumers buy only the cheapest product variety. Because foreign varieties include trade costs, the relative amount of domestic varieties bought by consumers is the higher, the higher the elasticity of substitution is. If consumers only buy varieties of their own region, peripheral firms have higher revenues than core firms, because there is less competition for local consumers in the periphery than in the core. Since this translates into higher wages for workers, relative wages are higher in the periphery, the higher the elasticity of

---

[19]   Amiti (1998) analyzes such cases. She shows that, if goods differ in their substitutability, the periphery can realize scale economies to a lesser extent than the core, due to a smaller home market. Thus, the periphery would be a net exporter of high-elasticity goods and a net importer of low-elasticity goods. In addition, she shows that the periphery would specialize in labor-intensive goods, if industries differ with respect to factor intensities. Furthermore, the periphery would specialize in the production of goods that are subject to lower trade costs, if industries differ with respect to trade costs.

substitution is, i.e., the lower the economies of scale are. Hence, Figure 3a shows a positive relationship between the elasticity of substitution and the relative real wage of the periphery.

Figure 3 — Relative Real Wage for Alternative Levels of Exogenous Parameters

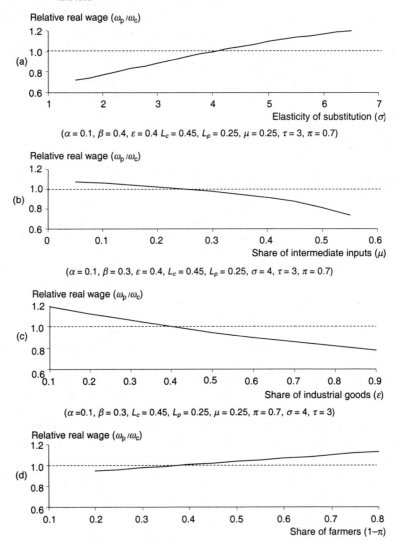

(a) Relative real wage (ω_p/ω_c)

$(\alpha = 0.1, \beta = 0.4, \varepsilon = 0.4\ L_c = 0.45, L_p = 0.25, \mu = 0.25, \tau = 3, \pi = 0.7)$

(b) Relative real wage (ω_p/ω_c)

$(\alpha = 0.1, \beta = 0.3, \varepsilon = 0.4, L_c = 0.45, L_p = 0.25, \sigma = 4, \tau = 3, \pi = 0.7)$

(c) Relative real wage (ω_p/ω_c)

$(\alpha = 0.1, \beta = 0.3, L_c = 0.45, L_p = 0.25, \mu = 0.25, \pi = 0.7, \sigma = 4, \tau = 3)$

(d) Relative real wage (ω_p/ω_c)

$(\alpha = 0.1, \beta = 0.4, L_c = \pi\, 45/70, L_p = \pi\, 25/70, \mu = 0.2, \sigma = 5, \tau = 2.2, \varepsilon = 0.75\ \pi)$

Figure 3b shows the impact of alternative shares of intermediate inputs in the production of goods on relative real wages. A higher μ means that firms use relatively more industrial goods and less labor. Thus, it shows the importance of forward linkages. Forward linkages are stronger in the core, where more domestically produced industrial goods are available. Consequently, Figure 3b shows that higher values of μ are associated with a lower relative real wage of the periphery.

Figure 3c shows the impact of alternative shares of industrial goods in total consumption on relative real wages. The higher the share, the lower the relative wage of the periphery. Essentially, the same argument as for the importance of industrial intermediate goods applies to the importance of industrial consumer goods. Since the periphery produces less varieties domestically than does the core, it also has to import a larger share of consumer goods. However, imported goods are subject to trade costs. Consequently, the higher the share of industrial goods in consumption, the higher the share of imported goods, and the higher the consumer price index. This, in turn, lowers the relative real wage of the periphery.

Figure 3d shows the relative real wage for alternative shares of farmers in the economy. Firms may choose to locate close to peripheral farmers, in order to be close to local consumer demand. Being close to local demand allows firms to avoid trade costs when selling their goods. The assumption that there are fewer firms per farmers in the periphery means that firms face less competition or higher demand per firm from local farmers. Thus, the demand of farmers is the centrifugal force of the model that explains, why not always all production takes place concentrated in the core. This force is the stronger, the more dispersed local demand is; i.e., the larger the share of farmers in the economy, the more important the farmers' demand for final goods is for firms, and the less important the demand from workers and other firms is. Thus, Figure 3d shows that the higher the share of farmers in the total labor force, the higher the relative wage of the periphery.

b. *The Impact of Trade Costs*

Trade between the two regions is subject to tariffs, transport costs, and other costs of overcoming economic distance. I have subsumed all of these under trade costs. The level of trade costs determines whether centrifugal or centripetal forces dominate and, consequently, determines where industries locate or where they relocate to. In Figure 4, one can see that for zero trade costs, which means $\tau = 1$, wages are the same in both regions. This holds independent from the level of the other exogenous parameters. This arises from the fact that location does not matter if nobody has to pay extra trade costs for importing intermediate or final

Figure 4 —   Alternative Levels of Trade Costs

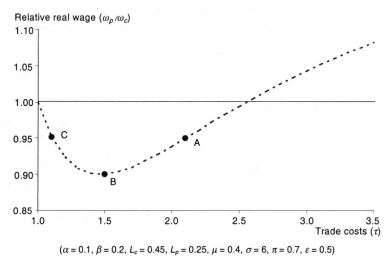

$(\alpha = 0.1, \beta = 0.2, L_c = 0.45, L_p = 0.25, \mu = 0.4, \sigma = 6, \pi = 0.7, \varepsilon = 0.5)$

goods. It does not matter where a firm produces its goods and whether it is close to other firms and consumers, because additionally, technologies and effective units of labor are assumed to be the same in all regions, and technological spill-overs are not considered. With relative wages equal to one, nobody has an incentive to move, and the distribution of industries is determined by the initial distribution of workers.

The higher the trade costs, the fewer trade takes place. Being in the periphery then means facing relatively less competition and having better access to local farmers' demand. Goods from the core, which include trade costs, are much more expensive than goods produced in the periphery, such that peripheral farmers mainly demand goods from peripheral firms. Because there are less firms in the periphery, each producer faces a larger proportion of peripheral farmers' demand for industrial goods than core firms face from core farmers. This translates into higher revenues of peripheral firms. Because all possible profits are distributed through wages, the peripheral region is able to pay higher wages than the core.[20] As a consequence, for prohibitive high trade costs, firms may want to be located in the periphery, while for zero trade costs, they are indifferent be-

---

[20]   Note that production costs remain higher in the periphery. This results from a higher price level for intermediate inputs. Thus, there is a tension between higher production costs on the one hand and better access to local farmers on the other hand. Similarly, consumers always face a higher consumer price level in the periphery. But for high trade costs, they also realize higher nominal wages, such that real wages are above those of the core.

tween the two locations. Since all possible profits are distributed in the form of wages, workers have the same preferences. For prohibitive high trade costs, workers realize higher real wages in the periphery, while for zero trade costs, real wages are the same in both locations. Hence, reducing trade costs from a prohibitive level to zero reduces the relative real wage of peripheral workers. However, it does not reduce them in a linear way. (If it would do so, core wages were always lower than peripheral wages and agglomeration could never be observed.)

If trade costs fall from a high to an intermediate level, core firms gain better access to the small market in the periphery, and peripheral firms gain better access to the large market in the core. However, this does not improve the position of peripheral firms. Peripheral firms now face more competition from a large number of core firms that each exports a small share of its production to the periphery. This reduces sales of peripheral firms in their own market. In order to match this loss in sales, they have to export to the core. However, they have to export a larger share of their production than core firms do, because a few peripheral firms have to match the sales of a large number of core firms. Thus, also a larger share of peripheral firms' output is subject to trade costs. This means that trade costs consume a larger share of revenues from peripheral firms than from core firms, which reduces relative wages in the periphery. If the total reduction of trade costs is sufficiently high, this leads to a situation in which the core is able to pay higher wages. This case happens for values of τ for which the curve in Figure 4 is below the dotted line. Centripetal forces then outweigh centrifugal forces and agglomeration results from an adjustment process. This effect is the stronger, the more one goes down the U-curve to point B, which is determined by the exogenous parameters of the model.

If trade costs are reduced to a level below point B, the demand of peripheral farmers becomes less important due to low trade costs. Peripheral farmers then can cheaply be served from the core. Peripheral firms then care more about the access to the large core market. A further reduction of trade costs improves the relative situation of peripheral firms, because it further reduces regional differences in the economic variables like input prices or the consumer price index. With zero trade costs, no cost differences between the two regions prevail, so that the relative wage converges to one. Thus, in an early integration process, the competition effect dominates and reduces relative wages in the periphery. With deeper economic integration, the competition effect peters out, and access to the core market and its intermediate input suppliers becomes more important. As a result, economic conditions as well as wages first diverge and later converge again.[21]

---

[21] Krugman and Venables (1995) suggest that this is a tentative explanation — though not the only one — why in the early globalization process, like in the 1970s, public

Figure 5 shows the real wages of the periphery and the core instead of the relative real wage as before, pointing to the absolute impact of trade liberalization
on real wages. The core region benefits continuously from trade liberalization,
because it only reduces costs from trade, and the competition of peripheral firms
is too small to much affect prices and wages in the core negatively. In relative
terms, trade liberalization may negatively affect core wages compared to the periphery for low trade levels. In absolute terms, it is always positive for the core.
In the periphery, one again finds a U-shaped curve, meaning absolute losses
from trade in an early integration process. This reflects that peripheral firms lose
market shares in their home market if trade costs decrease from a high or even
autarkically high level to an intermediate level. For high trade costs, they can
only partly match this loss by increased sales to the periphery and lower factor
input costs. Then, wages decrease in proportion to the lower value of sales. In
the Appendix, analytical solutions show the levels of trade costs for which a reduc-

Figure 5 —   Real Wages of the Periphery and the Core

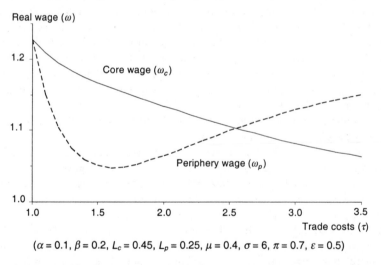

$(\alpha = 0.1, \beta = 0.2, L_c = 0.45, L_p = 0.25, \mu = 0.4, \sigma = 6, \pi = 0.7, \varepsilon = 0.5)$

debate mainly focused on the harm that reducing trade barriers might do to LDCs.
Nowadays the debate is reverse. Industrial countries fear competition from low-wage
LDCs. Figure 4 can give an explanation of this changing view. Let us assume that
the world is at point A in Figure 4 and consists of industrial countries (the core) and
LDCs (the periphery) only. A reduction of trade costs to point B leads to a fall in
relative wages in the periphery. Further reduction of trade costs to point C now hurts
the core in the sense that relative real wages in the core fall. Since aggregate real
wages still rise, this is not necessarily harmful. However, it can lead to a change of
comparative advantages in some sectors, such that an inevitably painful process of
structural change becomes necessary.

tion harms or benefits the periphery.[22] Absolute real wages start rising after some low level of trade costs is reached and approach values that are clearly higher than in the case of high trade costs, because of lower input costs and better access to the core market. They further approach core wages, the more trade costs go down. Hence, the consideration of trade costs in economic geography models means that trade liberalization does not have to be beneficial for peripheral regions in all cases. So far, all solutions to the model have been calculated for a fixed distribution of industries, where the core hosts 45 out of 70 firms. This means, the solutions are static equilibria for a given distribution of workers. They are not necessarily dynamically stable industry distributions, for which no migration would take place in the long run.

The next figures show the relative wage at different levels of trade costs for alternative industry distributions and the location of long-run (dynamic) equilibria. The horizontal axis exhibits the periphery's share of industry employment. The regions are of the same size for an industry share of 50 percent. Below that, the periphery is smaller; above that, the periphery is larger. For low trade costs (Figure 6a), the larger region always pays a higher real wage. Workers have an incentive to move from the smaller to the larger region, such that two stable equilibria exist, namely, those with complete concentration of all firms in either the core or the periphery. A distribution with an equal share of firms in both regions is an unstable equilibrium.

For high trade costs, Figure 6a shows the reverse situation. For reasons discussed above, with high trade costs, the smaller region always pays the higher wage. This yields an incentive for workers and firms to move from the larger to the smaller region until they are both of equal size. It follows that equal distribution of firms is a stable and the only equilibrium of the model.

For intermediate trade costs, Figure 6b shows five possible equilibria. An *SE* indicates a stable equilibrium, a *UE* indicates an unstable equilibrium. As in the case of high trade costs, equal distribution is a stable equilibrium. Workers and firms move to the smaller region until the two regions are of equal size, if they are of somewhat equal size initially. Then the better market access to local farmers in the smaller region outweighs the better forward and backward linkages in the larger region. However, for very unequal initial distributions of firms, the linkage effects are so much stronger in the larger region that the better access to farmers in the periphery cannot match the disadvantage of being far from other producers. This leads to three stable equilibria. Equal distribution as well as com-

---

22   Specifically, it can be shown that the total value of sales of peripheral firms increases with a marginal increase of τ, if the ratio of core to peripheral spending on industrial goods is smaller than $\tau^{2\sigma-2}$. Since the ratio is always larger than 1, it will exceed $\tau^{2\sigma-2}$ for τ close to one, and will be lower for large τ. See also Appendix II.

Figure 6 —   Industry Distributions for Alternative Levels of Trade Costs

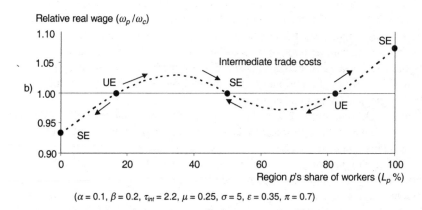

$(\alpha = 0.1, \beta = 0.2, \tau_{low} = 1.5, \tau_{high} = 4.5, \mu = 0.25, \sigma = 5, \varepsilon = 0.35, \pi = 0.7)$

$(\alpha = 0.1, \beta = 0.2, \tau_{int} = 2.2, \mu = 0.25, \sigma = 5, \varepsilon = 0.35, \pi = 0.7)$

plete concentration of firms in one region can result from a migration process, depending on the initial distribution of industries. Between these three stable equilibria there are two unstable equilibria with an unequal distribution of firms between the regions.

The existence of stable and unstable equilibria can also be illustrated in a bifurcation diagram (Figure 7). It shows the equilibrium size of the core for alternative levels of τ. Solid lines represent stable equilibria, dotted lines represent unstable equilibria. For high levels of trade costs, equal dispersion of industries is the only stable equilibrium. For intermediate levels of trade costs, multiple stable equilibria are possible. Agglomeration results, if the economy starts out very unequally distributed, while equal dispersion results, if the regions are of similar size.

Figure 7 — Stable and Unstable Equilibria

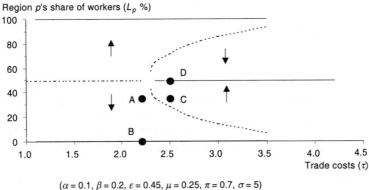

$(\alpha = 0.1, \beta = 0.2, \varepsilon = 0.45, \mu = 0.25, \pi = 0.7, \sigma = 5)$

This case illustrates the importance of the critical mass of firms for the development of regions and why a "big push" can bring about a cumulative process toward an equilibrium with a larger percentage of industrial workers that would not be possible with slow economic development of a region.[23] An industrial sector will only be able to survive in a region, if enough other firms start producing at the same time, or if the immobile demand is very high. Without the backward and forward linkages provided by the existence of other firms, the development of an industrial sector is not sustainable, as maximum wages that a firm can pay are lower than in the larger region at intermediate levels of trade costs. This means that a continuous or slow development of an industrial base cannot be successful for intermediate levels of trade costs. Only if the percentage of firms is that high that the distribution of industries is illustrated by a point above the dotted line, such as in point C, industrial activities are sustainable. Then, cumulative processes lead to a migration process of firms and workers until firms are equally distributed between the two regions, such as in point D. Below the dotted line and in the case of low trade costs, firms always end up completely concentrated in one region, such as in points A and B.

---

[23] See Rosenstein-Rodan (1943) and Murphy et al. (1989) for "big-push" theories. Last century's California may provide an illustrative example. For a long time, the region could not establish an industrial base. Because demand was so low, it was cheaper to transport industrial goods from the east than producing these goods with a very low scale of production. The exploration of gold in the area induced a big push that suddenly created enough domestic demand that sustainable industrial production was possible. Cumulative processes led to the further attraction of firms.

III.   The Augmented Model

1.   Congestion Effects

As is shown in Figures 6a and 7, the industrial production ends up completely concentrated in one region if trade costs are at a low level; for high levels of trade costs, an equal distribution of industries results from an adjustment process. For intermediate trade costs, both equal distribution or complete concentration can result (Figures 6b and 7). Hence, the prototype model comes to the same solutions as the original models by Krugman (1991b) and Krugman and Venables (1996).

The existing pattern of industry location in Europe and North America is very different, with several center-subcenter patterns. If the models are of any empirical relevance, then the level of trade costs between the most integrated regions like the US states and the regions in the European Union should be characterized as low or intermediate. However, for these levels of trade costs, the models predict a tendency toward complete concentration of firms in one region. This tendency is in line with Krugman and Venables' (1996) expectation that the European Union will look more like the regionally concentrated United States in the future. However, if anything, the empirically observable trend goes in exactly the opposite direction.

Molle and Boeckhout (1995) describe converging patterns of industrial location over the postwar period for Europe. This is confirmed by Molle (1997) who analyzes spatial concentration of different sectors and branches in the European Union between 1950 and 1990. He finds decreasing concentration of branches and specialization of regions. Cheshire (1995) points out the great variety of population patterns and trends in the European Union. He shows that some centers are gaining and others are losing around a general distribution with centers and subcenters.

For the United States, Kim (1995) finds indeed that regional specialization rose substantially until the turn of the century — a period during which trade costs were much higher than today. However, he reports that specialization flattened out in the interwar years and fell enormously since the 1930s — a period during which trade costs fell substantially. This is in line with the deconcentration of US employment, as observed by Chatterjee and Carlino (1997) for the postwar period. Their explanation for this trend is that densely populated areas are closer to the full capacity of local resources which increases the costs of production.

Thus, the prototype model can neither explain the observed existence of center-subcenter patterns, nor can it explain the current trend toward industry dispersion in Europe and the United States. Further centrifugal forces have obviously been neglected in the analysis so far. Up to now, the model has focused on the pecuniary transmission of advantages and disadvantages of economic agglomeration. However, there is a wide range of further factors that limit the size of economic agglomerations. While most of them can be included in a model, care should be taken on what the model shall explain. Therefore, in the literature, different weights have been assigned to different centrifugal forces.

Probably the first to write about the limits of regional concentration of the population were the ancient Greeks (Bairoch 1988: 74–75). Plato calculated the ideal republic to have exactly 5040 citizens. Aristotle emphasized the public function of cities and considered it to be vital that the citizens knew each other.[24]

However, also Greek cities quickly surpassed what Aristotle called "unsurpassable limits". But, ancient cities remained limited in size for a more basic reason, which was the supply of food to the city. Since food perishes in transit, people had to live close to food supplies. For instance, in the ancient Rome, a mere two percent of the empires' population lived in Rome itself, despite a rather centralist political system. The size of a city then depended on the quality of its soil and the size of its hinterland that could provide it with livestock and grain. The domestication of pack animals, improvements in the transport infrastructure, and the ability to store food increased the area that could supply a city with food such that cities could grow to larger sizes. Today, the supply of agricultural goods is no constraint to city growth anymore. Hence, it neither is an important centrifugal force. Therefore, the level of trade costs for agricultural goods is set at zero, for simplicity, in most economic geography models.[25]

Traditional location theorists mentioned a number of further centrifugal forces that can stop a trend toward agglomeration. Weber (1909) pointed out that higher land rents and wages might push industries out of the industrial core. Hoover (1948) added higher prices for raw materials in agglomerations. Isard (1956) mentioned higher land rents and a crowded transportation system as diseconomies of scale. Alonso (1960) formalized the relationship of land prices and distance in his concept of a bid-rent curve, where differences in land rents match differences in transport costs to a regional market. Negative externalities of economic agglomeration and crowding are further reasons why the core might be a

---

[24] In this context, "citizens" probably means male urban adults entitled to vote. For Plato and Aristotle, a city was constrained by the size that public meetings could have with all citizens present.

[25] This does not mean that trade costs for agricultural goods are negligible. Indeed, usually, they are higher than those for industrial goods. However, today, agricultural goods can be bought from all parts of the world so that their availability does not limit city growth anymore. Thus, they are negligible for the forces that an economic geography model should describe.

less attractive place than the periphery. Negative externalities are higher crime rates, pollution, traffic jams, and other bottlenecks in the infrastructure. These so-called congestion effects have been modeled by Kanemoto (1975), Henderson (1975; 1988: Chap. 7), and Dendrinos (1982) in the context of an optimal city size. Congestion effects seem to be of special relevance when looking at today's industrialized economies with a large number of cities that are exploding in size, and with their environmental, social, and traffic problems. Crime and pollution are much higher in large-scale agglomerations than in rural areas or small cities. Cullen and Levitt (1997) show that higher crime rates are an important centrifugal force. They estimate the impact of crime on urban flight for 137 US cities during the years 1976–1993. They find that each additional reported crime in a central city is associated with a net decline of about one resident.[26]

The decline of trade costs during the last two centuries (Vance 1986) has contributed to an increasing volume of traffic and congestion and ever larger urban agglomerations with numerous of them surpassing one million inhabitants (Table 1). This has significant external effects. Higher concentration leads to more severe traffic jams, which directly increase the costs of doing business in that location. Traffic congestion severely limits interactions within some cities. In Bangkok, average speed is about 5 miles per hour, and the average journey to work is 91 minutes (*The Economist* 1995). Just-in-time delivery is out of question in such a city. But also in other cities, like Bogota, Kingston, or Rio de Janeiro, the average journey to work takes more than an hour. The severity of traffic congestion and estimates of the external costs of traffic and congestion can be found in Hohmeyer et al. (1996), Maddison et al. (1996), and Mayeres et al. (1996). The data presented in these studies suggests an exponential congestion function. This is confirmed by Kirwan et al. (1995) who conclude that an exponential type of aggregate congestion function is empirically most satisfying.

Congestion effects can limit the attractiveness of being in the core in direct and indirect ways. They directly reduce the firm's advantages of being in the core if the costs of production increase through bottlenecks in the infrastructure, crime, or pollution. Congestion directly reduces the worker's advantages of being in the core if workers value "soft" location factors. Then, higher crime rates and pollution directly decrease the utility of the core as a residential location.

Beside these direct effects, congestion may have indirect effects if industry concentration leads to further rules and regulations that increase the costs of production. This may be the case if, for example, strong environmental pollution leads to public protest and hostility toward an expansion of industrial production, new airport runways, incinerating plants, power plants, etc. This may lead to political actions, for instance, tighter restrictions on residential housing, indus-

---

[26] See also Glaeser (1998) for further examples and references for congestion effects.

trial production, and pollutant emissions.[27] Such an internalization of external effects indirectly increases the costs of doing business at the more concentrated location. Societies that value environmental protection more, also regulate their industries more than others.[28] Congestion sensitivities might differ among regions for various reasons. One is the absolute level of pollution in a region. Another is that people in different regions have different rates of time preference. Future detrimental effects of pollution are considered more in some regions than in others. For instance, high-income regions might value environmental protection and cleanliness more than low-income regions, which have more basic concerns like nutrition, health care, or minimum social standards.[29]

Thus, congestion effects can influence the model in two ways. First, it can influence consumers' location utility if people make their moving decisions on the basis of real wages and "soft" location factors like in the model of Asilis and Rivera-Batiz (1994). In this case, real wages are adjusted by a term indicating the degree of pollution.[30] Second, congestion can influence firms' location utility by traffic jams, crime, social unrest, other bottlenecks in the infrastructure, and tighter regulations for industrial production like first formalized in an economic geography model by Brakman et al. (1996) and later used in Junius et al. (1995). This leads to higher production costs and lower real wages through the market process. Brakman et al. (1996) include congestion effects in the model of Krugman (1991b). Hence, my augmented model differs from their model in that it also considers an intermediate input sector. Despite different quantitative solu-

---

[27] See the volume by Tolley (1987) and Markusen (1996) for the severity of external effects of large-scale agglomerations and attempts to limit these effects through regional policy.

[28] In Williamson (1982), one finds an example for such different sensitivities. He analyzed disamenities and living conditions in 19th-century British towns. He found that the trade-off between private consumption and communal life quality was much different from what social reformers and historians have assumed, meaning that private consumption was much higher-valued by workers in that time.

[29] It can be observed that environmental concerns and regulations are higher in high-income countries. OECD (1991) suggests that public demand for environmental quality rises with income and induces a policy response to pollution. Grossman and Krueger (1995), World Bank (1996b), Selden and Song (1994) show that the relationship of environmental quality and per capita GDP takes the form of an inverted U across countries. For regional air pollution in US counties, Grossman et al. (1994) show a negative correlation with income levels. See Grossman (1995) and Stern et al. (1996) for surveys of this literature. The inverted U-shaped relationship of pollution and per capita GDP means that, ceteris paribus, high-income countries spend more money on pollution prevention technologies and abatement per output unit than low-income countries and, therefore, react more actively against the negative external effects of concentration.

[30] Similar to the first approach is the model by Ricci (1999), where the price of industrial goods that consumers perceive at a location depends exponentially on the size of the location.

tions, I come to the same qualitative solutions as Brakman et al. (1996), as will be shown below.

I use the Brakman et al. (1996) approach to model congestion for two reasons. First, it is more specific because it allows a separate analysis of the cases where congestion influences fixed and variable costs. Second, it seems that it is empirically the more realistic model. Brakman et al. (1996) assume that congestion effects depend on the amount of interactions in a region. These can be approximated by the number of firms (or alternatively workers) in a region. According to the above-cited empirical studies on congestion, and considering the fact that nature and people are able to absorb a certain degree of pollution and congestion with little harm, congestion effects rise exponentially with the number of firms (and, consequently, with the size of the population), so that they barely matter for a low number of firms and get increasingly important for a large number of firms per region. I consider two cases:

[16] $Z_{cj} = \alpha + \beta e^{\xi N_c} Q_{cj}$, and

[17] $Z_{cj} = \alpha e^{\xi N_c} + \beta Q_{cj}$,

where ξ is the sensitivity of the society toward congestion. In equation [16], the input demand function [3] is replaced by a function where congestion effects raise variable costs. In equation [17], congestion effects raise fixed costs. In both cases, increasing the number of firms (and hence workers) in a region has an ambiguous effect on the costs of production. Centrifugal as well as centripetal forces are dependent on the number of firms per region. As before, a higher number of firms increases the number of goods produced in that region and reduces the regional price level for intermediate inputs. However, the negative externalities associated with the production of goods rise as well and raise variable or fixed costs. At some point, the higher utility derived from the availability of differentiated products is offset by higher congestion costs.

a.   *Congestion Effects and Variable Costs*

Including variable-cost-congestion effects changes some other equations of the model. Congestion increases the price of goods by the same proportion as the costs of production. This reflects that more inputs have to be used for the same output. Instead of equation [5], the following pricing conditions have to be adopted:

[18] $p_{cj} = \beta e^{\xi N_c} + \alpha / Q_{cj}$ and

[19] $p_{cj} = (\sigma / \sigma - 1)\beta e^{\xi N_c}$.

This directly leads to a different output per firm, and equation [6] has to be transformed to:

[20] $Q_{cj} = (\sigma - 1)\alpha e^{-\xi N_c} / \beta$.

Equation [20] shows that firms try to accommodate higher variable costs by a lower scale of production. This reduction of output per firm does not increase the number of firms, because it is not accompanied by a reduction of inputs used per firm. Thus, the number of firms can still be described by equation [11]. Marginal costs, however, increase directly with the size of the congestion effects. Equation [10] has to be replaced by:

[21] $MC_c = w_c^{1-\mu} T_c^{\mu} \beta e^{\xi N_c} (1-\mu)^{\mu-1} \mu^{-\mu}$.

In turn, higher marginal costs raise the price index and lower the wage. Both can still be written as in equation [9] and [14].

Solutions to this model are illustrated in Figure 8, which shows the relative real wage of the periphery for alternative industry distributions and alternative levels of variable-cost-congestion effects. Trade costs are set at a low level, so that linkage effects provide the larger region with an advantage if congestion is not considered (see Figure 6a). For low congestion elasticities, the outcome of the model is not qualitatively distinct from Figure 6a. The larger region always exhibits

Figure 8 — Alternative Industry Distributions (Variable-Cost-Congestion Effects)

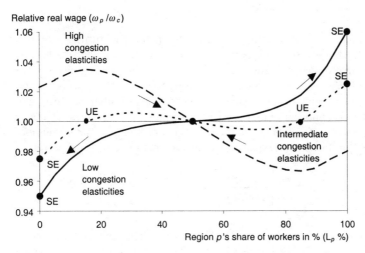

$(\alpha = 0.1, \beta = 0.4, \pi = 0.7, \mu = 0.2, \sigma = 4, \varepsilon = 0.4, \tau = 1.6, \xi_{low} = 0.17, \xi_{int} = 0.19, \xi_{high} = 0.23)$

a higher real wage. For high congestion elasticities, the pattern is reverse. The smaller region always exhibits a higher wage. For intermediate congestion elasticities, an interesting pattern emerges. For very small regions (to the left of the first unstable equilibrium and to the right of the second unstable equilibrium), wages are lower than in the larger region. In this case, lower congestion costs cannot outweigh the disadvantages of fewer industry linkages in the smaller region. However, if the regions are more similar, congestion matters and makes production in the core more expensive than in the periphery.[31]

b.   *Congestion Effects and Fixed Costs*

Including fixed-cost-congestion effects also changes some of the equations of the model. Instead of the pricing equation [5], one gets:

[22] $\beta + \alpha e^{\xi N_c} / Q_{cj} = p_{cj} = (\sigma / (\sigma - 1))\beta$.

Here, congestion affects fixed costs, so that average costs are higher than before for a given output. Under monopolistic competition, free entry of firms assures that firms produce output such that prices equal average costs. Since prices are also determined by the condition that marginal revenue equals marginal costs, and since congestion does not directly affect marginal costs, prices (in input terms) remain the same. This means that firms have to produce a higher output to accommodate higher fixed costs such that average costs equal the level they would have without congestion. Instead of equation [6], output per firm is then given by:

[23] $Q_{cj} = (\sigma - 1)\alpha e^{\xi N_c} / \beta$.

Because congestion is dependent on the number of firms per region, congestion effects raise fixed costs more in the larger than in the smaller region. This means that output per firm cannot be the same in both regions anymore. Equation [23] shows that the firms in the larger region produce with a larger scale of output than firms in the smaller region. A higher output per firm and a higher amount of inputs per output needed in the presence of congestion means that the fixed amount of inputs available in a region results in a smaller number of firms per region. Instead of equation [11], the number of firms is given by:

[24] $N_c e^{\xi N_c} = \dfrac{L_c}{\alpha \sigma}\left[\dfrac{\mu}{1-\mu}\dfrac{w_c}{T_c}\right]^{\mu}$.

---

[31] This suggests that for countries that are quite similar in size, lower congestion elasticities due to fewer environmental concerns, or a lower industry density in one country can lead to a relocation of firms and workers in the slightly smaller country.

Because congestion effects are lower in the smaller region, the number of firms declines relatively more in the larger than in the smaller region. Consequently, the regions are getting more similar in their economic variables that depend on the number of firms in a region, like the price index, the marginal costs, and the wages. These equations, however, can still be written as in equations [9], [10], and [14]. Solutions to this model are illustrated in Figure 9.

Figure 9 shows the relative real wage of the periphery for alternative industry distributions and alternative levels of fixed-cost-congestion effects. Again, trade costs are set at a low level, so that linkage effects provide the larger region with an advantage if congestion is not considered. Not surprisingly, for low congestion elasticities, there is a similar pattern as without them (see Figure 6a). Real wages in the peripheral region are lower than in the core. This can lead to complete concentration in the larger region. For a very high congestion elasticity, pollution abatement costs, regulation, crime, and other congestion effects are so high that the larger region always exhibits lower wages than the smaller region. This leads to an equal distribution of industries between regions.[32]

Figure 9 — Alternative Industry Distributions (Fixed-Cost-Congestion Effects)

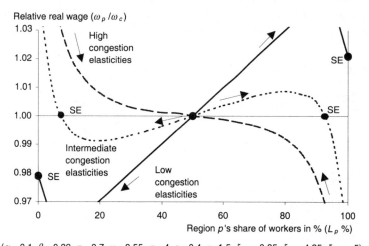

$(\alpha = 0.1, \beta = 0.32, \pi = 0.7, \mu = 0.55, \sigma = 4, \varepsilon = 0.4, \tau = 1.5, \xi_{low} = 0.35, \xi_{int} = 4.25, \xi_{high} = 5)$

---

[32] The empirical relevance of this case is questionable. Nevertheless, this argument has been widely used in policy debate. For instance, in the 1992 presidential campaign, Ross Perot warned American voters about the effects of NAFTA. He predicted that lower environmental standards in Mexico would lead to a strong movement of US jobs to Mexico unless wage costs converged.

In between these two cases, there is another pattern of relative wages. For intermediate levels of congestion elasticities, Figure 9 shows an S-shaped curve. In this case, there are three equilibria, two of which are stable. Complete concentration is no equilibrium anymore. In any long-run equilibrium, both regions produce industrial as well as agricultural products, although one region is larger than the other. Hence, for certain parameter constellations, the inclusion of congestion effects can explain a stable center-subcenter pattern of industry location as one finds it in most developed regions. Therefore, the prototype model extended by fixed-cost-congestion effects offers a theoretical possibility to explain existing patterns of industry agglomeration.

In Figure 10, I show the effects of trade liberalization when the effects of environmental regulation and congestion raise the fixed costs of production. Similar to Figure 4, a U-shaped curve is the result. Trade liberalization from a high level of trade costs reduces relative wages of the periphery, whereas trade liberalization from an intermediate level reduces relative wages of the core. In contrast to Figure 4, the curves do not show a relative wage of 1 for zero trade costs. For zero and close to zero trade costs, congestion effects raise wages in the periphery above those in the core. Whereas before, trade liberalization only reduced the size of the advantage of being in the core, now, it can even lead to a disadvantage of being in the core. As expected, the results of this section confirm the findings of Brakman et al. (1996).

Figure 10 — Alternative Levels of Trade Costs

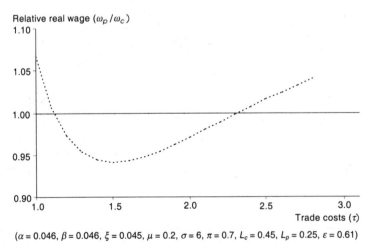

Relative real wage (ω_p / ω_c)

Trade costs (τ)

($\alpha = 0.046$, $\beta = 0.046$, $\xi = 0.045$, $\mu = 0.2$, $\sigma = 6$, $\pi = 0.7$, $L_c = 0.45$, $L_p = 0.25$, $\varepsilon = 0.61$)

2.   Land Rents and Commuting Costs

This section shall examine in how far other factors than congestion effects can describe partly dispersed, partly concentrated patterns of industry location. One alternative factor, mentioned in traditional location theory, is the argument that land rents are higher in inner cities than in the periphery. This might push workers and industries to the suburbs or rural areas. Krugman and Livas Elizondo (1996) incorporate this argument in an economic geography model. In their model, all production takes place at the central business district (CBD), and workers live along a straight line. The further they live from the CBD, the longer they have to commute. Commuting, in turn, reduces possible work time, so that a worker who lives δ units from the CBD works only $(1-\delta)$ hours. His income is δw times lower than that of a worker who does not have to commute. However, a worker has to pay land rents that exactly offset the opportunity costs of commuting. Hence, real wages in this economy are given by:

[25] $\omega = \dfrac{w}{T^\varepsilon}(1-\delta).$

Comparing two regions as in the prototype model, average commuting time and land rents are higher in the larger region. The smaller region has the advantage of its average travel distance to its CBD being shorter. Their workers save on commuting time but face lower wages and a higher price level. The level of trade costs determines which of the two effects prevails.[33]

Brezis and Krugman (1993) argue along similar lines in a slightly different model. They analyze the spatial effects of technological change for the case that a new technology is developed and produced in addition to an existing one. Productivities in production depend on the accumulated localized knowledge of all firms using that technology. Then, "new technology" firms do not gain from being located in the CBD and set up production in the periphery where commuting costs and land rents are lower. If the new technology is superior to the old one, this leads to the decline of the old core and to the rise of a new core. Thus, new technologies can explain the decline and rise of cities and a reversal of a cumulative process toward industrial concentration in one city.

These approaches remain unconvincing as an explanation of large-scale agglomerations for two reasons. First, although land rents might be a powerful ar-

---

[33] The most elegant model that includes land rents in an economic geography model is Fujita et al. (1999). They are able to describe the evolution of hierarchical spatial systems à la Christaller by an endogenous adjustment mechanism. Another approach has been adopted by Helpman (1995). He uses the nontradable good "housing" as a centrifugal force to show the impact of trade costs on the pattern of population distribution. In his model, high trade costs favor settlement in the core.

gument in an urban context to explain industry location, it is less obvious that they are also relevant in a regional or cross-country context.[34] For instance, intraurban land price differentials are known to be much higher than interurban or intraregional ones. Second, one implication of the suggested models is that high land rents push people with low income out of inner city districts, whereas workers with high opportunity costs of commuting should live closer to their work places. Since reality is different, as can be seen in almost all US cities,[35] there must be other disincentives of living in a densely populated area that outweigh commuting costs. Such disincentives could be higher crime rates in inner cities or higher pollution. These disincentives correspond with the urban congestion effects mentioned above. Therefore, I conclude that congestion effects as modeled in the previous section are a more decisive centrifugal force than land rents. Additionally, they are a more precise description of the centrifugal forces at work, since land rents are dependent on regional differentials in pollution, waste disposal, etc. The necessity to distinguish land rents and congestion effects becomes ultimately clear when analyzing the effects of economic development, for which the model will be extended in the next chapter. Let us imagine that, due to technological progress and higher per capita incomes, Chinese workers switch from driving bicycles to driving cars. Then, traffic in already crowded cities will completely break down. This might also increase inner-city land rents, but the primary cause of stronger centrifugal forces is higher congestion.

3.   Self-Fulfilling Expectations

Another reason why one cannot observe a tendency toward complete regional concentration of industries as implied by the prototype model could be that with

---

[34]   This means that if any, land rents are factor prices and thus dependent on the relative strength of centripetal and centrifugal forces or agglomeration economies and diseconomies. They are not an independent centrifugal force. Land rents may be an important factor to explain the location of single firms. However, in a model where all firms use the same technology and produce the same quality type of a differentiated good, land rents cannot explain the migration of a bunch of firms, because that would lower the equilibrium land rents in turn.

[35]   See Wheaton (1977) for empirical references. Alonso (1964) and Muth (1969) explain the increase in residents' income with greater distance to the city by assuming income elasticities that are higher for land consumption than for the cost of travel and commuting time. Wheaton (1977) tests and rejects their approach and concludes that other negative externalities of crowding play a more prominent role. In a mathematical model, Chatterjee and Carlino (1997) replicate the 297 metropolitan areas in the United States with the highest employment densities in 1951. The model shows that congestion costs alone are capable of explaining all of the postwar deconcentration without relying on theories about changes in preferences, technology, or government policies.

a different modeling of expectations, the dynamics of the model change and a different equilibrium is reached than the one suggested by the initial distribution of labor. It was assumed that workers and firms have static expectations with regard to wages and profits. That is, they believe that current wage differentials between the regions will persist in the future. If so, changes in regional employment are an increasing function of the wage gap. Then, the dynamics can be graphed as in Figure 6b and be described by a Marshallian adjustment mechanism:

[26] $-\dot{L}_p = \dot{L}_c = g\left(\omega_c - \omega_p\right), \quad g' > 0 ,$

where dots over a variable denote changes in time. Whenever workers realize differences in regional real wages, they move to the region that pays higher wages. The existence of forward and backward linkages leads to external economies of scale. Thus, the wage gap between the two regions is an increasing function of their relative size:

[27] $\omega_c - \omega_p = f\left(L_c - L_p\right), \quad f > 0 .$

For simplicity, I consider the case of low trade costs only, so that the core always pays higher wages than the periphery. Then, f is a continuos and strictly monotonic, increasing function, and the initial distribution of industries is the only determinant for the dynamic process that leads to complete concentration of industries in the initially larger region.[36]

The simplicity of this adjustment process crucially depends on the neglect of moving costs and self-fulfilling expectations. With their inclusion, the adjustment process is more difficult than above, and the dynamics can work in a different way. If moving is costly, workers are concerned about current and future wage differentials between the regions. However, they can only observe current wages. Since they are not sure about the underlying model of the economy and its parameters, they do not know which region pays higher wages in the future. Nevertheless, workers have some idea about the economy and form expectations on the base of their subjective view about it. This opens up the possibility of self-fulfilling expectations. If all people think that for some exogenous reason, region p is going to be the most attractive location for industries, they move there. This strengthens market linkages in that region until it eventually becomes the superior location, despite an initial disadvantage. Thus, one of the reasons

---

[36]   For high trade costs, the dynamics go in the opposite direction. This does not change the qualitative outcome of this section.

why cumulative processes might start or stop is just because people believe that they do so.[37]

To find out which one of the two — initial distribution of industries or self-fulfilling expectations — plays the decisive role for the dynamics of the economy, one has to formalize the above arguments regarding the calculus of workers.[38]

Workers are assumed to be able to borrow and lend freely at interest rate r and to live infinitely. They maximize the present value of expected life-time wages, which at time t_0 can be expressed as:

[28] $\int_{t_0}^{\infty} \omega(t)e^{-rt}dt$.

Workers will move to the other region if the benefits of being there exceed the moving costs. In order to ensure that workers move smoothly, moving costs are assumed to rise with the squared number of workers moving per period. If $1/\gamma$ is a measure of these moving costs, γ indicates the speed of moving. Besides this technical speed of moving, the number of workers moving at a point of time ($\dot{L}_c$) depends on the value of working in the region of choice (q):

[29] $\dot{L}_c = q\gamma$.

At time t_0, the present value of working in the region of choice depends on all current and future wage differentials and the discount factor (r):

[30] $q(t_0) = \int_{t_0}^{\infty} \left(\omega_c(t) - \omega_p(t)\right)e^{-r(t-t_0)}dt$.

---

[37]   If moving is not costly, but workers form expectations about future wages, the initial distribution of industries is irrelevant because moving is reversible without any costs. Workers then move toward the region that they believe pays higher wages. They move again if their expectations do not materialize or their expectations for wages in the next period favor another region. For instance, political events or technological change can raise positive or negative expectations toward a region. An example might be the accession of Hong Kong to China that might have increased uncertainty about its future prospects as a financial center. This could lead some firms to the believe that future profits would fall in Hong Kong. Such a development would strengthen the relative attractiveness of alternative locations such as Singapore. Hence, some movement would strengthen linkage effects in Singapore. A cumulative process would raise relative profits in Singapore and indeed lower them in Hong Kong, even if China had not changed its policy. Only self-fulfilling expectations would lead to Hong Kong's relative decline.

[38]   For the seminal paper that this section draws on see Krugman (1991c), and see Matsuyama (1991) for a similar analysis.

Because moving is subject to moving costs, being in the region of choice is an asset decision and moving is an investment decision. The equilibrium return per time period on the asset of being in the region of choice should equal the difference of wages plus the capital gain on this asset:

[31] $rq = (\omega_c - \omega_p) + \dot{q}$.

Without any loss in the economic content, equation [27] is respecified by:

[32] $\omega_c - \omega_p = \theta L_c$, $\theta > 0$ and $\omega_c = \omega_p = 1$ if $L_c = L_p$,

where θ indicates the degree of external economies of scale. As a consequence, [31] and [32] can be simplified to:

[33] $\dot{q} = rq - \theta L_c$.

Equations [29] and [33] constitute a dynamic equation system in the (q, L_c) space.[39] The qualitative solution of the dynamic system can be graphed in a phase diagram (Figure 11).[40] The objective of a phase diagram is to translate the dynamics implied by two differential equations into a system of arrows that describes the qualitative behavior of the economy over time.

The horizontal axis of Figure 11 shows region c's share of workers. The vertical axis shows the value of being in region c rather than in region p. Each point in the phase diagram represents a position of q and L_c at a given point in time. To construct the phase diagram, I first determine the $\dot{L}_c = 0$ and $\dot{q} = 0$ schedules. The $\dot{L}_c = 0$ schedule shows all combinations of L_c and q, where L_c does

---

[39]   Fukao and Bénabou (1993) criticize the formulation of q as in equation [30] in their comment on Krugman (1991c). Instead of integrating over an infinite life span, one should integrate until a finite point of time, at which concentration of all workers in one region is reached. Then, the last movers have an incentive to avoid moving costs by waiting until everybody else has moved to the region of choice. The interpretation of equation [29] then is that the moving costs equal what workers are willing to pay for moving at a point t rather than at the finite point in time, when moving is not linked to any costs. This would lead to different terminal conditions and to equilibrium paths of the economy toward the full concentration points. This approach is not adopted here because it invalidates the arbitrage condition [33], besides the different interpretation of equation [29]. This means that in Fukao and Bénabou's formulation of the model, there is no value associated with being in the fully concentrated region of choice, so that $q = 0$ for $L_c = 100$ percent, which I consider to be a problematic economic implication.

[40]   See Chiang (1984) or the mathematical appendix of Barro and Sala-i-Martin (1995) for a comprehensive explanation of the working of phase diagrams.

Figure 11 — Initial Distributions Determine the Adjustment

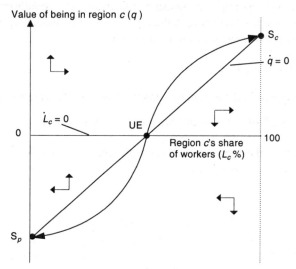

Source: Krugman (1991c: 660).

not change over time, i.e., where no migration between the two regions takes place. Equation [29] suggests that this is only the case for $q = 0$. If the value associated with being in another region is zero, no migration takes place. The $\dot{L}_c = 0$ schedule, therefore, equals the horizontal axis.

The $\dot{q} = 0$ schedule shows all combinations of L_c and q where q does not change over time, i.e., where the value of the asset q remains constant. Equation [33] determines that this is only the case if the wage gap between the regions equals the interest rate times the asset q. Since the wage gap equals zero if the regions are of equal size, $L_c = 50$ percent; $q = 0$ can be determined as one point of the schedule. Solving equation [33] for q at $\dot{q} = 0$ gives $q = (\theta / r)L_c$. Then the slope of the schedule is given by $dq / dL_c = \theta / r$, and the schedule can be drawn as in Figure 11.

The $\dot{q} = 0$ and the $\dot{L}_c = 0$ schedules intersect at the point ($L_c = 50$ percent; $q = 0$). This is an intertemporal equilibrium point. At any other point, either q, L_c, or both change over time. The direction of these changes can be calculated and expressed by the laws of motion indicated by the little arrows.

Horizontal arrows indicate how L_c changes for a given q. An arrow pointing to the right means that L_c grows, i.e., workers move from region p to region c. An arrow pointing to the left means that L_c falls, i.e., workers move to the region p. Because workers move to region c if q is positive, arrows are pointing to the right above the $\dot{L}_c = 0$ schedule. Because workers leave region c if q is negative, arrows are pointing to the left below the $\dot{L}_c = 0$ schedule.

Vertical arrows indicate how q changes for a given L_c. An arrow pointing upward means that q increases, i.e., the asset of being in region c rises over time. An arrow pointing downward means that q falls, i.e., the asset of being in region c falls over time. The direction of the arrows can be determined by the derivative of the $\dot{q}$ schedule with respect to q, i.e., $d\dot{q}/dq = r > 0$. This means that $\dot{q}$ steadily increases with a higher q. If one moves continually from the bottom to the top of the phase diagram crossing the $\dot{q} = 0$ schedule, $\dot{q}$ must pass through the three stages negative, zero, and positive. This means that vertical arrows point downward below the $\dot{q} = 0$ line and point upward above it. The economic interpretation is that above the $\dot{q} = 0$ schedule, the wage differential between the regions is lower than the interest rate times the asset of being in region c. For this to hold, the expected gain on the asset of being in region c must be rising (see equation [31]).

The dynamics of the system consistent with the laws of motion can take the shape of an S, as in Figure 11. For values of $L_c < 50$ percent, the dynamics lead to a stable equilibrium (S_p) with zero percent workers in region c. For values of $L_c > 50$ percent, the dynamics lead to a stable equilibrium (S_c) with full concentration of all workers in region c. Thus, the initial distribution of industries determines which equilibrium is reached.

However, two interlocking spirals as in Figure 12 are also consistent with the laws of motion. In this case, the dynamics can lead to the complete concentration of industries in either region. This means that the economy can end up fully concentrated in the region that initially was smaller and paid lower wages. Consequently, self-fulfilling expectations instead of initial industry distribution can determine which equilibrium is reached.

In order to analyze when the initial distribution only and when also expectations can determine the long-run equilibrium, I determine the local stability of the system at the intersection point of the $\dot{q} = 0$ and the $\dot{L}_c = 0$ schedules.[41] Thus, one has to find solutions for:

---

[41] A local stability analysis only determines which equilibrium is reached from a specific point. From any other point, a different equilibrium could result. However, Fukao and Bénabou (1993) show that the global behavior of this system equals its local behavior, and that the economy indeed hits a boundary at $L_c = 0$ or $L_c = 100$ percent in finite time. Therefore, I need to analyze the local stability only.

Figure 12 — Expectations Can Determine the Adjustment

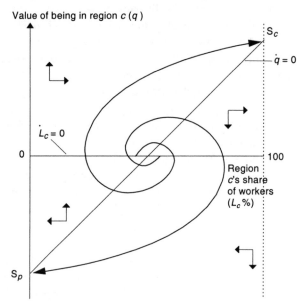

Source: Krugman (1991c: 661).

[34] $\begin{bmatrix} 1 & 0 \\ 0 & 1 \end{bmatrix} \begin{bmatrix} \dot{q} \\ \dot{L}_c \end{bmatrix} + \begin{bmatrix} -r & \theta \\ -\gamma & 0 \end{bmatrix} \begin{bmatrix} q \\ L_c \end{bmatrix} = \begin{bmatrix} 0 \\ 0 \end{bmatrix}.$

$q(t) = \overline{m}e^{bt}$ and $L_c(t) = \overline{n}e^{bt}$ are possible general solutions for such a system.[42] It follows that $\dot{q} = b\overline{m}e^{bt}$ and $\dot{L} = b\overline{n}e^{bt}$. Then, equation [34] can be transformed to:

[35] $\begin{bmatrix} b & 0 \\ 0 & b \end{bmatrix} \begin{bmatrix} \overline{m} \\ \overline{n} \end{bmatrix} + \begin{bmatrix} -r & \theta \\ -\gamma & 0 \end{bmatrix} \begin{bmatrix} \overline{m} \\ \overline{n} \end{bmatrix} = \begin{bmatrix} 0 \\ 0 \end{bmatrix},$

which equals:

[36] $\begin{bmatrix} b-r & \theta \\ -\gamma & b \end{bmatrix} \begin{bmatrix} \overline{m} \\ \overline{n} \end{bmatrix} = \begin{bmatrix} 0 \\ 0 \end{bmatrix}.$

---

[42]   See Barro and Sala-i-Martin (1995: 468–471).

In order to find a nontrivial solution for $\overline{m}$ and $\overline{n}$, the determinant of the first matrix has to equal zero:

[37] $b^2 - br + \theta\gamma = 0$.

From that, one gets the characteristic roots of the system that equal:

[38] $\dfrac{r \pm \sqrt{r^2 - 4\theta\gamma}}{2}$.

The characteristic roots indicate what form the dynamics of the system take, i.e., if they directly lead to one of the two stable equilibria at S_p and S_c, if they lead to one of the equilibria after fluctuating around the initial equilibrium point (at the intersection of the $\dot{q} = 0$ and $\dot{L}_c = 0$ schedules), or if they never reach an equilibrium. In principle, six cases can be distinguished.[43] In the present context, two cases matter. The real parts, which equal r, are positive in any case because only positive interest rates have to be considered. Therefore, the system has two positive roots for $r^2 > 4\theta\gamma$, and two complex roots for $r^2 < 4\theta\gamma$.

With two positive roots, no fluctuation of the system is possible. It approaches directly its long-run equilibria. Then, the adjustment process can be described by Figure 11, where the economy always ends up in the initially larger region and expectations play no role.

With two complex roots, the economy evolves in an oscillating manner. The positive real parts assure that the system fluctuates in widening oscillations. This means that the economy diverges from the initial equilibrium and ends up concentrated in one region. Due to the fluctuations around the initial equilibrium point, the system can end up concentrated in the initially smaller region. Then, the adjustment process can be described by Figure 12. If the economy ends up concentrated in the initially smaller region, self-fulfilling expectations must have played a role. Hence, expectations matter if $r^2 < 4\theta\gamma$.

---

[43]   If the roots are real numbers and positive, the initial equilibrium point is unstable, and the dynamics lead directly to concentration in one of the two full concentration equilibria. If the roots are real numbers and negative, the initial equilibrium point is stable, and the dynamics lead always to equal distribution of industries between the two regions. If the roots are real numbers but of opposite sign, the system is saddle-path stable. If the roots are complex with negative real parts, the economy converges to the initial equilibrium point in an oscillating manner, and equal industry distribution results. If the roots are complex with positive real parts, the economy diverges from the initial equilibrium point in an oscillating manner, and concentration in one of the regions results. If the roots are complex with zero real parts, the system does not approach any equilibrium but infinitely circles around the initial equilibrium point.

The role of self-fulfilling expectations thus depends on the relationship of r, θ, and γ. Self-fulfilling expectations are possible if the interest rate (r) is low, economies of scale (θ) are high, and the adjustment process (γ) is fast. The reason is that workers discount their future wages relatively little if interest rates are low. Expected future wages then matter quite a lot. If economies of scale are large, the interdependence of workers' expectations and decisions is relatively strong. Finally, if the speed of adjustment is fast, expectations matter relatively more because the initial distribution of workers is less decisive for the determination of the wage levels of future periods.

Based on the analysis of Krugman (1991c), this section has shown that self-fulfilling expectations can stop cumulative processes and explain a movement of industries and workers out of the initially advantaged region. Self-fulfilling expectations can play a role if the rate of time preference and moving costs are low and external economies of scale are high. If so, cumulative causation will not necessarily lead the economy to concentration in the initially larger region. It can approach any equilibrium. In how far self-fulfilling expectations actually play a role in explaining the observed trends of industry distribution in the United States and Europe is questionable. I assume that self-fulfilling expectations play a more decisive role in the determination of lower-scale agglomerations, which means at an urban rather than at a regional level. In any case, self-fulfilling expectations fail to explain a center-subcenter pattern of industry location. I conclude that congestion effects are the most obvious centrifugal force to be included in the prototype model in order to explain large-scale center-subcenter patterns.

IV.   The Development Model

1.   Industrial Concentration and Economic Development

In the introduction of this study, I presented some stylized facts (Table 1) that suggest that not all countries converge to the same specific spatial structure. Moreover, also within countries, it seems that spatial structures do not remain constant over time. In this section, I try to explain the changing pattern of spatial concentration of countries over time. Therefore, I further extend the previous economic geography model by taking into account the effects of economic development. The model will show that the relationship of industrial concentration and economic development takes the form of an inverted U-curve, where industrial concentration first increases and then decreases with continuing economic development.[44] Hence, different patterns of economic concentration between countries and the changing pattern of concentration within countries in the course of economic development can be explained.

In order to adjust the model for the effects of economic development, I consider two typical features of economic development: nonhomothetic demand and technological change. They explain that in the course of economic development, production usually shifts from the primary sector to the industrial sector (Syrquin 1989). That means the model has to take account of sectoral structural change.

Therefore, I respecify the input demand function:

$$[39] \quad Z_{cj} = \alpha(1-\rho)^t + \beta(1-\rho)^t e^{\xi N_c} Q_{cj},$$

where t is the level of economic development. In the course of economic development, productivity increases in a Hicks-neutral way and is assumed to reduce fixed and variable input requirements per period (t) by ρ percent. Congestion effects increase the variable input requirements of production due to bottlenecks in the infrastructure, like traffic jams, prevention of crime, and pollution prevention and abatement. As before, congestion effects are dependent on the number of firms in a region. Marginal costs and prices now read:

$$[40] \quad MC_c = w_c^{1-\mu} T_c^{\mu}(1-\mu)^{\mu-1}\mu^{-\mu}\beta(1-\rho)^t e^{\xi N_c},$$

$$[41] \quad p_{cj} = \frac{\alpha(1-\rho)^t}{Q_{cj}} + \beta(1-\rho)^t e^{\xi N_c}, \quad \text{and}$$

$$[42] \quad p_{cj} = \beta(1-\rho)^t e^{\xi N_c}\frac{\sigma}{\sigma-1}.$$

As before, the agricultural sector produces with constant returns to scale. Labor in the form of farmers is the only factor of production and, for simplicity, underlies the same technical progress as industrial goods. By choosing adequate units, marginal products and wages can be normalized to one at any time, so that income in the agricultural sector always equals its labor share, $1 - \pi$. Since land is equally distributed between the regions, and trade costs for agricultural products are zero, the amount of farmers and, consequently, total farmers' income equals $1 - \pi/2$ per region.

---

[44] Initially, the model has been described in Junius (1996b).

Farmers can only work on farms of their original region, since land in the other region is occupied by other farmers already. However, I relax the standard assumption of most economic geography models that farmers are immobile between sectors over longer time spans as well. It is necessary to relax this assumption in order to account for the fact of rural-urban migration in the course of economic development and structural change. Therefore, I assume that they may switch sectors if relative demand for agricultural products declines. This happens in the course of economic development because the higher income elasticity of demand for industrial goods reduces relative demand for agricultural goods. As a reaction, the number of agricultural workers decreases instantaneously such that demand equals supply of agricultural products again. This leads to a change of the production structure toward industrial goods. When leaving their farms, the former farmers can seek employment in the industrial sector of the periphery or the core region. I assume that they first settle in proportion to the existing distribution of industries between the regions. This keeps the previous ratio of core to periphery industrial employment constant.

In order to consider nonhomothetic demand, the previous utility function is transformed into a Stone–Geary function by introducing a subsistence level of agricultural products, A_s.

[43] $U = M^\phi (A - A_s)^{1-\phi}$, $0 < \phi < 1$.

ϕ is the marginal propensity of income to spend on industrial goods, M is again an aggregate of a larger number of products. $1 - \phi$ is the marginal propensity to spend on agricultural goods, after the subsistence level of agricultural goods is consumed. From this, the average share of income in the core and in the periphery spent on industrial and agricultural goods can be calculated and is expressed as ε and $1 - \varepsilon$:

[44] $\varepsilon_c = \phi(RGDPC_c - A_s)/RGDPC_c$ and

$1 - \varepsilon_c = 1 - \phi(RGDPC_c - A_s)/RGDPC_c$,

where $RGDPC$ is real per capita income. This type of utility function assures that a higher income shifts consumption from agricultural toward industrial goods. Real per capita income is defined as the total regional income divided by the price level and the population in a region:

[45] $RGDPC_c = \dfrac{Y_c}{T_c^\varepsilon (L_c + 0.5(1-\pi))}$,

where Y is total regional income, which is still determined as in equation [12].

Total regional income times average spending on industrial goods in a region gives total consumer spending on industrial goods (S):

[46] $S = \varepsilon_c Y_c + \varepsilon_p Y_p$.

I normalize total nominal income in both regions to one, i.e., $Y_{c+p} = 1$. Out of this, farmers earn a total income of $1 - \pi$, which equals the share of farmers in the labor force because farm wages are set to one. It follows that total income generated in the industrial sector equals π. I further reduce the analysis by assuming that, on average, workers earn a nominal wage of one, such that the share of income generated in the industrial sector (π) equals the share of the labor force that is working in the industrial sector.[45] Now, the share of labor that is working in the industrial sector can be easily determined. Total spending on industrial goods was determined in equation [46]. A share μ of total revenues is always spent on intermediate inputs. This implies that the wage sum of industrial workers in both regions is determined by:

[47] $S(1 - \mu) = w_c L_c + w_p L_p$.

Since the share of income generated in the industrial sector equals the share of labor working in the industrial sector, equation [47] displays the endogenous distribution of labor between the two sectors. If technological progress increases productivity and, hence, real incomes, the nonhomothetic utility function ensures that total spending on industrial goods increases. This induces instantaneously some farmers to work in the industrial sector, such that average wages in the industrial and agricultural sector remain the same. Thus, total spending on industrial goods determines employment in the industrial sector:

[48] $\pi = w_c L_c + w_p L_p$.

Solving the equation system simultaneously for both regions further determines price levels, number of firms, income, sales, and wages per region. Again, the relative wage indicates the relative strength of centripetal and centrifugal forces. Centripetal forces outweigh centrifugal forces if core wages are higher

---

45   This implies that, on average, farmers and industrial workers earn the same wage. This contrasts empirically observable urban-rural wage gaps, but reduces the analysis substantially. Above that, defining that industrial wages are always some multiple of rural wages would not change the qualitative results of the model. This simplification has the disadvantage that in one region wages in the industrial sector can be lower than in the agricultural sector. Again, restricting the parameters that this is not the case does not change the qualitative results but alters the simplicity of the algebra.

than peripheral wages. In the next section, I solve the model and determine under what conditions centripetal forces prevail. I focus on the effects of trade
costs, economic development, and the initial distribution of industries in order to
explain why the pattern of industry distribution varies across countries in the
course of economic development.

2.   Mechanics of the Model

Figure 13 shows the effects of economic development on the real wage ratio.[46]
The ratio shows a U-shaped pattern, which is drawn for various initial industry
distributions, indicated by v, the percentage of industries in the core. $v - 1$ implies complete concentration, while $v = 0.5$ implies equal distribution of industries. Productivity increases over time, so that higher values of t in Figure 13 indicate a higher level of economic development and a higher real per capita GDP.
At a low level of economic development, e.g., $t = 0$, relative wages are more or
less the same for all industry distributions because of low linkage effects and
low congestion effects. With increasing t, a higher income elasticity of industrial
goods than that of agricultural goods induces a shift from agricultural production

Figure 13 — Alternative Industry Distributions and Economic Development

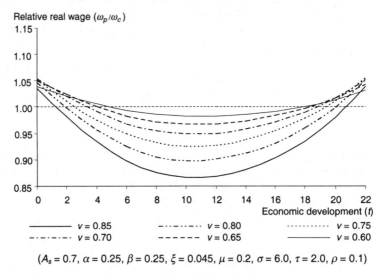

$(A_s = 0.7, \alpha = 0.25, \beta = 0.25, \xi = 0.045, \mu = 0.2, \sigma = 6.0, \tau = 2.0, \rho = 0.1)$

---

[46]   See also Appendix II for an analytical exploration of the model.

toward industrial production.[47] This reduces the relative importance of being close to the demand of farmers and increases the relative importance of forward and backward linkages. Since linkage effects are stronger in the core, Figure 13 shows that core firms mainly benefit from the structural change such that the relative wage of the periphery declines.[48]

However, after a certain point of development, the relative wage of the periphery rises again, indicating stronger centrifugal forces. Economic development increases the overall amount of economic activity and, consequently, also the congestion effects. This leads to higher costs of production. With congestion being more prone in the core than in the periphery, congestion effects increase production costs relatively more in the core than in the periphery. The relative strength of centrifugal forces rises, and raises the relative wage of the periphery. Thus, for high levels of economic development, the advantages of stronger linkage effects in the core are increasingly counterbalanced by congestion effects such that wage ratios converge again. This leads to a U-shape relationship between the relative wage of the periphery and economic development. Thus, on balance, centrifugal forces are highest for low and high levels of economic development and lowest for intermediate levels.

I have not modeled the dynamics of worker migration explicitly, because not enough is known about the adjustment and migration process. Especially, the time that the migration process takes in comparison to the process of technological and, hence, structural change and to the reduction of trade costs is unknown. However, I can conclude that concentration results from an adjustment process whenever centripetal forces are higher than centrifugal forces. This means that the U-curve of peripheral to core wages implies the inverted U-curve of industrial concentration and economic development.

The curve is more pronounced for more unequal initial industry distributions, indicated by a higher v. The reason is that from low to intermediate development stages, linkage and home market effects are the dominant determinants of industry location, and at high development stages, congestion effects matter more. Therefore, a region first benefits the more, the larger it is, and later it suffers from higher congestion effects, the larger it is.

---

[47] For instance, for the parameter values used in the calculations of Figure 13, the agricultural share in GDP declines from 69.7 percent at $t = 0$, to 47.1 percent at $t = 10$, to 35.5 percent at $t = 22$.

[48] Since industrial production takes place in cities, higher levels of development mean higher levels of urbanization. However, urbanization does not imply concentration. In the model economy, the number of possible sites is reduced to two, the core and the periphery. If urbanization increases the relative number of firms in the core, it also increases concentration. If urbanization increases the relative number of firms in the periphery, it decreases concentration. In the first case, urbanization strengthens centripetal forces, in the second case it strengthens centrifugal forces.

Without structural change, technological progress would benefit the periphery more strongly, because congestion effects constitute a bigger problem in the core. In this case, the regions would converge in their economic structure. Without congestion effects, cumulative causation would suggest that the regions diverge until complete concentration of all industries is realized in the core. Consequently, the shift of the relative importance of linkage and congestion effects in the course of economic development prevents the lock-in of the pattern of industry distribution and accounts for the diversity and changing patterns of industry concentration.

The results do not depend on the neglect of income when determining the effects of congestion, as other simulations have shown. Including the effect that higher real income increases the sensitivity toward congestion and pollution and, thereby, leads to higher production costs, as argued in Section B.I.1, does not change the qualitative results presented in this section.

To summarize, centrifugal forces dominate during low and high levels of economic development while centripetal forces dominate during the intermediate level of economic development, as indicated by the real wage ratio. Thus, the model suggests a U-shaped relationship between economic development and the relative strength of centrifugal and centripetal forces, which means that industrial concentration follows the shape of an inverted U in the course of economic development.

3.   Simultaneous Changes of Parameters

Considering that trade costs may fall in the course of economic development, it is important to check whether the effects of a change in the parameters cancel each other out or reinforce each other. Simultaneous changes of the two variables are shown in the surface plot of Figure 14. Starting at the lower right corner of Figure 14, declining trade costs (τ) and increasing economic development (t) first lower the relative wage of the periphery, i.e., the relative wage of the core rises. However, high levels of economic development and low levels of trade costs again lead to a higher relative wage of the periphery.

The figure shows that the two variables reinforce each other such that simultaneous changes also lead to a U-curve pattern where centripetal forces are highest for intermediate values of trade costs and economic development, such that an inverted U-curve between economic development and economic concentration would result from an adjustment process.

Figure 14 — Simultaneous Variations of Trade Costs (τ) and Economic Development (t)

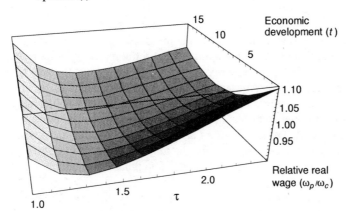

$(A_s = 0.7, \alpha = 0.25, \beta = 0.25, \xi = 0.025, \mu = 0.2, \phi = 0.7, \sigma = 6.5, v = 0.65, \rho = 0.1)$

4.   Initial Conditions and the Distribution of Industries

The model so far predicts that industrial concentration varies with the level of economic development. However, when looking at current and previous primacy ratios, there seem to be more differences than different GDP levels can explain. Especially, it seems that industry patterns are more equally distributed in most European countries than in most developing countries (DCs) at comparable income levels.

I propose that the pattern of industry concentration is systematically different in European countries than in DCs because the country groups have industrialized at different times and with different initial population distributions. The combination of higher trade costs and a more equal distribution of the population at the beginning of the industrialization in the last century favored a more balanced pattern of industry distribution in Europe.

Before the industrial revolution in Europe in the 19th century, the urban population was relatively equally dispersed (Bairoch et al. 1988). Some industrial or manufacturing production had been established at several places already. Locally dispersed resources ensured that production was dispersed as well. One could find, for instance, high-skilled glass production in Bavaria, Bohemia, and Lorraine, which were surely not the major agglomerations of their countries. Other production was equally dispersed according to natural deposits or traditional skill advantages. Craftsmanship developed slowly in accordance with local demand and later transformed into manufacturing and industrial production.

Skilled labor was not only found in the capital, but was distributed according to traditional manufacturing production. This means that initial conditions at the outset of the industrial revolution did not extremely favor any particular region in terms of human capital. Home market effects might have favored the major agglomerations of that time. During the industrialization of Europe, productivity rose, trade costs fell, and some industry concentration indeed took place. But this concentration did not necessarily take place in the primate cities. None of the European capitals like Amsterdam, Brussels, Berlin, or Paris became a major center of modern industry (Mokyr 1995).[49] Instead, heavy industrial production was attracted to the Ruhr area, Manchester, and Silesia, where in the first place the abundance of natural resources attracted the location of industries. Less developed transport technologies made the transport of natural resources to the existing population centers too costly to develop industrial production concentrated in these places.

The conditions in today's DCs are considerably different. First, industrialization has taken place later, during a time when transport technologies have been more advanced and thus trade costs have been lower, which has favored concentrated production. Second, the initial distribution of production was less dispersed.[50] Most of the DCs are former colonies. For administrative and safety reasons, the colonial powers concentrated most economic activities in one city, from which also trade with the home country was conducted. In these countries, skill levels and formal education were very unequally distributed, too. Colonization led to a dual economy with an administrative, relatively highly skilled productive center in an otherwise sometimes feudal economy. Relevant technologies of production were adopted from the colonial powers. Skilled immigrants and colonial administrators were concentrated in the capital. This prevented the spread of their knowledge and the development of an own functional system of cities. The native and rural population was poorly skilled compared to the immigrants. This means that human capital was concentrated where immigrants arrived. This was almost always the major harbor like Buenos Aires or Rio de Janeiro. Thus, colonization led to high disparities between the capital and the hinterland in terms of human capital and income levels. Later, this has been strengthened by import substitution policies. This also meant that the demand of the peripheral population did not constitute an important centrifugal force compared to the large home market effects in the capital and the importance of the transport links to the colonial powers.

---

[49] See also Pollard (1981) for an extensive description of the European industrial revolution. Williamson (1995) provides an overview of some stylized facts and alternative explanations on the relationship of industrialization and urbanization in developed and developing countries.

[50] See Bairoch (1988: 436–440) and United Nations (1995a).

Figure 15 — Simultaneous Variations of Trade Costs (τ) and the Initial Distribution of Industries (υ)

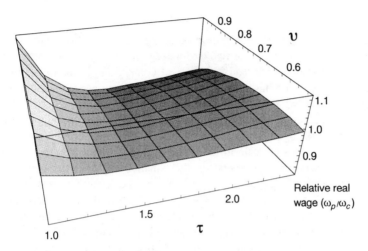

$(A_s = 0.7, \alpha = 0.25, \beta = 0.25, \xi = 0.045, \mu = 0.2, \sigma = 6.0, t = 16, \rho = 0.1)$

In conclusion, one can say that the conditions at the outset of the European industrialization were associated with higher trade costs and a more equal population distribution than in today's DCs. To illustrate the effects of these different conditions, I solve the model for simultaneous variations of trade costs and the initial distribution of industries. The simulations are reported in the surface plot of Figure 15, where υ indicates the percentage of industries that initially reside in the core, and τ indicates trade costs.

The lower right corner of Figure 15 indicates high trade costs and relatively equal distribution of industries. Moving from this corner toward the upper center indicates conditions of developing countries at the beginning of their industrialization. As the figure suggests, the European conditions favor much stronger centrifugal forces to become effective than the DCs' conditions. Thus, they triggered the development of a more balanced distribution of industries in European countries than in developing countries.

V.   Deriving Testable Hypotheses from the Theoretical Model

In this chapter, I presented a prototype economic geography model to explain industrial location patterns for two trading regions. The model considers internal economies of scale which lead to imperfect competition in the industrial sector. Imperfect competition has the implication that goods prices are location-specific. Together with forward and backward linkages in the industrial sector, this leads to external economies of scale. The demand of a dispersed immobile part of the population works against this centripetal force. The trade-off between the realization of economies of scale in the larger region and the need to pay for trade costs when serving consumers in the smaller region determines whether centripetal or centrifugal forces prevail. As in other economic geography models, centrifugal forces prevail for the case of high trade costs, and centripetal forces prevail for the cases of intermediate and low trade costs. This means that for high trade costs, a cumulative process leads to an equal distribution of industries. For low trade costs, complete concentration in the initially larger region results.

As complete concentration of industries can rarely be observed and often center-subcenter patterns of industry distribution appear quite stable, I included congestion effects in the prototype economic geography model, as first formalized by Brakman et al. (1996). This leads to a greater diversity of possible spatial structures that the model can explain. As shown in the introduction, not all countries converge to the same center-subcenter structure which then remains fixed over time. Therefore, in a second step, the effects of economic development are included in the model. Initially, economic development strengthens centripetal forces by an increase of demand for industrial products. This strengthens the advantages of being in the larger region. In later development stages, higher levels of congestion balance the distribution of industries again.

The economic geography approaches can be empirically tested in various ways. I concentrate on three topics which I consider most important at this stage of the life cycle of the models. The first two topics concern the empirical relevance of two important assumptions on which economic geography models rely. These are that EOS and trade costs are important and sizable phenomena. Unfortunately, there is not much consensus among economists that EOS matter, and the current debate on the effects of the so-called globalization suggests that also trade costs cease to matter empirically. Therefore, I will assess the empirical relevance of EOS and trade costs. Only if both turn out to be empirically important phenomena, it makes sense to further analyze the third topic which is testing the predictions of the economic geography models concerning the spatial distribution of economic activities.

The main point of the prototype model is that, depending on their level, trade costs can enhance spatial concentration or spatial dispersion. The main point of the augmented model is the inclusion of congestion effects in the prototype model. The hypothesis that can be derived from this model is that densely populated and industrialized countries should be spatially less concentrated. The main point of the development model is that spatial concentration and economic development have the relationship of an inverted U-curve. The testable hypothesis is that spatial concentration depends positively on per capita GDP and negatively on its squared value. Furthermore, the model suggests that also historic developments can have long-run impacts on the spatial pattern of economic activities. These hypotheses will be tested in the third section of Chapter C.

C. Economic Geography: Empirics

The theoretical models rest upon the interplay between EOS and trade costs. In the larger region, EOS can be realized to a larger extent. This comes with the disadvantage that trade costs have to be paid for the shipment of goods to the smaller region. The model has shown that high EOS and low trade costs favor spatial concentration, and low EOS and high trade costs favor spatial dispersion. If both EOS and trade costs are of small magnitude or nonexistent, then congestion effects outweigh home market effects. This does not necessarily mean that the theoretical reasoning of economic geography models is wrong, it just means that it is empirically irrelevant, because the endogenous spatial forces that the models describe are negligible. As a consequence, the spatial distribution of industries and the international division of labor have to be explained by traditional models, with differences in technologies and factor endowments, and with technological rather than pecuniary externalities.

Hence, the assumption that EOS and trade costs are of sizable magnitude is vital for the relevance of the economic geography approaches. Only if both matter, then the spatial distribution of production and trade may be explainable by the models of Chapter B. Unfortunately, there is no consensus among economists whether EOS matter or not. Despite their important impact on economic theory, empirical evidence on EOS remains elusive and stays behind the theoretical contributions to this topic. Although many empirical studies exist, so far no clear conclusion has emerged from the literature. Part of the reason for the lack of consensus is that the different levels of aggregation and the different approaches to estimate EOS are not clearly distinguished in the literature. In the first section of this chapter, I try to give an overall picture of the empirical relevance of EOS. This cannot be done by a single specific estimation but only by a review of the vast amount of approaches and studies of EOS. Therefore, I survey the empirical literature on EOS and assess their empirical relevance instead of estimating one specific form of EOS for a specific industry, region, or year. This shall show whether the departure from the assumption of constant returns to scale, which is necessary for economic geography models, is justified or not.

A similar ambiguity as with EOS exists for the empirical relevance of trade costs. Despite their important theoretical impact, their nature and magnitude are not well understood. The current debate on the effects of the so-called globalization even suggests that trade costs are increasingly negligible for trade flows. Therefore, in the second section of this chapter, I proceed by assessing the relevance of trade costs in two parts. In a first part, I give an overview over several types of trade costs and their magnitude. In a second part, I test the hypothesis that declining transport costs and tighter economic integration have made distance less important in the past decades. I do so by estimating the effects of distance on international trade flows between 45 countries in a gravity model for the years 1967–1995.

After having established that both EOS and trade costs matter empirically, I can conclude that the economic geography approaches provide an adequate framework for analyzing spatial patterns of production and trade. Still, this does not imply that the predictions and implications of economic geography models in general, and specifically my development model, are empirically valid. Therefore, I proceed by estimating the specific features of my economic geography model in the last section of this chapter. I test the economic geography model by applying it to a question that has long been analyzed in regional and urban economics, i.e., the explanation of the degree of spatial concentration within countries. I test whether spatial concentration is influenced by trade costs, population density, GDP per capita, and initial conditions. Thereby, the main hypothesis is that spatial concentration and economic development have the relationship of an inverted U-curve.

I.   The Empirical Relevance of Economies of Scale

1.   A Framework for the Analysis

In order to come to an overall assessment of the empirical relevance of EOS, I have already mentioned that it is crucial to distinguish the different levels on which EOS can occur. I distinguish internal and external, and static and dynamic EOS. Internal EOS (InEOS) arise on the level of the single firm. External EOS (ExEOS) arise on the level of the industry or the region. Static EOS raise productivity levels. Dynamic EOS raise productivity growth rates. Internal EOS lead to imperfect competition. External EOS lead to agglomeration economies. Hence, both are crucial elements of economic geography models. Making a difference between the different types of EOS is important, since their origin and economic effects are different.[51]

---

[51]   Some authors use the terms internal and external economies of scale differently. The crucial difference is the level of aggregation at which the dividing line is drawn. If the industry is the main object of study, then internal EOS arise on the industry level and external EOS arise on the regional level. In this survey, I distinguish EOS on the firm level, the industry level, and the regional level. I use the term internal EOS with reference to the single plant or firm only. This has the advantage that internal refers

Static InEOS reduce the unit costs of the plant or firm with an increase of its own current output at that point in time. InEOS prevail if the elasticity of costs with respect to firm output is less than one. This means that unit costs fall with an increase in output at any point in time because of decreasing marginal costs or the existence of fixed costs in production. InEOS can have several sources. An important source are indivisibilities or the spreading of fixed costs over a larger scale of output. Additional sources may be laws of nature or of technical-physical relationships (Berndt 1991: 61), economies of increased dimensions, and economies of specialization. With a higher output, workers can specialize more narrowly on a special task that they may perform better than if they devoted only a fraction of their working time to that task.[52]

Dynamic InEOS reduce the unit costs of the firm with an increase in its cumulative output. They are also called learning effects. An increase in firm output may lead to higher productivity through learning such that unit costs decrease over production time. Additionally, the spreading of certain costs like costs for patents, for product development, and for capital equipment and plant construction decrease unit costs over time. They are independent of the scale of production but necessary for any productive activity. Further sources are improvements in organizational structures, capacity of workers to work more productively, and technological improvements. These improvements may be different in different stages of production. Firms in new industries are more likely to exhibit larger learning effects than in mature industries.

To sum up, static InEOS lead to a downward movement along the average cost curve if current output increases at a given point in time. Dynamic InEOS lead to a downward shift of the average cost curve if cumulative output increases.

External EOS (ExEOS), also called positive external effects, externalities, or agglomeration economies, mean that firms benefit from being close to other firms because of backward and forward linkages in the production of goods, labor market pooling, sharing of common assets like infrastructure, and knowledge- or technological spillovers. Static ExEOS result in a higher productivity level, whereas dynamic ExEOS result in a higher productivity growth rate.

---

to those EOS that can be influenced by the action of a single economic agent. External EOS then refers to those EOS that cannot be influenced by a single economic agent. They arise on the industry level or regional level, which are aggregates of economic agents that usually do not form a unit of economic decision making.

[52] See Scherer et al. (1975: Chap. 4) for an overview and further discussion of the sources of InEOS, its limits, and its offsetting forces. Scherer et al. (1975) and Scherer and Ross (1990) provide numerous references on early theoretical and empirical work. Jorgenson (1986) discusses econometric issues concerning the modeling of producer behavior under increasing returns to scale.

Static ExEOS prevail if the elasticity of unit costs of a firm with respect to industry or regional output is less than one. They reduce unit costs of a firm through an increase in the output of other firms. The increase may take place on the level of the industry or the region, depending on the origin of the external effects. If the origin of the externalities lies within the firm's own industry, they are called localization externalities (LocEOS). Then, unit costs decrease with the output of all firms of the industry. Localization advantages are, for instance, labor market pooling, asset sharing, and the availability of more specialized intermediate input suppliers. If the origin of the externalities lies within the region or the city where the firm is located, they are called urbanization externalities (UrbEOS). Then, unit costs decrease with the output of all firms in the region. An urbanization advantage is, for instance, the proximity to consumers, which reduces transport and marketing costs.

Dynamic ExEOS increase growth rates of an industry. They arise because geographic concentration of firms leads to knowledge and technology spillovers between firms. A distinction has been made to stress differences in the nature of the externalities. Following the influential study of Glaeser et al. (1992), dynamic ExEOS are called Marshall–Arrow–Romer externalities (MAREOS) if they are of an intraindustry nature. They are called Jacobs externalities (JaEOS) if they are of an interindustry nature. That is, dynamic MAREOS correspond to static LocEOS, and dynamic JaEOS correspond to static UrbEOS. Glaeser et al. (1992) argue in favor of this distinction that Jacobs (1969, 1984) suggests the most significant spillovers to come from outside the own industry, even if they are rarer, while Marshall (1920), Arrow (1962), and Romer (1986) are supposed to assume that most learning and knowledge spillovers take place within individual industries. This distinction seems somewhat artificial and overstylized, since, for instance, Arrow considers only one industrial sector, where inter- and intraindustry spillovers cannot be distinguished. Nevertheless, in order to comply with the literature, I also adopt the terms MAREOS and JaEOS. Figure 16 summarizes the definitions.[53] The respective estimation equations for each of the different types of EOS are derived in the Appendix III in a production and cost function framework. The following presentation of the empirical literature is structured according to the disaggregation of Figure 16.[54]

---

[53] The distinction between localization and urbanization economies goes back to Isard (1956: 182–188); the one between internal and external EOS goes back to Marshall (1920). The literature often does not clearly distinguish between static and dynamic ExEOS. Therefore, one often finds that localization and MAREOS are used synonymously, because both are intraindustry externalities. Similarly, often urbanization and JaEOS are used synonymously, because both are interindustry externalities.

[54] In this survey, two concepts of increasing returns are not considered. First, I leave out the distinction between EOS on the plant level and on the firm level, that is the

Figure 16 — Classification of Economies of Scale

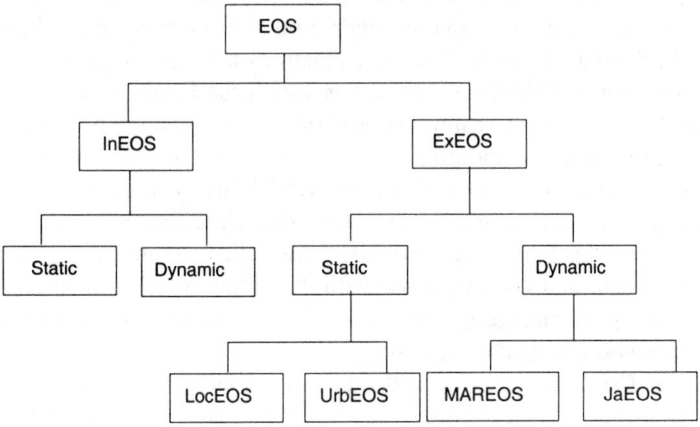

2.   Internal Economies of Scale

a.   Estimating Static Internal Economies of Scale

In order to measure static InEOS accurately, unit costs should be measured at different levels of output within a firm at a point in time. Of course, the length of the production run cannot be extended or reduced for experimental purposes. Thus, the estimation of static InEOS faces severe difficulties. To avoid those difficulties, auxiliary measures are often taken instead of econometric estimates as an assessment of the importance of InEOS. Strong InEOS favor large firms, oligopolistic market structures, and the concentration of production. Hence, the following four indicators are often used as an indirect measure of the strength of EOS in an industry: The *Price-Cost Margin,* also called the *Lerner Index,* is calculated as price minus marginal costs divided by average costs. It indicates the degree of market power of a firm within an industry. The *N-Firm Concentration Ratio* shows the proportion of total sales in the industry accounted for by the *N*-largest firms. The *Herfindahl-Hirschman Index* is the sum of the squared market shares of all firms in the industry and increases with higher concentration of production. The *Minimum Efficient Plant Size* (MES) is the size of the firm at

---

distinction between economies of *scale* and economies of *scope*. Instead, I assume a broader product definition such that each firm produces one product type only, which allows me to focus on InEOS rather than economies of scope and to set equal plant and firm level EOS. Second, I leave out network externalities, that are EOS on the demand side.

which the long-run average cost curve starts being flat such that a doubling of output leads to an insignificant reduction of unit costs, say by less than 5 percent. The MES is a measure of EOS, because high MES points to a reduction of unit costs over a large range of output.

Comparability of firm-level EOS is complicated if firms operate with a different scale of production at which the degree of EOS is estimated, because the degree of EOS varies with the level of output at which they are measured. In the presence of fixed costs, the average cost curve is downward-sloping even for constant marginal costs, because average fixed costs decline. Then, the reduction of unit costs from increasing output by a given absolute level is highest at low levels of output. If so, scale economies may be more relevant for small firms and may already be more exploited by large firms. Therefore, Bain (1956) suggested to measure the degree of InEOS at a fixed point of the long-run average cost curve. This could be 1/3 or 1/2 of the MES. The degree of InEOS is then measured by the increase of unit costs from the MES to 1/3 or 1/2 of MES.

The three approaches most commonly used to assess and estimate direct or indirect measures of static InEOS are the survivor technique, econometric estimates of profit and cost functions, and engineering estimates. In this section, I focus mainly on econometric and engineering estimates, since these approaches are able to yield exact estimates about the size of InEOS. In contrast, the survivor technique is often used as a first measure to assess the size structure in an industry before more rigorous econometric approaches are applied. The survivor technique has been suggested by Stigler (1958). He argues that instead of estimating potential costs at different levels of output, it would be more appropriate to check whether firms at different sizes are able to survive. The optimal firm level could then be seen from the growth rates of firms at different size groups. He suggests: "Classify the firms in an industry by size and calculate the share of industry output coming from each class over time. If the share of a given class falls it is relatively inefficient and in general is more inefficient the more rapidly the share falls" (Stigler 1958: 54). If a class of firms is able to survive, it will have at least MES. The survivor technique has the advantage that its costs are much lower than that of other approaches. This is true for data collecting as well as data processing. The problem that Stigler himself found is that a large range of firm sizes passes the survivor test for various other reasons than only low InEOS.[55]

---

[55] Stigler applies the test to 48 3-digit US industries and calculates optimum firm sizes for each of them. He finds that the optimum size has a fairly wide range. This lets him conclude that the average cost curves for firms are horizontal over a long range of firm sizes. Saving (1961) finds that over half of US industries, for which he has made survivor tests for 1947–1954, have a maximum MES of 1 percent of the industry size, which also indicates an early flattening out of the average cost curve. Other

Econometric Estimates

One part of the econometric literature on InEOS relies on Hall (1988, 1990). Hall observes that prices differ substantially from marginal costs in US industries, and that the Solow residual fails to be uncorrelated with product demand and factor price movements. He discusses several possible explanations of the failure of this invariance property. Hall concludes that the most likely explanations are monopolistic competition and increasing returns, both of which contradict the crucial assumptions of Solow's approach to measure productivity growth. He develops a method to derive an index of returns to scale and estimates of markups over marginal costs. Using value-added data for US manufacturing, he estimates markups for 26 2-digit industries and finds returns to scale to exceed 1.5 in all of them but services.[56] His approach has been adopted and further developed by Caballero and Lyons (1989, 1992), Caballero et al. (1990), and Bartelsman et al. (1994).

Caballero and Lyons include a measure for aggregate manufacturing in Hall's approach. This enables them to distinguish between internal and external EOS. In their studies, internal EOS refer to productivity increases due to industry-wide output expansion, thus capturing something in between InEOS and LocEOS in my classification. They find no increasing internal returns but a positive correlation between productivity in a specific industry and overall industrial activity.

---

applications of the survivor technique can be found in Weiss (1964), Shepherd (1967), Rees (1973), and Rogers (1993). Hibdon and Mueller (1990) show that using annual data over the period 1947–1984 changes Stigler's results in the petroleum refining industry and leads to a declining long-run cost curve. Eisen (1994) studies the optimal firm size in the life insurance business. He finds that the optimal firm size is stretched over a fairly large range, which contradicts the hypothesis that scale economies determine firm size in the insurance business. He notes that regional markets, specialization of small firms on specific products, and market niches may explain why firms of different sizes are able to survive. The survivor test is criticized because it cannot control for other influences than size by including further explanatory variables like heterogeneity of inputs or the quality of the management. Similar to the specialization of production, optimal firm size is also an increasing function of the size of the market, reflecting trade costs rather than scale efficiency (Berry 1992). Also, the process of firm shrinkage and growth is a very gradual one. As firms generally start out small and then grow, the size structure in an industry also reflects its historical life pattern, and not only its possibility to survive. It may also be that the optimal technology varies with other characteristics of a firm, and optimal size is a function of technology. If also firm size varies in the product cycle, there might be firms with non-frontier technologies that should not change their size until the existing technology has been depreciated, which might bias firm size classes further. See MacPhee and Peterson (1990) for a comparison of the results of engineering, econometric and survivor approaches for specific US industries over the years 1958 to 1982.

[56] See Domowitz et al. (1988) and Shapiro (1987) who also report strong market power in numerous US industries and significant departures of perfect competition.

They conclude that external EOS rather than internal EOS are the most important reason for the failure of the invariance of the Solow residual. The use of value-added data in these studies has been criticized by Basu and Fernald (1997). They show that with imperfect competition, value-added data biases the estimates upward, so that one finds large apparent externalities even if they do not exist. Instead, output data should be taken. Using gross output data for 21 2-digit US manufacturing industries, they find little or no significant effects of an increase of output in one manufacturing sector on the productivity of other sectors.[57] Hall's approach has been further developed by Röger (1995) who controls for the possible presence of imperfect competition. By considering positive markups over marginal costs, he is able to show that over 90 percent of the difference between primal and dual productivity measures can be explained by imperfect competition. As a by-product, he gets markup estimates for US manufacturing industries. His estimates are considerably lower than Hall's and lie between 15 percent in apparel and 214 percent in the electric, gas, and sanitary services industry.

Oliveira–Martins et al. (1996) further extend Röger's method by including intermediate inputs. This makes it possible to estimate markups by using output instead of value-added data. This removes the upward bias of the estimation with value-added data (Basu and Fernald 1997). Oliveira–Martins et al. (1996) use the OECD Stan-database to estimate markups for 19 OECD countries and 36 manufacturing sectors at the 3–4-digit level. Figure 17 summarizes their results. It can be seen that markups vary considerably between industries and countries. Highest markups were estimated for tobacco products, drugs and medicines, and office and computing machinery, while lowest markups were estimated for footwear, wearing apparel, and motor vehicles. I will use these estimates in Chapter C.II.2.c to analyze the interplay of the sectoral market structure and trade costs in explaining sectoral trade flows.

Other econometric methods of estimating InEOS are the comparison of costs or profits of firms in an industry at different scales of output on the basis of cross-section, time-series, or panel data. For these studies, no common methodo-

---

[57] However, Oulton (1996) confirms the results of Caballero and Lyons by the use of gross output data for the United Kingdom. He finds externalities of an expansion of aggregate manufacturing output, but no externalities of sectoral output. On the industry level, returns to scale appear to be constant.

Burnside et al. (1995) and Burnside (1996) argue that the evidence for increasing returns based on Hall's approach is not convincing because they do not control for the cyclical variation in the utilization of capital and impose unjustified cross-industry equality restrictions on the parameters. Burnside's most robust evidence suggests that the typical US manufacturing industry displays constant returns with no external effects. However, he acknowledges that there is significant heterogeneity across industries.

Figure 17 — Estimated Sectoral Markups for 14 OECD Countries

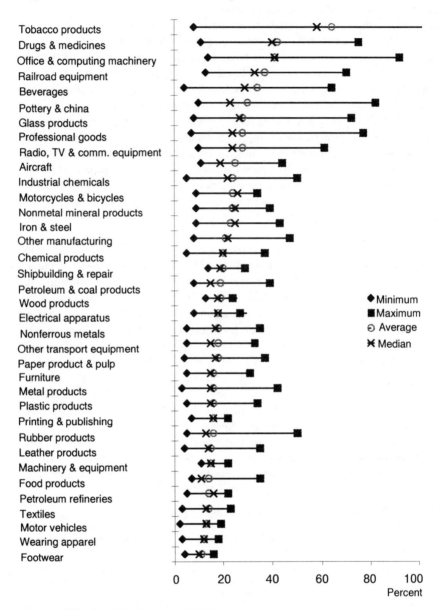

Source: Oliveira–Martins et al. (1996).

logical framework can be presented. They explore InEOS in several single industries. Probably the best-studied industrial sector is the electric power generation, where most studies find considerable InEOS. These, however, may change over time. For instance, Christensen and Green (1976) analyze InEOS with cross-section data for US electric power firms. While significant unrealized scale economies could be found in 1955, most firms were operating at the flat part of the average cost curve in 1970.[58]

Griliches and Ringstad (1971) and Ringstad (1978) analyze manufacturing industries in Norway. From the data on more than 5000 firms, they find evidence for small economies of scale in the range of 4 percent that are not very sensitive to the production function used and show little differences across industries. The authors point out that the estimates may be uncertain, i.e., they may be either too low or too large. Baldwin and Gorecki (1986) estimate cost and production functions for Canadian industries on the 4-digit level. For 1979, they find returns to scale to average approximately 10 percent for 107 manufacturing industries. Highest InEOS are found in tobacco, nonmetallic mineral goods, and food and beverages, whereas low InEOS are found in clothing manufacturing, knitting, leather, and textiles.

Panel data analyses are used by Westbrook and Tybout (1993) and Tybout and Westbrook (1992) to analyze scale effects in Chilean and Mexican manufacturing firms in different 3-digit industries. Westbrook and Tybout (1993) find returns to scale to vary between 0.8 and 1.2. However, the coefficients are not statistically different from 1, i.e., they are constant returns to scale. These estimates abstract from fixed costs, which may be a strong source of InEOS. Tybout and Westbrook (1992) find scale effects of more than 2 percent in only 3 of 20 industries. They use several estimators, notably OLS, between estimators, within estimators, j^{th} difference estimators, each with and without instrumental vari-

---

58   There is a large number of further studies which cannot all be discussed in detail in this chapter. For instance, Owen (1983) estimates InEOS using price and cost data for the European car, truck, and consumer durables industries. He finds cost reductions due to an increase of output, but does not distinguish between static and dynamic InEOS. Little et al. (1987) analyze the relationship between firm size and factor productivity in five Indian industries. With the exception of machine tool manufacturing, no InEOS can be found, once technical efficiency is controlled for by the average experience of the labor force, the age of the capital stock, the experience of the entrepreneur, and the level of capacity utilization. Scherer (1980: 92) presents profit rates for small and large US firms for the 1960s and the 1970s. He finds evidence that larger firms have higher profit rates, but these estimates may be biased upward due to variations across size categories in the accounting conventions involving depreciation. Marcus (1969) finds no clear relationship between size and profitability in the United States. Some industries are characterized by positive, others by negative, and others by no relationship between size and profitability. Surveys of estimates in electric power industries are provided by Cowing and Smith (1978) and Jorgenson (1986: 1893–1897).

ables. The properties of these estimators are discussed at length in Westbrook and Tybout (1993) and are summarized in Table 2. The table suggests that instrumental variable estimators — including method-of-moments estimators — are the most appropriate estimators, because they consider sunk costs, and they are not biased by unobserved plant effects and measurement errors. Unfortunately, it is usually hard to find appropriate instruments.

Using census data to estimate the relationship of costs or profitability on the one side and the scale of output on the other side has several further drawbacks. The definition of most census trades includes the production of a broad range of goods for which InEOS and other characteristics like market size and growth may vary substantially. The estimates may also reflect influences of varying relative factor prices at different output levels. An omitted variable problem arises when trying to sort out cost savings associated with scale effects from those due to other possible sources. For example, lower costs and higher profits may also be caused by higher monopoly power of larger firms. Profits are often lower in smaller firms not because of lower efficiency but because owner-managers pay themselves higher salaries in order to avoid double taxation. Small firms do better in booms than large firms and less well in throughs, reflecting a less diversified product and consumer structure, and larger firms have more possibilities to smooth reported earnings in their accounts. For the empirical analysis, the main problem is how to measure a cost decrease. Actual observations also include the impact of other variables like product heterogeneity, differences of capital vintages between firms within an industry, and the quality and prices of the factors of production. Cost data may understate InEOS, because competitive pressure eliminates a higher share of actual or latent smaller firms than larger ones. Since only the most efficient small firms are able to survive, the

Table 2 —   Sources of Biases for the Estimators

Estimator	Capture sunk costs	Biased due to unobserved plant effects	Biased due to measurement errors
OLS	yes	yes	yes
Between	yes	yes	yes, but attenuated
Within	no	no	yes, possibly exacerbated
j^{th} difference	no	no	yes, possibly exacerbated
Instrumental variables, OLS	yes	no	no
Instrumental variables, between	yes	no	no
Instrumental variables, within	no	no	no
Instrumental variables, j^{th} diff.	no	no	no

Source: Tybout and Westbrook (1992: 14).

sample is biased, which leads to a weaker observed size-cost relationship than that implied in the technology.[59]

Summing up, various econometric studies have found positive economies of scale so far. However, there are several difficulties with econometric estimates, and returns to scale vary widely between industries. Estimates of markups seem to yield robust evidence for the departure from perfect competition and marginal cost pricing, which supports the hypothesis of the importance of InEOS.

Engineering Estimates

In order to circumvent the problems that arise with real data, the engineering approach takes hypothetical data for costs at different output levels in order to construct engineering cost functions. In this approach, estimates of cost levels at different scales of production made by managers, engineers, economists, and accountants are assembled. Scientific laws, experimental data, and process costs are taken together to estimate a relationship of unit costs and the scale of production. This gives a calculation of probable costs of enterprises of different sizes. The advantage of this approach is that it is able to focus on the specific production process where it can abstract from influences other than scale, such as relative prices and learning effects. The concentration on the technical aspects of an increase in output makes it more reliable in the sense that it is not biased by other influences.

The construction of engineering production functions goes back to Chenery (1949). Since then, several specific industry studies have been performed. These are surveyed in Wibe (1984) and further discussed in Smith (1986) and Wibe (1986). One of the first more comprehensive studies of InEOS using engineering data was Pratten (1971). He examines plant size EOS on the basis of firm data from 28 manufacturing industries in the United Kingdom and concludes that considerable EOS exist. These, however, vary substantially for different industries. The most comprehensive evidence on InEOS was collected again by Pratten (1988). He summarizes numerous studies, out of which the most important may be Pratten (1971), Scherer (1980), Müller and Owen (1985), Weiss (1976), and Connor et al. (1984). Since his estimates are still the most often cited, the main results of his study are presented in Tables 3–5. Table 3 shows branches of manufacturing industry ranked by their approximate size of InEOS, which are measured at 1/2 MES. Very high degrees of InEOS are found in motor vehicles, other means of transport, chemicals, machinery and instrument manufacturing, and paper and printing.

---

[59] See Berry (1993) for a thorough discussion of the complications when relating firm size and economic efficiency.

Emerson (1988) concludes in his report on the completion of the EC single market that InEOS are an important characteristic in the production of EU industrial goods, since over 50 percent of the EC 12's industrial production takes place in these branches. This is confirmed by Pratten's (1988) calculations of the percentage of MES of UK and EC output. From this percentage, the sustainable number of firms in an industry can be concluded. High percentages indicate high InEOS, independent of the elasticity of output to an increase in inputs at MES. Pratten (1988) shows that for several industries, MES are too high to support more than a few firms in the United Kingdom. 27 percent of EC output is produced in industries whose MES is above 5 percent of the whole EC market. Consequently, in the long run, these industries support at most 20 firms EC-wide.[60]

Table 3 —   Branches of Manufacturing Industry Ranked by Size of Economies of Scale

NACE Code	Branch	Cost gradient at half MES (percent)	Remarks
35	Motor vehicles	6–9	Very substantial EOS in production and in development costs.
36	Other means of transport	8–20	Variable EOS: small for cycles and shipbuilding (although economies are possible through series production level), very substantial in aircraft (development costs).
25	Chemical industry	2.5–15	Substantial EOS in production processes. In some segments of the industry (pharmaceutical products), R&D is an important source of EOS.
26	Man-made fibers	5–10	Substantial EOS in general.
22	Metals	>6	Substantial EOS in general for production processes. Also possible in production and series production.
33	Office machinery	3–6	Substantial EOS at product level.
32	Mechanical engineering	3–10	Limited EOS at firm level but substantial in production.
34	Electrical engineering	5–15	Substantial EOS at product level and for development costs.
37	Instrument engineering	5–15	Substantial EOS at product level, via development costs.
47	Paper, printing, and publishing	8–36	Substantial EOS in paper mills and, in particular, printing (books).

---

[60] In contrast to these findings is the study by Lyons (1980). He estimates MES of firms in 118 UK trades. He finds that for most trades, MES is below 250 employees, which indicates rather small InEOS.

Table 3 continued

NACE Code	Branch	Cost gradient at half MES (percent)	Remarks
24	Nonmetallic mineral products	>6	Substantial EOS in cement and flat glass production processes. In other branches, optimum plant size is small compared with the optimum size for the industry.
31	Metal articles	5–10 (castings)	EOS are lower at plant level but possible at production and series production level.
48	Rubber and plastics	3–6	Moderate EOS in tire manufacture. Small EOS in factories making rubber and molded plastic articles, but potential for EOS at product and series production level.
41–42	Drink and tobacco	1–6	Moderate EOS in breweries. Small EOS in cigarette factories. In marketing, EOS are considerable.
41–42	Food	3.5–21	Principal source of EOS is the individual plant. EOS at marketing and distribution level.
49	Other manufacturing	n.a.	Plant size is small in these branches. Possible EOS from specialization and the length of production runs.
43	Textile industry	10 (carpets)	EOS are more limited than in the other sectors, but possible EOS from specialization and the length of production runs.
46	Timber and wood	n.a.	No EOS for plants in these sectors. Possible EOS from specialization and the length of production runs.
45	Footwear and clothing	1 (footwear)	Small EOS at plant level but possible EOS from specialization and longer production runs.
44	Leather and leather goods	n.a.	Small EOS.

Source: Pratten (1988), cited from Emerson (1988: 129).

InEOS are lowest or nonexistent in the branches of leather and leather goods, footwear and clothing, timber and wood as well as the textile industry. Low InEOS prevail in food, drink and tobacco, and rubber and plastics. Table 3 also shows that the cost reductions at 1/2 MES vary substantially in different subsectors of the branches. Table 4 shows the distribution of extra costs in percent that arise from a firm size below 1/2 of MES. The table shows that InEOS are in the range of 2–15 percent for most of the 45 firms for which a cost gradient was available. Product groups on the 3-digit level of the NACE Code for which InEOS are superior or equal to 10 percent are shown in Table 5. The highest levels of InEOS can be realized in books, bricks, dyes, and aircraft.

Table 4 —   Supplementary Costs Borne for a Plant Size below 50 Percent of the
Minimum Efficient Size (MES)

Extra costs (percent)	Distribution of sample (percent)
0–2	4
2–5	36
5–10	29
10–15	24
15–20	2
20–25	2
25 and over	2

Source: Pratten (1988: 82).

These estimates are not a fixed technical relationship or a common law. MES
firm sizes change over time and are different in different countries. For example,
Sands (1961) finds increasing MES in the first half of the century. Schwalbach
(1988) shows that average firm size in Germany, Italy, and the United Kingdom
is considerably smaller than the MES, which leads to higher production costs of
up to 25 percent. As a result, the gains from completing the EC single market
have been found to depend on how far these EOS are realized. If production can
indeed be expanded to MES, productivity gains will be huge.

Table 5 —   Products for Which the Cost Slope below 50 Percent of the Minimum Efficient Size (MES) Is Superior or Equal to 10 Percent

NACE Code	Product	Cost gradient at 1/2 MES
473	Books	20–36
241	Bricks	25
251	Dyes	17–22
364	Aircraft	20
251	Titanium oxide	8–16
242	Cement	6–16
251	Synthetic rubber	15
342	Electric motors	15
471	Kraft paper	13
251	Petrochemicals	12
26	Nylon	12
311	Cylinder block castings	10
311	Small cast-iron castings	10
438	Carpets	10
328	Diesel engines	10

Source: Pratten (1988: 74).

The disadvantage of engineering estimates is the lack of familiarity of managers and engineers with what happens if firms operate at a different size than the one being used. Thus, they are subjective to a certain extent. It is also often difficult to get reliable and comparable information. Since the sources are interviews and questionnaires, the approach is associated with high costs both for the person seeking information and for the informant. It lacks the rigor of other approaches that use statistical and econometric methods. Additionally, engineering data tend to show greater cost reductions with size than do cost or profit data. Berry (1992) argues that engineers may hold constant the technology across size of potential firms, although lower-cost technologies may exist for lower or higher levels of output. This may bias cost estimates for output levels above the current output level of the firm.

b.   *Estimating Dynamic Internal Economies of Scale*

Empirical studies of dynamic InEOS or learning effects go back to Wright (1936). He finds that the productivity of aircraft production increases with firm cumulative output. The semiconductor industry is often cited as the prime industry for learning-by-doing effects. Irwin and Klenow (1994) use quarterly firm data for the period 1974–1992 to assess learning effects of seven semiconductor generations. They find that the fall in unit costs due to an increase in cumulative output is as high as 10–27 percent. Intergenerational spillovers are weak or nonexistent, indicating that a comparative advantage in the production of one semiconductor generation does not imply a strategic asset in the sense that it may lead to a long-lasting competitive advantage in future semiconductor generations. Additionally, Irwin and Klenow (1994) find that firms learn three times more from an increase in their own cumulative production than from an increase in other firms' cumulative production.

Learning curve effects have also been surveyed by Argote and Epple (1990) and Ghemawat (1985).[61] Ghemawat compiled 97 studies that analyze learning effects for 102 manufacturing products. A summary of these studies is given in Table 6. The average elasticity of unit costs with respect to cumulative output is 0.31, which translates into a slope of the learning curve of 0.81. Consequently, unit costs decline on average to 81 percent of their previous level if cumulative output doubles.

Learning effects vary according to different sectors. Table 7 shows sectors where the highest learning effects can be realized according to Emerson (1988: 138). These are electronic components and microcomputing. As it seems, learning effects are the stronger, the higher the share of labor, especially skilled labor,

---

[61] See also Berndt (1991: 66) for further references on the estimation and interpretation of learning curve effects.

Table 6 —   Learning Curve Elasticity Estimates for Manufacturing Products

Number of products	Learning curve elasticity ($-\alpha_c$)	Learning curve slope (d)
3	0.62–0.74	0.60–0.65
3	0.51–0.62	0.65–0.70
10	0.41–0.51	0.70–0.75
23	0.32–0.41	0.75–0.80
30	0.24–0.32	0.80–0.85
26	0.15–0.24	0.85–0.90
6	0.08–0.15	0.90–0.95
1	0.00–0.08	0.95–1.00
Average	0.31	0.81

Source: Ghemawat (1985: 146).

and the lower the share of machinery costs in manufacturing. Ghemawat (1985: 144) concludes that "manufacturing activities encounter steeper learning curves than raw materials purchasing, marketing sales, or distribution". This reflects that the most significant gains of cumulative production usually take place in the early stages of a product's life cycle.[62]

Table 7 —   Examples of Total Unit Cost Reduction Observed for Various Activities as a Result of Doubling Cumulative Production

Industry or service sector	Fall in unit costs as a result of cumulative production being doubled (percent)
Electric components	30
Microcomputing	30
Ball-bearings	27
Industrial plastics	25
Equipment maintenance	24
Life insurance	23
Aerospace	20
Electricity	20
Starters for motor vehicles	15
Oil refining	10

Source: Emerson (1988: 138).

---

[62] See also Emerson (1988: 137–140).

c. Internal Economies of Scale and the Economic Geography of Production and Trade

Despite many methodological reservations, the previous two sections have documented that the assumption of strictly constant returns on the firm level and perfect competition in economic geography models is not unfounded. The question remains whether the inclusion of EOS adds to the explanation of the spatial phenomena under study. Therefore, some papers test hypotheses concerning the impact of internal economies of scale in economic geography models or intraindustry trade models on which they rely. One hypothesis is that larger countries have a larger home market, so that they can exploit scale economies to a larger extent. This should give them a comparative advantage in the distribution of scale-intensive products. Torstensson (1998) tests this hypothesis with OECD data for 23 countries, product groups at the 4-digit level of ISIC, and different proxy variables to measure the degree of InEOS. He finds no clear evidence that countries with larger domestic markets are net exporters in industries that are characterized by InEOS. In contrast, Brülhart and Torstensson (1996) find employment in scale-intensive industries to be concentrated in the center of the European Union, supporting the importance of InEOS for the location of industries and trade patterns. This suggests that home market effects play a role.

In two other studies, Davis and Weinstein (1996, 1999) nest an economic geography model with InEOS into the neoclassical Heckscher–Ohlin framework in order to assess the relative impact of comparative advantages and increasing returns to scale on the production structure and on trade. In the earlier study, they use the framework for explaining the structure of OECD production. They find that 90 percent of the explainable trade specialization can be traced back to endowment differences, and at most 10 percent may be due to economic geography. In the second study, they analyze the regional production structure of nineteen Japanese industries. In eight out of these, they find economically significant evidence for sizable home market effects. These industries are transport equipment, iron and steel, electrical machinery, chemicals, precision instruments, nonferrous metals, textiles, and paper and pulp. Davis and Weinstein (1999) conclude that economic geography is very important for understanding the regional structure of production, while it may explain little of the international structure of production.

Another part of the literature tests the hypothesis that the volume of intraindustry trade rises with the degree of InEOS. Most empirical studies find no robust relationship between scale and intraindustry trade.[63] Leamer (1992) finds

---

[63] See Leamer and Levinsohn (1995) and Hummels and Levinsohn (1995) for an overview of the empirical literature on international trade theory. They report little evidence that scale economies provide an important determinant of trade. This may partly be due to the low robustness of possible determinants of intraindustry trade.

that constant returns to scale cannot generally be ruled out. Then, trade can also be explained by Armington preferences, where consumers simply distinguish between home and foreign consumer goods. However, Harrigan (1994) argues in a widely quoted paper that most empirical evaluations of intraindustry trade models are misleading because of incorrectly regressing Grubel and Lloyd indices on various proxies for scale economies. He argues that the Grubel and Lloyd index does not necessarily vary with the degree of EOS. Instead, he proposes a model to distinguish between an Armington-type explanation for intraindustry trade and increasing-returns-type explanations. Using the four different measures for InEOS discussed in the beginning of Section 2.1. and 1983 OECD data for 26 countries, Harrigan (1994: 327) finds some evidence that the volume of trade is higher in sectors with high InEOS. However, his results are also sensitive to the choice of the proxy of InEOS. Nevertheless, he concludes that "...product differentiation by location of production is an important cause for trade, and that international exploitation of scale economies may also contribute importantly to the volume of trade." Hence, it is fair to say that the empirical evidence is mixed with regard to the relevance of InEOS in explaining patterns of production and trade across countries. Further studies are clearly needed to identify the origin and extent of home market effects and the spatial level on which they may occur.

3.   External Economies of Scale

a.   *Estimating Static External Economies of Scale*

Static ExEOS explain the agglomeration of industries, i.e., why some of them cluster while others do not. Estimating static ExEOS can answer three questions. First, whether concentration of economic activities of certain industries and in certain areas is advantageous at all; second, whether the advantages result from the mere urbanization or from the localization of certain industries; and third, how much productivity increases due to the agglomeration of industries.

The first question tests whether agglomeration economies exist or not. Such papers are, for instance, Carlton (1983) and Wheeler and Mody (1992). In estimating investment and location decisions of US firms, they include a term approximating agglomeration economies. They find that industrial concentration is advantageous for the location of further firms.[64] More specific are two other pa-

---

Torstensson (1998) performs a sensitivity analysis of possible intraindustry trade determinants and finds that most variables are rather fragile and sensitive to different specifications and measurements.

[64]   Similar approaches have been adopted by Carlino (1979), Hay (1979), Moomaw (1981), and Shefer (1973), who also find evidence for agglomeration economies.

pers. Head et al. (1995) analyze investment decisions in the United States. They try to sort out endowment differences of different states in order to isolate spillover effects. They find that Japanese manufacturing investment is likely to be located near other Japanese firms of the same industry, and does not simply mimic the geographical pattern of US firms in their industry. They also find that the observed spillovers do not stop at state borders. Smith and Florida (1994) come to similar results, analyzing the location of Japanese affiliated manufacturing establishments in automotive-related industries. They find that these firms reveal strong preferences for locations with other Japanese automotive assemblers, holding constant several other determinants. From this, they conclude that backward and forward linkages are important sources of agglomeration economies.

The finding that there are agglomeration economies seems obvious for every one living in a city whose economic structure is not oriented toward the extraction and exploitation of natural endowments. Therefore, a second group of papers analyzes the nature of agglomeration economies, that is, the relative impact of urbanization and localization economies. This is important in order to assess whether specialized or diversified cities lead to the most efficient division of production. For instance, the former socialist countries apparently believed in localization economies and, therefore, created large monostructured regions. However, they did not consider that localization economies may peter out after some level of production, which led as well to an inefficient allocation of resources (Siebert 1994: 102).

One paper that estimates whether urbanization or localization economies prevail, is Henderson (1986). He analyzes cross-sectional data for the United States and Brazil to estimate the nature and extent of ExEOS. He finds that ExEOS are in general rather due to localization than to urbanization. The specialization of a city leads to localization externalities, which, however, peter out for larger city sizes. Since ExEOS peter out, one should expect small and medium size cities to be more specialized than larger cities. Nakamura (1985) goes further and analyzes the relative impact of localization and urbanization externalities for different industries. Localization economies are more important for "heavy industries", whereas urbanization economies are more important for "light industries".[65] Von Hagen and Hammond (1994) focus on the effects of localization economies. They argue that if localization externalities exist, "...the correlation of employment changes should be stronger among firms of the same local industry than among firms pertaining to different local industries..." (1994: 7). They find that this is indeed the case. Two commonly cited sources of localization ex-

---

Moomaw (1983), Segal (1976), and Sveikauskas (1975) estimate the impact of urban size on industrial productivity, which comes out to be positive up to a certain city size.

[65] Two further papers that assess the relative importance of urbanization and localization economies are Greytak and Blackley (1985) and Sveikauskas et al. (1988).

ternalities are asset sharing and labor market pooling effects. Von Hagen and Hammond (1994) find that the former dominates in more mature labor markets and the latter in regionally growing labor markets.

Agglomeration occurs because the factors of production can realize higher prices if they are spatially concentrated. Given the existence and nature of agglomeration economies, a third group of papers analyzes how much productivity or factor prices rise depending on agglomeration economies. The three measures used to proxy agglomeration economies are the density of economic activity, travel time to a regional center, and the distance to a regional center.

The most important recent paper on the relationship of productivity and the density of economic activity is the one by Ciccone and Hall (1996). They find evidence that spatial density leads to aggregate increasing returns for US states. According to their study, labor productivity rises by about 6 percent for a doubling of employment density. Thus, more than half of the variation of output per worker can be traced back to local ExEOS. Above that, they find that increasing returns to density describe productivity differences better than increasing returns to size. The paper by Kanemoto et al. (1996) follows the same line. They estimate aggregate Cobb–Douglas production functions for Japanese metropolitan areas in 1985 and different city size classes. Possible productivity increases due to a doubling in size are 25 percent for cities between 200,000 and 400,000 residents, 1 percent for cities below 200,000 residents, and 7 percent for cities with more than 400,000 residents.

Sveikauskas et al. (1985) estimate the effect of travel time to the center of São Paulo city on the productivity of newly built manufacturing firms in São Paulo State in eight different industries. They include skill levels, learning effects, and InEOS in a Cobb–Douglas production function. On average, a doubling of travel time is associated with a Hicks-neutral 15 percent decline in overall productivity. Hanson (1996) confirms these results with Mexican data on regional wages in the clothing industry. Distance to Mexico City, as measured by travel time, accounts for 41.4 percent of the variance in regional wages.

Several papers estimate the effect of distance to a regional center on productivity levels. Hansen (1990) uses the same framework as Sveikauskas et al. (1985) to estimate the effects of agglomeration economies on productivity and wages in São Paulo. He finds that Hicks-neutral productivity decreases by 0.11 percent per 1 percent increase in distance from the city center. He also finds a positive impact of InEOS, with size measured by workers per firm. Losses in firm productivity due to a larger distance from the center of São Paulo are almost totally matched by lower wages. On average, firm productivity declines by 8.9 percent, and wages decline by 8.7 percent, due to a doubling of distance from São Paulo City. Henderson (1994) sets up a model of industry location and estimates its determinants. He uses 1970 data of auto components and agricultural machinery for Brazil and the United States. A doubling of distance to a regional market center from the average of 290 km lowers profits by 6 percent. Profits per firm rise with industry scale but peak after a certain size. This is probably due to market size effects because the peak shifts out with larger urban size.

b. Estimating Dynamic External Economies of Scale

Empirical work on dynamic ExEOS broadly focuses on two questions. The first is whether local spillovers between firms in a region or in an industry can be identified, because these may lead to dynamic ExEOS. The second question is whether variables that are associated with such spillovers do account for different growth rates of industries or regions.

The most obvious form of spillovers may exist in R&D. Firms may not be able to internalize all the returns to their research such that social returns are higher than private returns to R&D. Jaffe (1986) finds evidence for local R&D spillovers in a sample of 432 US firms. The number of patents per R&D spending are higher for firms that locate in areas with above-average R&D spending. He finds that patents would increase by 20 percent if every single firm increased its R&D efforts by 10 percent. However, profits and market value of low-R&D firms would decrease with high-R&D neighbors. Jaffe (1989) studies the effects of university research spending on corporate patents. He finds evidence that geographical proximity increases the number of patents, after controlling for corporate R&D. Bernstein and Nadiri (1988) analyze the effects of inter- and intraindustry R&D spillovers in five US high-tech industries for 1958–1981. They find that spillovers result from a narrow range of industries and that there are significant differences in the size of the spillovers between industries. These findings are confirmed by an analysis of the social rates of return of R&D, which are found to be higher than the private rates of return.

Jaffe et al. (1993) find evidence for local knowledge spillovers by looking at US patent citations. They analyze whether patents are more likely to cite old patents originating in their own region than the ones originating in another region. Controlling for other reasons than technological spillovers, they find that this is the case. They also find that around 40 percent of a patents' citation come from outside their own technological environment, pointing to the importance of cross-fertilization between different research areas. Analyzing the biotechnological industry, Audretsch and Stephan (1996) find knowledge spillovers to be important, but unlikely to be locally restricted. They conclude that the geographic dimension of spillovers has been overstated in the literature. By contrast, Audretsch and Feldman (1996) find evidence for the localization of knowledge spillovers within an industry. Industries tend to cluster locally if proxies for knowledge spillovers such as local university research, R&D intensity, and skilled labor are important factor inputs. It turns out that knowledge-intensive industries have a greater propensity to cluster their innovative activities than knowledge-extensive industries. Branstetter (1997) uses panel data of US and Japanese firms for the years 1983–1989 in five industries with above-average R&D-sales ratios. He finds that knowledge spillovers are primarily intranational rather than international in scope. There is only a small effect for Japanese firms benefiting from research of American firms, while a positive effect for American firms from Japanese research could not be identified at all.

Irwin and Klenow (1994) and Coe and Helpman (1995) come to different conclusions. Irwin and Klenow (1994) show that international borders are no impediment for spillovers in the semiconductor industry. Coe and Helpman (1995) show that a country's total factor productivity (TFP) also depends on the R&D stocks of its trading partners. They find that the more open a country is to international trade, the stronger the effects of foreign R&D are on domestic productivity. They derive these findings by exploiting the cointegration relationship between TFP and R&D stocks. Hence, they estimate levels instead of changes of the two variables, as most other studies do. They show that in large countries, the elasticity of TFP with respect to domestic R&D stocks is larger and the elasticity of TFP with respect to foreign R&D stocks is smaller than in small countries. Engelbrecht (1997) extends the analysis of Coe and Helpman (1995) by including a human capital variable. This reduces the coefficient of domestic R&D capital and international R&D spending, which nevertheless remain highly statistically significant. Coe et al. (1997) analyze international R&D spillovers, when considering human capital as measured by secondary school enrollment rates. For a group of 77 developing countries, they find that a developing country's total factor productivity is larger, the greater its foreign R&D capital stock, the greater its openness toward trade with industrial countries, and the more educated its labor force is.

Concluding, one can say that a vast amount of papers shows the existence of spillovers, which are the origin of ExEOS in many dynamic models. Regarding the spatial scope, the evidence is mixed whether these externalities are restricted regionally or not.[66] Griliches (1979, 1992) surveys part of this literature in detail and discusses the econometric difficulties related to this topic. He concludes that "...many of these studies are flawed and subject to a variety of reservations, but the overall impression remains that R&D spillovers are both prevalent and important..." (Griliches 1992: 29).

The second part of the literature on dynamic ExEOS tests whether variables associated with spillovers indeed foster growth rates of cities, regions, or countries. It also evaluates the relative importance of MAREOS and JaEOS. For data reasons, most studies focus on the city level.

---

[66] For further studies on R&D and spillovers see Bode (1998), Maurer (1998), Ács and Audretsch (1990), Ács et al. (1992, 1994), Feldman (1994), Bernstein and Nadiri (1989), Anselin et al. (1997), and those surveyed in Griliches (1992).

One of the most influential studies is Glaeser et al. (1992). They analyze the determinants of city growth between 1956 and 1987 of 170 US cities. They find that industry employment growth rates in individual industries depend positively on the degree of competition in each industry and the shares of other industries in the region. The influence of the share of the own industry is either insignificant or negative. This confirms the view of Jacobs rather than that of Marshall–Arrow–Romer, although the analysis might be biased by the focus on large and mature cities. Therefore, the analysis cannot rule out that intraindustry spillovers are important for industries in early life cycle stages. This supposition is confirmed by Henderson et al. (1995). They find evidence for MAREOS as well as JaEOS, analyzing data for eight manufacturing industries in 1970 and 1987. For more mature capital goods industries, MAREOS but no JaEOS are prevalent. However, new high-tech industries are more likely to locate in diversified cities. This is consistent with the theory on urban specialization and product cycles that more mature industries move to smaller and more specialized cities, while new industries need the diversity of a large city. Using a more intensive data set than Glaeser et al. (1992), Miracky (1995) confirms the view of Jacobs in two ways. First, he finds that industry growth is highest in cities where, on average, other industries have small establishments. He interprets this to reflect "...spillovers of knowledge across firms producing young products..." (p. 74). Second, he finds that spillovers occur in cities rather than in larger areas such as US states.

This finding is confirmed in a more general approach by Bostic et al. (1997). They estimate that specialization has a negative impact on productivity growth for a sample of 79 US cities between 1880 and 1890. Urbanization is negatively correlated with capital growth, positively correlated with labor growth, and uncorrelated with output growth. The most advanced of all these studies is Henderson (1997). While all previously mentioned studies analyze the employment patterns across locations at two points in time, Henderson analyzes panel data on county employment in five United States industries from 1979–1990. He argues that initial conditions may have important effects on dynamic externalities, but that these effects may die out after a certain time. Therefore, it is important to analyze the lag structure of the externality variables instead of analyzing the impact of the initial industry mix over 10, 16, or 30 years. He finds that MAREOS show their largest impact after three to four years and die out after five to six years. By contrast, JaEOS seem to persist till the end of the time horizon of the data, which is eight years.

To conclude this section, this review of the empirical literature of EOS shows that there is abundant evidence that both internal and external EOS matter. Thus, the assumptions of economic geography models, that increasing returns exist on the firm level and agglomeration economies exist on the regional level, can be empirically justified.

II.   The Empirical Relevance of Trade Costs

Chapter B has shown the theoretical relevance of trade costs. They play a key role for the qualitative solution of economic geography models. Their level determines the relative strength of centripetal and centrifugal forces, which influences the pattern of industrial production between peripheral and core regions.[67] This chapter shows the empirical relevance of trade costs.

There are surprisingly few "hard" facts about the exact nature and magnitude of the costs of overcoming economic distance, despite their important theoretical impact, and despite the fact that it has become fashionable to discuss likely consequences of the so-called globalization caused by declining tariffs and trade costs. It is not entirely clear what kind of costs really impede trade between countries in a time when world-average tariff rates plus cif-fob (cost-insurance freight free on board) differences of industrial goods prices have fallen — as will be documented — to less than 10 percent of import values.

Therefore, this chapter analyzes two questions. The first is, in how far trade costs still matter for the spatial pattern of production and trade, and whether their influence has declined in the last decades. The second is, what kind of costs are behind these trade costs that make business costly across space.

The chapter starts with a descriptive part. It summarizes different kinds of trade costs and reports trends in their magnitude. I do not aim at providing synthetic measures of global trade costs in a coherent framework in terms of time, sectoral coverage, and geographical coverage, as this would be a larger research project in its own. Rather, I collect fragmentary evidence that aims to be suggestive instead of complete. I find that several costs of overcoming distance have declined in the last decades, which would suggest that distance plays a smaller role for trade and the location of production than in previous years. The implication for economic geography models would be that patterns of industry location and trade flows become increasingly indeterminate.

In order to identify whether distance still matters, in the second part of this chapter, I estimate its impact on the trade volumes of 45 countries in a gravity model of international trade. The model is estimated for each year between 1967 and 1995. In order to detect what kind of costs might impede trade, I test for the relative importance of transport costs and search costs by constructing sectoral

---

[67]   Furthermore, trade costs play a distinctive role in international trade models. In traditional trade models, they determine the borderline between traded and nontraded goods (Dornbusch et al. 1977). In intraindustry trade models, the inclusion of trade costs leads to home market effects that can explain wage differentials across countries despite similar factor endowments and technologies (Krugman 1980).

samples where the one or the other are likely to prevail. The impact of the sectoral market structure on international trade is estimated in further disaggregated
samples.

1.   Trends in the Costs of International Trade

Trade costs go far beyond tariffs and transport costs. They also include capital
transfer costs, communication and information costs, insurance costs, and the
costs of nontariff trade barriers (NTBs). Figure A1 shows the most important
types of trade costs. Some authors mention further trade-reducing effects, like
psychological barriers to trade. "Typically, trade begins close to home and then,
as experience and confidence grows, expands 'like rings in the water'"
(Nothdurft 1992: 39). Additionally, Siebert (1997: 12) mentions that the recent
political stability between major political blocs, the abolishment of apartheid,
and the decline in the number of wars have trade-cost-reducing and trade-en-
hancing effects. The nature of these costs makes it hard to quantify the overall
costs of overcoming economic distance. Therefore, this section picks out some
of these costs and shows the importance of them in order to get an idea about
their magnitude and their hypothesized decline in the last decades.

a.   *Tariffs and NTBs*

In the course of eight rounds of multilateral trade negotiations, average industrial
goods tariffs of OECD countries have been reduced from above 40 percent in
the late 1940s to a level of 3.9 percent after the Uruguay Round concluded in
1994.[68] Since the first GATT round in Geneva in 1947, the number of countries
involved in the negotiations increased from 23 to 123 in the Uruguay Round.
Now, US$4,180 billion or 99 percent of world exports are covered by the vari-
ous agreements under the multilateral trade negotiations.

Table 9 shows average tariff levels of developed countries before and after
the implementation of the Uruguay Round agreements. Average tariffs vary between sectors, but, except for the textiles and clothing sector, they amount to less
than 10 percent. Thus, compared to previous levels, tariffs of developed countries do not constitute major impediments to international trade.[69]

---

68   See Table 8 for an overview and Finger et al. (1996) for details.

69   Tariffs of developing countries are considerably higher. For industrial goods, the
weighted average tariff in developing countries amounts to more than 19 percent and
will still be 14 percent after the implementation of the Uruguay Round agreements.
For the African developing countries, the weighted average for industrial goods will
even remain 21 percent, which will slow down the integration of these countries into

Table 8 —   Overview of Results of GATT Multilateral Trade Negotiations

Round (Year)	Countries involved	Merchandise trade covered		Average tariff cut[c]	Average final tariff [c]
		Current[a] US$	Percent of world exports[b]		
Geneva (1947)	23	10	20	35	–
Annecy (1949)	33	–	–	–	–
Torquay (1950–51)	34	–	–	25	–
Geneva (1955–56)	22	3	3	–	–
Geneva (1960–62)[d]	45	5	4	–	–
Geneva (1964–67)[e]	48	40	21	35	8.7
Geneva (1973–79)[f]	99	300	19	34	4.7[g]/6.3[h]
Geneva (1986–94)[i]	123	4180[j]	99[j]	35	3.8[g]

[a]Billion US$. — [b]World exports taken from IFS (1972: xii–xiii and 1996: 114–115). — [c]In percent. — [d]Dillon Round. — [e]Kennedy Round. — [f]Tokyo Round. — [g]Weighted average in world's nine major industrial markets. — [h]Manufactured imports into industrialized countries. — [i]Uruguay Round. — [j]Note that this is only the goods part of the UR results. On top of this figure which is total merchandise trade, come the results from all the services now integrated or to be integrated into the WTO. To be comparable with the prior figures, it should be adjusted for those countries not yet being WTO members. However, since most of those not in the WTO have applied for membership, it will soon become relevant.

Source: Spinanger (1997: 27).

While tariffs could be reduced successfully, protectionism in the form of NTBs seems to have increased prior to the Uruguay Round as far as the product coverage of NTBs is concerned. This may have offset or exceeded the lower import duties in the two decades before the Uruguay Round.[70] Early estimates of the importance of NTBs for the period 1966–1986 are reported by Laird and Yeats (1990a). They show that the share of imports of developed countries that is subject to NTBs increased from 25 to 48 percent in that period. Reasons for the increase were mainly the common agricultural policy in the European Union and protectionism of textiles and clothing, food products, and ferrous metals. Other NTBs are for instance voluntary export restraints (VERs), safeguards, countervailing duties, anti-dumping procedures, and technical barriers to trade, like product regulations and standards that have the objective to ensure that products are safe for consumers to use and environmentally clean. Table A1 gives an overview over the different kinds of NTBs. For a detailed presentation

---

the world trading system (Piazolo 1998). See also Frankel (1997) for further data on trade costs.

[70] However, Harrigan (1993) shows that NTBs of OECD countries have only small effects. He calculates tariff equivalents of OECD import restrictions and finds that those are lower than tariffs or transport costs in 1983.

Table 9 — Uruguay Round Tariff Reductions of Developed Countries by Industrial Product Group (percent)

Product category	Average tariff			World imports (value in bill. US$)
	After UR	Before UR	Reduction in percent	
All industrial products[a]	3.9	6.3	38	736.9
Textiles and clothing	12.1	15.5	22	66.4
Metals	1.5	3.7	59	69.4
Mineral products, precious stones and metals	1.1	2.3	52	72.9
Electric machinery	3.5	6.6	47	86.0
Leather, rubber, footwear, and travel goods	7.3	8.9	18	31.7
Wood, pulp, paper, and furniture	1.1	3.5	69	40.6
Fish and fish products	4.5	6.1	26	18.5
Nonelectric machinery	2.0	4.8	58	118.1
Chemicals and photographic supplies	3.9	6.7	42	61.0
Transport equipment	5.8	7.5	23	96.3
Manufactured articles n.e.s.	2.4	5.5	56	76.1
[a]Excluding petroleum.				

Source: GATT (1994: 11).

of the methodology of calculating NTBs and a detailed survey of the existing literature, see Laird and Yeats (1990b).

NTBs continue to exist, although the Uruguay Round has achieved a tariffication of quantitative restrictions in agricultural products. Low and Yeats (1995) report NTBs facing developing countries after the Uruguay Round. Reductions are most noticeable in textile and clothing sectors, which are agreed to phase out until 1st January 2005. VERs are also phased out. Low and Yeats report the NTB-trade coverage ratio to have fallen by 3/4 of their previous level, with an above-average decrease in countries with a high share of textiles in exports. NTB-trade coverage ratios of the OECD countries average 18 percent of developing country imports and 10.9 percent of industrial country imports. Amjadi and Yeats (1995) describe NTBs facing Africa before and after the Uruguay Round. The ratio of all non-fuel exports of Sub-Saharan Africa that faced NTBs declined from about 11 percent before to only 3 percent after the Uruguay Round.

b.   *Transport Costs*

Average transport costs declined throughout the last decades to fairly low levels (see Table 10) although the average shipping distance has increased steadily since 1960 (Frankel 1997). In 1994, freight costs for total world trade amounted to only 5.4 percent of import values. Due to a poorer infrastructure and lower trade volumes, they were about twice as high in developing countries than in developed market economies. But even in developing countries, freight costs on average amounted to less than 10 percent of import values.

Freight and insurance rates have been collected by the WEPZA Research Center (1991). This study reports freight charges and freight weights for 120 product groups to the United States from 206 countries excluding Canada and Mexico. Freight and insurance rates for 4,281,555 tons of air freight averaged US$0.87/kilo. For 414,224,656 tons of vessel imports, they averaged US$0.03/kilo. Lowest rates are found in the sector chemicals and related products, since these are relatively heavy products. If these products are excluded, freight and insurance rates averaged US$0.12/kilo for the remaining 107,247,119 tons of imports. Obviously, these rates are much higher for landlocked countries and for countries with low trade volumes.[71]

Table 10 — Estimates of Total Freight Costs[a] in World Trade by Groups (millions of US$)

Country group	Estimate of total freight costs of imports		Value of imports (cif)		Freight costs (percentage of import value)	
	1980	1994	1980	1994	1980	1994
1. World total	123,264	219,317	1,856,834	4,063,338	6.64	5.40
2. Developed market economy countries	78,286	125,252	1,425,979	2,922,810	5.49	4.29
3. Developing countries, of which in:	44,978	94,065	430,855	1,140,528	10.44	8.25
Africa	10,432	10,660	77,757	96,453	13.42	11.05
America	10,929	17,438	123,495	219,350	8.85	7.95
Asia	21,979	64,156	211,089	805,203	10.41	7.97
Europe	1,320	1,331	16,037	15,600	8.23	8.53
Oceania	318	480	2,477	3,922	12.84	12.24

[a]Derived from IMF cif/fob factors and IMF input data. The estimate for the world is not complete, since data for countries that are not members of the IMF are not included.

Source: UNCTAD (1996: Table 38).

---

[71]   See Amjadi et al. (1996) for the problem of landlocked African countries. They display data that show that most African countries face higher transport costs to American markets than their competitors from other continents. See Frankel (1997: Table 3.1) for calculations of ad valorem transportation and insurance costs of US imports by single countries.

Table 11 — Weight and Freight Charges to the US in 1989 for 10 Major Trading Partners Excluding Canada and Mexico Using Air Transport

Country	Tons	US$/kg
Japan	2,764,351	0.28
West Germany	156,906	1.47
United Kingdom	120,368	1.57
Colombia	118,987	0.45
Italy	99,490	2.67
Taiwan	96,433	3.28
Hong Kong	80,563	3.18
France	71,331	1.61
Korea	69,765	2.85
China	56,826	3.01

Source: WEPZA Research Center (1991: 63).

In Table 11, I display freight and insurance rates for 10 major US trading
partners. I report air freight instead of vessel freight and insurance rates, since
differences in the latter rates mainly reflect differences in the sectoral composition of countries' exports to the United States, which were especially low for
countries producing petroleum or chemicals and related products. Freight
charges per kilo were lowest for mass-exporting Japan and close-by Colombia. It
is also striking that Italy faces much higher freight charges to the United States
than the other West European countries, namely, West Germany, the United
Kingdom, and France.

Table 12 and Table 13 show the evolution of freight rates. Table 12 shows liner
freight rates since 1985. The table shows declining rates, which amounted in 1995
to only 71 percent of their 1985 values. Table 13 displays freight rates for wheat on
North-Atlantic routes in 1980 in US dollars per ton. The table shows a decline in
the 1986–1990 period to levels that were about half of the 1953–1955 level.
Absolutely lower levels were observed in the 1981–1985 period.

Table 12 — Liner Freight-Rate Index (1985 = 100)[a]

1985	1989	1990	1991	1992	1993	1994	1995
100	84	75	79	78	76	74	71

[a]UNCTAD Liner Index compiled by the Ministry of Transport in Germany. Freight
rates on cargoes loaded or discharged by liners of all flags at ports in Antwerp/Hamburg
range.

Source: UNCTAD (1992, 1994, 1996).

Table 13 — Freight Rates for Wheat on North Atlantic Routes in 1980 (US$/ton)[a]

1953 –1955	1956 –1960	1961 –1965	1966 –1970	1971 –1975	1976 –1980	1981 –1985	1986 –1990
30.9	24.3	21	18	15.7	15.3	10.8	14.6
23.2	18.2	15.8	13.5	11.7	11.5	8.1	11.0

[a]The first row refers to rates for vessels under 20,000 t; the second row refers to rates for vessels over 20,000 t.

Source: Roehner (1996: 353).

For technical reasons, transport costs may vary for different products, since the transportability of goods varies due to weight, value, and consistence. Yet, apart from technical determinants of differences in transport costs, there are also institutional determinants. Rauch (1999), for instance, calculates insurance and freight costs as percentage of customs values of US imports from Japan. He divides products into three commodity categories, depending on whether they are traded in an organized exchange, whether they have a quoted reference price, or whether none of the two applies. He translates these categories into homogeneous, near-homogeneous, and differentiated products. He uses two methods of aggregation for his goods, which he calls conservative and liberal.[72] Both methods yield similar results, as Table 14 shows. Transport costs are about twice as high

Table 14 — Transportability of Commodity Categories[a]

Method	Category	1970	1980	1990
Conservative aggregation	Organized-exchange	15.59	12.45	13.51
	Reference-priced	13.06	13.19	12.05
	Differentiated	6.58	6.40	5.88
Liberal aggregation	Organized-exchange	16.04	12.67	13.89
	Reference-priced	11.24	11.03	10.74
	Differentiated	6.51	6.38	5.86

[a]Based on insurance and freight as percent of customs value of US imports from Japan or comparably distant country.

Source: Rauch (1999: Table 2).

---

[72] The conservative method of aggregation minimizes the number of 3- and 4-digit commodities, which possibly can be classified as organized-exchange or reference-priced, while the liberal method maximizes these numbers. Under the liberal method, in 1990, organized-exchange had a 16 percent share of commodities in value of total trade, reference-priced one of 19.5 percent, and differentiated products one of 64.6 percent.

for homogeneous and near-homogeneous than for differentiated goods. Comparing 1990 values with those in 1980 and 1970, one finds a moderately declining trend.

c.   *Communication and Information Costs*[73]

"The Death of Distance" and "A Connected World" are the titles of two surveys on the development of telecommunications presented in *The Economist* by Cairncross (1995, 1997). These titles reflect the large impact of the evolution of new technologies, the shift toward global competition in international telecommunication services, and the privatization of state-owned telecommunication monopolies in several countries. These developments have improved the quality and the extent of services and have led to a reduction of prices of telecommunication services. They have led to a situation where international boundaries are getting increasingly unimportant for the handling of international communication.

International treaties, recommendations, and agreements are doing their part to facilitate trade in telecommunications.[74] So far, international telecommunications have been operated on a bilateral basis — the so-called accounting rate system. Since this system is generally regarded as rewarding inefficiencies and preventing or retarding price reductions, there is increasing pressure to create a multilateral system with settlement payments set closer to actual costs.

Further pressure on telephone charges is coming from alternative calling procedures such as calling cards, call re-origination, call-back services, and international resale services. Another alternative is voice-over-data networks with the Internet telephony as its most popular form. While this technology so far has only approximately 50,000 users, technological improvements are expected to increase its use substantially. The attraction of this service lies in the flat-rate fee which is not dependent on usage time, distance, or international boundaries.

Table 15 shows that standard international tariffs toward other OECD countries have decreased by 20–30 percent in most countries during the 1991–1996 period. Since competition in the US telecommunication sector had already been introduced in the 1980s, the slide in the US prices is not reflected in the data for the nineties. It should also be taken into consideration that competition in the US market is mainly based on discount schemes such that the presented standard

---

[73]   For an intensive discussion of the impact of various types of communication and information costs on the spatial pattern of international trade, see also the early work of Herrmann et al. (1982). In their empirical analysis, they consider, for instance, variables like common languages, religions, colonial ties, and preferential trading arrangements.

[74]   See ITU (1997: 90) for the 11 major treaties concerning trade in telecommunications.

tariffs exceed applied charges by one-third to one-half. It should also be noted that US-, Canada-, New Zealand- and Australian tariffs appear absolutely higher, because these countries are on average further away from most of the other OECD countries. Turkey, Italy, and Norway have experienced the highest tariff reductions when calculated in international prices. Norway now has the lowest prices toward its OECD partners.

Table 15 — OECD Trends in Collection Charges[a]

	1991	1992	1993	1994	1995	1996	1991–1996 Exchange rates (percent)	1991–1996 Local currency (percent)
Australia (Telstra)	1.38	1.37	1.30	1.12	1.25	1.26	−8.42	−7.26
Austria	1.23	1.20	1.28	1.18	0.94	1.06	−13.76	−23.58
Belgium	1.13	1.10	1.12	0.76	0.77	0.88	−22.34	−28.33
Canada	1.37	1.29	1.22	1.00	0.94	0.96	−29.76	−19.47
Denmark (Tele Dan.)	0.80	0.74	0.82	0.77	0.69	0.62	−21.84	−24.48
Finland (Telecom Fin.)	0.99	0.93	0.69	0.63	0.63	0.58	−41.72	−9.34
France	1.14	1.13	1.02	0.88	0.81	0.89	−21.54	−26.12
Germany	1.00	0.97	0.97	0.91	0.93	0.65	−34.88	−32.19
Greece	1.36	1.18	0.97	0.81	0.78	0.81	−40.15	−10.12
Iceland	1.54	1.52	1.35	1.09	1.25	1.11	−28.14	−19.45
Ireland	1,43	1.30	1.37	0.79	0.81	0.84	−41.30	−41.76
Italy	1.44	1.36	1.37	0.87	0.77	0.69	−52.27	−34.21
Japan (KDD)	2.19	2.36	2.51	2.85	2.77	2.16	−1.59	−38.83
Luxembourg	1.26	1.04	0.97	0.96	0.81	0.80	−36.68	−33.81
Mexico[b]	n.a.	n.a.	n.a.	2.96	2.78	2.03	−31.21	32.91
Netherlands	1.01	0.99	0.97	0.92	0.89	0.78	−23.34	−18.46
New Zealand (TCNZ)	1.66	1.54	1.36	1.38	1.48	1.64	−0.93	−9.79
Norway	0.93	0.72	0.71	0.58	0.55	0.49	−47.07	−36.94
Portugal	1.39	1.37	1.56	1.25	1.14	0.97	−30.22	−19.71
Spain	1.77	1.73	1.57	1.25	1.03	1.08	−39.05	−27.16
Sweden (Telia)	1.06	1.04	1.08	0.80	0.70	0.66	−38.26	−20.33
Switzerland	1.17	1.14	1.00	0.90	0.94	0.79	−32.55	−38.85
Turkey	2.74	2.11	2.35	1.78	1.28	0.83	−69.60	n.a.
UK (BT)	0.89	0.79	0.78	0.66	0.59	0.61	−31.13	−19.48
US (AT&T)	1.34	1.33	1.33	1.40	1.42	1.57	16.84	10.74
OECD average	1.34	1.26	1.24	1.06	1.01	0.95	−29.46	−23.00

[a]The average of a one-minute tariff in peak time based on (1 initial minute + 3 additional minutes)/4. OECD average is a simple average. All calculations are in exchange rates 1990–95, except for the last column. Average in last column is average of the reduction rate of each country. All averages in local currency exclude Turkey. — [b]Mexico is excluded from the OECD average or as a destination country. Mexican data are for 1994–96.

Source: OECD (1997: 119).

Figure 18 — Number of OECD Internet Hosts (in 1,000 in July)

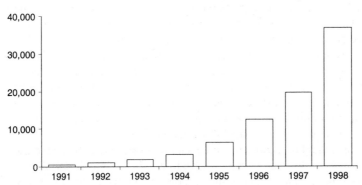

Source: OECD (1997: 56) and http://nw.com/zone/www/report.html.

The most significant impact on the decline in communication costs is expected to result from the use of Internet technology. It allows almost costless communication and the transmission of data and information within minutes from the most remote place as long as they have a telephone line. Therefore, the number of Internet hosts has increased exponentially since its first use in 1981. In January 1997, there were 14.94 Internet hosts per thousand inhabitants in the OECD average (OECD 1997: 58). This led to a tremendously high demand for additional lines from business and residential users. Many of them are installing second lines for Internet usage. Figure 18 shows its expansion since 1991.

With traded goods shifting from bulk and raw material trade to more heterogeneous and differentiated goods, the specific needs and the production process of the importing party are becoming increasingly important. This goes hand in hand with a higher service share in internationally traded goods. Both make information and communication between trading partners more important. Especially for financial institutions that increasingly operate in a globalized market, telecommunications are crucial for the delivery of services. The importance of telecommunications is reflected in their inclusion in the Annex to the General Agreement on Trade in Services (GATS) negotiated during the Uruguay Round. 48 countries made commitments to open their markets for basic telecommunications under the GATS.[75] Liberalization of telecommunication markets is bringing new investments, skills, and innovative technologies, which all lead to a reduction of the costs of communication and information.

---

[75]   In February 1997, 69 WTO members agreed upon further liberalization commitments in the basic telecommunications area, which have been entered into force on January 1, 1998. The agreements cover more than 90 percent of global telecommunication revenues.

To summarize, the prices for international communication have seen a dramatic fall, while the services offered have improved significantly in the last decades. The trend of decreasing telecommunication prices has been initiated and is expected to continue for four reasons: 1) the formation of global alliances between telecommunication companies; 2) overcapacities, particularly in undersea cables; 3) the convergence of traditional voice and data communication leading to significant economies of scale in switching and transmission technologies; and 4) digitalization of telecommunication services, which leads to economies of scale in transmitting data, because a multitude of telecommunication services can be routed through the same infrastructure.[76]

To conclude this section, it can be said that there are still sizable trade costs, but all of them declined in the observed periods. Although not all of them are related to the distance between them, their decline facilitates international trade in general, while declining distance-dependent costs, like transport costs and the costs of international communication and information, facilitate especially trade between distant countries.

2.   A Gravity Model Approach

Another way to look at the spatial impact of the costs of international trade is to estimate the specific impact that these costs have for international trade flows. Therefore, I estimate a gravity model for each year between 1967–1995. This analysis has two goals. The first is to establish that distance matters. For economic geography models to make sense, a sizable and significant distance effect is expected. The second is to analyze whether distance matters as much as it did 30 years ago.

Since distance does not change over time, a declining regression coefficient of geographic distance would indicate a decline in the marginal effect of distance between trading partners, i.e., a change in the marginal costs per percentage point of increase in distance. It should be noted that it would not reflect a decline in the average trade costs. See also Frankel (1997: 74) for a discussion of this point. My hypothesis is that trade costs incur a labor-intensive fixed cost element like loading and unloading and a technology-intensive variable cost element like communication or transportation. Then technological progress, like the Internet, would reduce costs of long-distance trade more than costs of short-distance trade. This would be reflected in a lower regression coefficient of the distance variable.

---

[76]   See also ITU (1997: Chap. 6) for details on the changing telecommunication environment.

Previous results concerning the changing impact of the marginal effect of distance are ambiguous (Frankel 1997: 70–74). Most of the studies find that distance elasticities do not show a trend, although they do show great variation from one year to another. This means that so far no clear downward trend could be identified, such that distance elasticities are lower nowadays than in previous decades. Frankel et al. (1995) estimate a gravity model for every fifth year since 1965. If anything, distance elasticities rise (in absolute values) with 1985 as an outlier. These results are in line with Bröcker and Rohweder's (1990) estimates for the years 1968, 1972, 1976, 1980, and 1983. So far, Boisso and Ferrantino (1997) is the only study of my knowledge that calculates distance elasticities for each year over a longer period of time. Overall, they cannot identify a declining trend for distance elasticities for the observed period from 1960 to 1985 either.

My results show that the mid-1980s were a particularly bad period to end such a study. The oil price shock and the large overvaluation of the US dollar distorted trade flows and data greatly. I show that distance elasticities can vary enormously from year to year, such that looking at these elasticities every fifth or tenth year, like several studies do, only gives an incomplete picture of their evolution. Therefore, my study covers every single year from 1967 to 1995. In contrast to previous findings, it shows that distance elasticities have declined by around 20 percent throughout that period. Nevertheless, distance remains one of the most important impediments to international trade.

The next section reviews the literature on the theoretical setting of the gravity model and refers to previous applications. In a further section, I present the data used in my regressions. The last section in this part presents my results.

a.   ***The Theoretical Specification of a Gravity Equation***

Linnemann (1966) was among the first to propose gravity models as a pragmatic way to determine bilateral trade flows as a result of supply conditions at the origin, demand conditions at the destination, and trade-stimulating or trade-restricting forces between two countries. These determinants are usually approximated by the exporter's and importer's GDP, their per capita incomes, and their distance. The term "gravity model" refers to the similarity to Newton's law. Trade-stimulating forces are, for example, a common language, customs unions, trade bloc participation, former colonial ties, and direct land borders. Trade-restricting forces are trade costs because they drive a wedge between supply and demand. Trade costs are typically approximated by the distance between trading partners, which shall combine 1) transport costs, 2) transport time — representing problems of perishability, adaptability to market conditions, and irregularities in

supply, and 3) psychic distance — representing familiarity with laws, institutions, and habits.[77]

The attraction of the gravity equation lies in the robustness of its empirical results and the simplicity of its functional form. It has gained popularity in recent
years after a microeconomic foundation was developed by Anderson (1979), Bergstrand (1985), Helpman and Krugman (1985: Chap. 8), Bröcker (1987), and
Thursby and Thursby (1987). Helpman (1987) derives a structural form of a gravity equation out of an international trade model with imperfect competition. He shows
that the larger the similarity in factor compositions, the larger the share of intraindustry trade, and that changes over time in relative country size can explain rising
trade-to-income ratios. Bergstrand (1989, 1990) combines Heckscher–Ohlin elements, Chamberlinian monopolistic competition, and the Linder hypothesis in his
model. Using a nonhomothetic utility function, he gives a microeconomic explanation of the gravity equation that is extended by a complex price term and various
endowment and factor intensity variables. Deardorff (1995: 26) derives the gravity
equation out of a Heckscher–Ohlin approach. However, he also shows that the equation is consistent with other trade theories. Therefore, he argues that the gravity
model is not suitable for testing or falsifying any theory. Evenett and Keller (1998)
address this identification problem and construct a large number of samples according to differences in factor endowments between country pairs. Consequently,
they are able to identify samples in which Heckscher–Ohlin trade is likely to matter
more, and other samples where trade in differentiated goods is likely to matter
more. They find that the gravity equation scores much better in samples that suit
the monopolistic competition model of trade rather than the competitive one.

Most of the applied papers estimate the following simple version of a gravity
model:

$$[49] \quad \begin{aligned} \log(EX_{xm}) &= \alpha + \beta_1 \log(GDP_x \cdot GDP_m) + \beta_2 \log(GDPC_x \cdot GDPC_m) \\ &\quad + \beta_3 \log(Distance_{xm}) + \beta_4(Conditional\ Variables), \end{aligned}$$

where EX_{xm} are exports from country x to m, GDP is gross domestic product,
and $GDPC$ is GDP per capita. Entering GDPs and GDP per capita in multiplica-
tive form can be justified by modern trade theory that predicts larger trade volumes between more similar countries in terms of size and income or factor en-

---

[77] Recent findings of large border-effects and a strong home bias in international trade
as found by McCallum (1995), Wei (1996), Helliwell (1996), Nitsch (1997), and
Cyrus (1997) suggest that there are other important trade costs besides those that are
approximated by the physical distance between trading partners. For instance,
McCallum reports that Canadian provinces trade with each other 20 times more than
with equidistant US states. Therefore, dummy variables for a common language,
trade bloc participation, colonial ties, or exchange rate volatilities are often used to
proxy further (or lower) trade costs in addition to the mere distance between trading
partners.

dowments. Using conditional variables, the gravity model has been applied to several questions.[78] In the following, I concentrate on the effects of distance, *GDP*, *GDPC*, common land borders, a common language, and different trade bloc participation.[79]

b. Data

Export data, population data, and GDP data are taken from the CHELEM CD-ROM (CHELEM 1995), published by the Centre d'Etudes Prospectives et Informations Internationales. This data base combines data from different original data sources like the UN, IMF, World Bank, OECD, etc. Since data from these sources are often fragmented and incoherent, CHELEM is an attempt to supply complete and harmonized accounts on trade and the world economy. Thus, exports (fob) of country x to country m always equal imports of country m from country x. Also, trade data exists for a larger number of country pairs and years than in other sources.

Still, for a few country pairs and years reported exports are zero, because they are below the lowest reported volume of one thousand US dollars or not available. Including these observations leads to the problem that the log of these values cannot be calculated such that the common log-linear form of equation [49] cannot be estimated.

---

[78] See also the survey in Oguledo and MacPhee (1994) and the book by Frankel (1997). Wang and Winters (1992), Havrylyshyn and Pritchett (1991), Piazolo (1997), Schumacher et al. (1997), and Hamilton and Winters (1992) have used the model to estimate the trading potential of East European countries. Other authors have used the model to estimate whether there is a trend toward regionalization of world trade (Frankel 1993; Frankel and Wei 1993; Frankel et al. 1995).

Some studies have used the gravity equation to analyze whether exchange rate volatility affects bilateral trade flows and come to mixed results. Rohweder (1989), Thursby and Thursby (1987), and papers cited therein find support for the influence of exchange rate volatility on bilateral trade flows. Bröcker and Rohweder (1990) report strong trade-impeding effects of exchange rate uncertainty for a sample of 86 countries and small effects for a subsample of industrial countries. Wei (1996) finds no effects for the 1982–1994 period, and Eichengreen and Irwin (1995) find little effects in the pre-World–War II period. Frankel and Wei (1993) report changing positive and negative effects for EU trade, depending on the year. Overall, the effects are small. The literature is surveyed by Sapir et al. (1994: 39). They conclude that "...empirical studies on the impact of exchange rate volatility on trade do not reach a consensus...". The results of the studies with the most negative effect of exchange rate volatility on trade suggest that even eliminating volatility in 1990 would only have increased world trade by 3 percent and EU trade by 0.15 percent. While this does not imply that the existence of exchange rates may not have a trade-reducing effect, it shows that their volatility is not the major obstacle to trade. Hence, they are not considered in my further empirical analysis.

[79] Additionally, some authors use dummy variables for each exporting and importing country to single out country-specific effects (Herrmann et al. 1982).

Four methods have been used to deal with this problem. Most authors simply exclude these zero-observations (McCallum 1995, Helliwell 1996, Hamilton and Winters 1992, Brada and Méndez 1985, Bikker 1987, and Frankel and Wei 1993). Obviously, this method has the drawback that it leads to a sample selection bias and does not use the information about why exports may be low in these cases.

Therefore, Linnemann (1966) and Wang and Winters (1992), among others, suggested to substitute the zeros by a very small number like half of the minimum reported trade volume. This is clearly an ad hoc procedure. However, it makes it possible to estimate the transformed sample by OLS. A third, similarly ad hoc procedure is to add 1 to all dependent observations and to estimate the log-linear form by OLS (Eichengreen and Irwin 1995, 1998).

Another way to deal with zero trade flows is to use the Tobit estimation procedure. It has been used to estimate gravity models by Balassa and Bauwens (1988), Havrylyshyn and Pritchett (1991), Eaton and Tamura (1994), and Boisso and Ferrantino (1997). The Tobit procedure is the only one to consider that exports are limited dependent variables censored at zero.[80] Especially for sectoral trade flows between developing countries, zero observations are often made. Then, a large bias can arise by using the OLS procedure. Greene (1981) shows that the bias can be expressed as one divided by the sample proportion of non-zero observations. However, higher computational costs of the Tobit procedure may outweigh the disadvantage of a bias of the OLS procedure if only a few observations equal zero in the sample.[81]

In this study, I use export data for the years 1967–1995 and a sample of 45 major countries.[82] This means that there are 1,980 observations per year. Only a small fraction of these are zero (for instance, 43 in the year 1980, and 24 in 1995). I accept a small bias of my estimates and substitute the zero entries by half of the minimum reported export values. To check for the sensitivity of this procedure, I use alternative minimum export volumes.[83]

---

[80]   See Rohweder (1988) for a detailed description.

[81]   See also Frankel (1997: 145–147) for a discussion of several strategies to deal with zero-valued trade flows. With the exception of Rauch (1999), most authors report that exclusion or inclusion of missing values made little substantive difference to their results.

[82]   The sample is listed in Table A1 in the Appendix. The country sample represents around 90 percent of world output and trade. From the original sample South-Africa is excluded, as trade volumes were long-depressed due to political boycott. Several East European countries are excluded because trade was not reported for bilateral trade.

[83]   In the sectoral samples of OECD countries, there are even less zero observations. Out of 20 sectors, there are only 3 sectors with 1, 2, and 3 zero observations, respectively. I also tried the Tobit procedure and found, that the coefficients usually did not change in the first two digits after the dot. To check for the sensitivity of the OLS procedure, I

I further use a dummy for adjacent countries (*ADJ*), i.e., countries with a common land border. This distinguishes country pairs with the same geographic distance between their commercial centers but likely different trade volumes, like the United States and Mexico on the one hand, and Greece and Sweden on the other hand, because a common border increases the familiarity with the culture, institutions, and preferences of the trading partner.

I use a dummy for countries that have a common language (*LAN*), because speaking the same language facilitates the communication between trading partners. Hence, a common language reduces the search costs of international trade. In order to analyze different effects between different languages, I construct three dummy variables to distinguish country pairs that have English, Spanish, or French as a common language.[84] The distance between countries has been calculated by Schumacher et al. (1997).[85] I also use dummies for the participation in the following regional trading arrangements[86]: EC12, EFTA, Mercosur, Andean, NAFTA, East Asian Economic Caucus, and ASEAN. For a better comparability of the results, I follow Frankel et al. (1995) and use the same dummies for all years, even though not all of the trade blocs had been formed in the earlier years under study. I expect insignificant dummy coefficients in these years. The trade bloc participation of each country is reported in Table A1.

c.   *Results*

All Sectors

I estimate the gravity model in the form of equation [49] separately for each year. The results are displayed in Figures 23 to 28. The first regression estimates equation [49] with the log of GDP (ln*GDP*), the log of per capita GDP (ln*GDPC*), the log of the distance (ln*DIS*), and dummies for adjacency, a common language, and a joint-trade-bloc participation as the explanatory variables. All variables, with the

---

tried using several minimum values ranging from 1/10th to 100 times of the reported one. The results did not change much.

[84]   A dummy for German-speaking country pairs was removed, because all these countries also share a common border. Above that, even when excluding the common border dummy, the coefficient of a common German language is insignificant for several years and was negative in all of them. A dummy for Portuguese-speaking countries was also excluded, because only two countries in the final sample speak Portuguese and a significant coefficient cannot be identified for all specifications and years.

[85]   He uses the shortest distance between the capitals of two countries. In the following cases, the geographic or commercial centers were taken: Canada (Montreal), United States (Kansas City), Australia (Sydney), West Germany (Frankfurt am Main), Brazil (Rio de Janeiro), Pakistan (Karachi), and India (Bombay).

[86]   For simplicity, I will use the term free trade area (FTA) for all groups even if some groups may be preferential trade arrangements while others may be even customs unions or economic unions.

exception of adjacency, are statistically significant at the one percent level for all 29 years. The $\overline{R}^2$ lies between 0.56 and 0.66, depending on the year. In the second regression, reported in Table 16, I distinguish three different languages and six different FTAs by using single dummies for each of them. I report White-heteroskedasticity-consistent standard errors (White 1980).

Table 16 — Regression Results of the Gravity Model, All Sectors 1967–1995

	1967	1968	1969	1970	1971	1972	1973
Constant	−18.36***	−18.89***	−19.47***	−19.63***	−19.88***	−18.25***	−18.65***
	(0.81)	(0.82)	(0.83)	(0.82)	(0.86)	(0.87)	(0.86)
lngdp	1.02***	0.99***	0.98***	0.97***	1.00***	0.94***	0.96***
	(0.03)	(0.03)	(0.03)	(0.03)	(0.03)	(0.03)	(0.03)
lngdpc	0.64***	0.69***	0.72***	0.73***	0.70***	0.61***	0.60***
	(0.04)	(0.04)	(0.04)	(0.04)	(0.04)	(0.04)	(0.04)
lndis	−1.06***	−1.00***	−0.99***	−0.98***	−0.98***	−0.91***	−0.94***
	(0.06)	(0.07)	(0.07)	(0.07)	(0.07)	(0.07)	(0.06)
Adjacency	−0.39	−0.37	−0.31	−0.27	−0.34	−0.30	−0.37
	(0.27)	(0.29)	(0.29)	(0.30)	(0.30)	(0.31)	(0.32)
English	0.86***	0.86***	0.82***	0.64***	0.60***	0.76***	0.87***
	(0.23)	(0.23)	(0.23)	(0.22)	(0.23)	(0.21)	(0.20)
Spanish	1.44***	1.55***	1.60***	1.61***	1.53***	1.16***	1.11***
	(0.18)	(0.19)	(0.18)	(0.18)	(0.17)	(0.16)	(0.19)
French	0.45*	0.44*	0.54**	0.52*	0.53**	0.50**	0.47**
	(0.25)	(0.25)	(0.26)	(0.27)	(0.26)	(0.24)	(0.23)
EC12	−0.64***	−0.52***	−0.54***	−0.56***	−0.54***	−0.38***	−0.39***
	(0.15)	(0.15)	(0.15)	(0.15)	(0.15)	(0.14)	(0.14)
EFTA5	−0.12	−0.05	0.02	0.06	0.13	0.22	0.08
	(0.22)	(0.22)	(0.21)	(0.21)	(0.21)	(0.22)	(0.22)
Mercosur2	1.82***	1.95***	1.87***	1.89***	1.60***	1.12***	0.58
	(0.30)	(0.32)	(0.32)	(0.32)	(0.36)	(0.35)	(0.38)
Andean4	0.31	0.47	0.42	0.57	0.96	1.06*	1.19*
	(0.53)	(0.48)	(0.58)	(0.56)	(0.59)	(0.56)	(0.67)
NAFTA3	−0.96***	−0.87***	−0.92***	−0.94***	−0.95***	−0.55*	−0.40
	(0.30)	(0.31)	(0.31)	(0.29)	(0.27)	(0.29)	(0.31)
EastAsian8	3.79***	3.82***	3.79***	3.81***	4.02***	3.66***	3.47***
	(0.22)	(0.22)	(0.22)	(0.21)	(0.21)	(0.20)	(0.19)
$\overline{R}^2$	0.63	0.62	0.62	0.62	0.62	0.63	0.64
SEE	2.23	2.24	2.26	2.23	2.28	2.13	2.11
F-Test	258	251	250	255	252	256	269

Table 16 continued

	1974	1975	1976	1977	1978	1979	1980
Constant	−18.99***	−19.92***	−19.89***	−21.70***	−20.79***	−21.27***	−20.22***
	(0.92)	(0.94)	(0.92)	(0.97)	(0.94)	(1.01)	(0.95)
lngdp	0.96***	0.97***	0.96***	0.96***	0.95***	0.97***	0.96***
	(0.03)	(0.03)	(0.03)	(0.03)	(0.03)	(0.03)	(0.03)
lngdpc	0.60***	0.58***	0.62***	0.69***	0.63***	0.59***	0.58***
	(0.04)	(0.04)	(0.04)	(0.04)	(0.04)	(0.04)	(0.04)
lndis	−0.94***	−0.84***	−0.91***	−0.83***	−0.85***	−0.81***	−0.91***
	(0.06)	(0.06)	(0.06)	(0.06)	(0.06)	(0.07)	(0.06)
Adjacency	−0.45	−0.24	−0.38	−0.46	−0.50*	−0.53	−0.14
	(0.33)	(0.31)	(0.30)	(0.31)	(0.30)	(0.32)	(0.23)
English	0.87***	0.83***	1.02***	0.95***	0.99***	1.08***	1.09***
	(0.20)	(0.21)	(0.21)	(0.21)	(0.21)	(0.21)	(0.19)
Spanish	1.18***	1.82***	1.53***	1.84***	1.78***	1.60***	1.10***
	(0.21)	(0.24)	(0.24)	(0.20)	(0.19)	(0.20)	(0.22)
French	0.59**	0.42*	0.24	0.21	0.03	0.19	−0.07
	(0.23)	(0.23)	(0.25)	(0.27)	(0.26)	(0.27)	(0.25)
EC12	−0.30**	−0.30**	−0.24*	−0.22	−0.25*	−0.16	−0.40***
	(0.14)	(0.14)	(0.14)	(0.14)	(0.14)	(0.14)	(0.12)
EFTA5	0.08	0.01	−0.15	−0.10	−0.12	0.07	−0.30*
	(0.23)	(0.23)	(0.23)	(0.24)	(0.25)	(0.26)	(0.18)
Mercosur2	0.22	1.45***	1.15***	1.54***	1.34***	1.33***	0.59**
	(0.35)	(0.37)	(0.33)	(0.33)	(0.36)	(0.34)	(0.24)
Andean4	1.25**	0.67	1.00*	1.11**	0.92**	1.19***	1.19***
	(0.63)	(0.53)	(0.56)	(0.51)	(0.44)	(0.44)	(0.37)
NAFTA3	−0.32	−0.47	−0.50	−0.13	0.01	0.01	−0.25
	(0.34)	(0.32)	(0.31)	(0.33)	(0.34)	(0.37)	(0.27)
EastAsian8	3.37***	3.47***	3.34***	3.42***	3.25***	3.41***	3.22***
	(0.19)	(0.19)	(0.19)	(0.20)	(0.19)	(0.20)	(0.18)
$\bar{R}^2$	0.61	0.60	0.61	0.61	0.61	0.59	0.59
SEE	2.14	2.18	2.16	2.17	2.15	2.22	2.16
F-Test	244	233	238	236	236	221	220

Table 16 continued

	1981	1982	1983	1984	1985	1986	1987	1988
Constant	−19.53***	−20.06***	−19.29***	−19.69***	−19.84***	−19.82***	−19.39***	−19.36***
	(0.90)	(0.88)	(0.89)	(0.91)	(0.91)	(0.90)	(0.88)	(0.86)
lngdp	0.99***	0.99***	0.99***	0.98***	0.95***	0.94***	0.95***	0.96***
	(0.03)	(0.03)	(0.03)	(0.03)	(0.03)	(0.03)	(0.03)	(0.02)
lngdpc	0.56***	0.57***	0.54***	0.59***	0.59***	0.50***	0.44***	0.41***
	(0.04)	(0.04)	(0.04)	(0.04)	(0.04)	(0.03)	(0.03)	(0.03)
lndis	−1.03***	−1.00***	−1.02***	−1.04***	−0.94***	−0.78***	−0.75***	−0.73***
	(0.06)	(0.05)	(0.06)	(0.06)	(0.06)	(0.06)	(0.05)	(0.05)
Adjacency	−0.25	−0.19	0.01	0.12	0.10	0.11	0.04	0.43***
	(0.25)	(0.24)	(0.17)	(0.17)	(0.21)	(0.24)	(0.24)	(0.14)
English	1.06***	0.88***	0.81***	0.72***	0.64***	0.60***	0.68***	0.59***
	(0.18)	(0.18)	(0.18)	(0.18)	(0.18)	(0.19)	(0.17)	(0.17)
Spanish	0.83***	1.17***	1.05***	1.18***	1.44***	1.59***	1.51***	1.57***
	(0.21)	(0.20)	(0.27)	(0.25)	(0.25)	(0.22)	(0.22)	(0.21)
French	0.03	0.00	0.16	0.28	0.16	−0.09	−0.09	0.30
	(0.28)	(0.28)	(0.19)	(0.19)	(0.25)	(0.29)	(0.30)	(0.19)
EC12	−0.37***	−0.27**	−0.16	−0.10	−0.01	0.07	0.06	0.01
	(0.12)	(0.12)	(0.12)	(0.13)	(0.12)	(0.12)	(0.11)	(0.11)
EFTA5	−0.38*	−0.41**	−0.42**	−0.56***	−0.49***	−0.30*	−0.25	−0.34**
	(0.19)	(0.20)	(0.17)	(0.16)	(0.16)	(0.18)	(0.18)	(0.14)
Mercosur2	0.40	1.14***	0.86***	0.87***	1.07***	1.12***	1.12***	0.76***
	(0.27)	(0.24)	(0.27)	(0.24)	(0.21)	(0.27)	(0.24)	(0.13)
Andean4	0.94***	0.50	0.10	0.08	0.06	0.20	0.72***	0.60*
	(0.36)	(0.36)	(0.48)	(0.45)	(0.53)	(0.39)	(0.27)	(0.31)
NAFTA3	−0.54**	−0.43	−0.49	−0.76**	−0.67**	0.16	0.29	0.04
	(0.23)	(0.29)	(0.31)	(0.30)	(0.28)	(0.30)	(0.30)	(0.27)
East Asian8	2.88***	2.75***	2.67***	2.54***	2.56***	2.71***	2.74***	2.61***
	(0.18)	(0.18)	(0.18)	(0.17)	(0.18)	(0.19)	(0.18)	(0.17)
$\bar{R}^2$	0.58	0.59	0.59	0.58	0.58	0.61	0.64	0.64
SEE	2.18	2.13	2.15	2.25	2.18	2.04	1.96	1.93
F-Test	212	219	219	208	215	243	268	276

Table 16 continued

	1989	1990	1991	1992	1993	1994	1995
Constant	−19.15***	−19.03***	−17.90***	−17.84***	−17.61***	−17.51***	−17.43***
	(0.84)	(0.88)	(0.84)	(0.84)	(0.84)	(0.84)	(0.80)
lngdp	0.93***	0.94***	0.95***	0.95***	0.97***	0.97***	0.96***
	(0.02)	(0.02)	(0.02)	(0.02)	(0.02)	(0.02)	(0.02)
lngdpc	0.43***	0.39***	0.32***	0.30***	0.30***	0.31***	0.29***
	(0.03)	(0.03)	(0.03)	(0.03)	(0.03)	(0.03)	(0.03)
lndis	−0.72***	−0.70***	−0.74***	−0.72***	−0.77***	−0.81***	−0.77***
	(0.05)	(0.05)	(0.05)	(0.05)	(0.05)	(0.05)	(0.05)
Adjacency	0.49***	0.48***	0.50***	0.53***	0.43***	0.39***	0.37***
	(0.14)	(0.14)	(0.14)	(0.14)	(0.14)	(0.14)	(0.14)
English	0.48***	0.65***	0.76***	0.85***	0.85***	0.74***	0.55***
	(0.17)	(0.17)	(0.17)	(0.16)	(0.16)	(0.16)	(0.16)
Spanish	1.68***	1.51***	1.32***	1.33***	1.16***	1.23***	1.40***
	(0.19)	(0.19)	(0.18)	(0.17)	(0.17)	(0.16)	(0.16)
French	0.31	0.32	0.41**	0.40**	0.39**	0.42**	0.52***
	(0.21)	(0.20)	(0.19)	(0.19)	(0.19)	(0.18)	(0.18)
EC12	0.06	−0.05	−0.07	−0.08	−0.10	−0.18*	−0.13
	(0.11)	(0.11)	(0.11)	(0.11)	(0.11)	(0.11)	(0.10)
EFTA5	−0.43***	−0.42***	−0.38***	−0.28**	−0.17	−0.27	−0.26
	(0.14)	(0.14)	(0.14)	(0.14)	(0.16)	(0.17)	(0.17)
Mercosur2	1.14***	0.55*	0.84***	1.09***	1.06***	0.92***	1.01***
	(0.31)	(0.31)	(0.14)	(0.25)	(0.17)	(0.14)	(0.17)
Andean4	0.46	0.96***	1.07***	1.16***	1.25***	1.16***	1.14***
	(0.29)	(0.26)	(0.27)	(0.24)	(0.27)	(0.30)	(0.27)
NAFTA3	−0.09	−0.05	−0.18	−0.07	−0.13	0.04	0.67**
	(0.26)	(0.27)	(0.30)	(0.26)	(0.26)	(0.25)	(0.29)
East Asian8	2.49***	2.55***	2.33***	2.21***	2.01***	1.89***	1.92***
	(0.16)	(0.16)	(0.16)	(0.16)	(0.17)	(0.17)	(0.16)
$\overline{R}^2$	0.66	0.65	0.65	0.65	0.65	0.65	0.67
SEE	1.84	1.88	1.86	1.81	1.81	1.79	1.65
F-Test	299	286	282	289	284	286	313

*Significant at 10 percent level, **significant at 5 percent level, ***significant at 1 percent level. — Number of observations: 1,980; White-heteroskedasticity-consistent standard deviations in parentheses.

Source: Own calculations.

Figure 19 — The Evolution of the Distance Coefficient

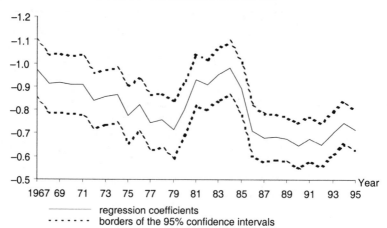

The coefficient of ln*DIS* is significant for all years. In 1995, an increase in the marginal distance of trading partners of one percent reduces trade volumes by 0.71 percent (regression one). Consequently, there is a sizable effect that distance matters for international trade. Hence, economic geography models are right to consider the costs of economic distance as a main determinant of spatial patterns of production and trade. Figure 19 shows the regression coefficients (solid line) and the 95 percent confidence intervals (broken lines) over the 29-year period. Since the gravity equation has been estimated separately rather than jointly, no joint hypothesis can be tested. Still, it can be seen that the 1967 and the 1995 confidence intervals do not overlap. This supports the overall observable downward trend in absolute values over the whole period, which is only interrupted in the beginning of the 1980s. Starting with a value of −0.97, the distance elasticity falls (in absolute values) under fluctuations to −0.72 in 1979, before it rises (in absolute values) sharply to −0.98 in 1984. From then on, it falls again (in absolute values) and remains more or less stable around −0.70 from 1986 onward. The temporary decline at the end of the 1970s and in the beginning of the 1980s was most likely caused by the oil price shock which made long-distance transportation more costly (Siebert 1997: Figure 1.4). Long-distance trade might have been substituted by short-distance trade. This view is supported by the sharp rise of the adjacency coefficient after 1979 (Figure 22).

The higher distance coefficient during the mid 1980s was probably caused by the huge appreciation of the US dollar. This also led to a substitution of short-distance trade for long-distance trade. The overvaluation of the US dollar increased US (and Canadian) imports and decreased their exports. If those countries that had a trade surplus with the United States substituted some imports from close-by countries for imports from the United States, which is by its location for most countries a long-distance trading partner, then average shipping distance declined. This is reflected in a larger distance elasticity. This view is supported by the decline of export-weighted mean physical distance between 1980 and 1983, reported in Boisso and Ferrantino (1997: Figure 1).

Most of the ln*GDP* coefficients are below but not statistically different from one, which means that there is only a small tendency for countries to be increasingly inward-oriented with larger size (Table 16). The real appreciation of the US dollar has probably distorted comparative advantages and trade patterns in the early 1980s. Above that, it distorted the data for the gravity equation. This is reflected in the coefficients of ln*GDP*. They are especially high at that time. As all variables are measured in current US dollars, GDP values of other countries appear much smaller than only some years ago compared to the United States. This results in higher GDP coefficients for these years. Using PPP-adjusted GDP data does not help to reduce the distortion, as export data are measured in current US dollars as well, and hysteresis effects reduce trade volumes only sluggishly.

The coefficient of ln*GDPC* declined from around 0.6 at the end of the 1960s to around 0.25 in the early 1990s (Figure 21). This means that in the beginning of

Figure 20 — The Evolution of the GDP Coefficient

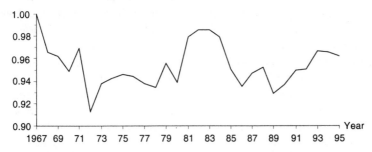

Figure 21 — The Evolution of the GDP per Capita Coefficient

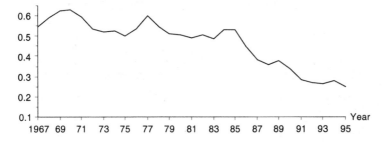

Figure 22 — The Evolution of the Adjacency Coefficient

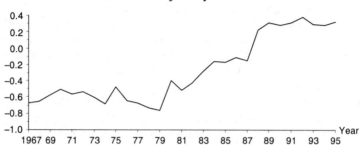

the sample period, a one percent increase of the per capita income of trading partners — ceteris paribus — increased exports by 0.6 percent. The declining export elasticity of per capita income might reflect a shift to more open trade policies of developing countries over the reported period and their increasing shares in world trade of manufactures.

Contrary to my intuition, the common land border coefficient (*ADJ*) is significantly negative for most of the years until 1987. It is significantly positive since 1988 only. In 1995, neighboring countries traded 1.38 times (= exp 0.32)[87] more than nonneighboring countries with the same distance (Figure 22).

The dummy for a common language is significant at the 1 percent level for almost all years and lies between 0.63 and 1.04 (Figure 23). This means that a common language increased trade volumes up to 2.8 fold (= exp 1.04). This substantiates that communication plays a crucial role in explaining trade flows. Not speaking the same language is a strong impediment to communication and trade and increases the costs of economic distance. In the second regression, I distinguish between countries that have English (*English*), Spanish (*Spanish*), or French (*French*) as a common language in order to analyze whether some languages have become more or less important. These results are reported in Table 16, besides Figure 23. For all years, the English and Spanish language dummies are significant at the 1 percent level, while the French dummy is often insignificant. This might be due to the fact that French is spoken in no country besides

---

[87] For the interpretation of the coefficient, the exponential form has to be taken, because the dependent variable is expressed in natural logarithms, while the border dummies enter the regression in absolute values. The unexpected negative coefficient of adjacency before 1987 could point to a misspecified functional form of the distance variable. Therefore, I tested the gravity equation in some other functional forms and with several combinations of the dependent variables. The results were not sensitive to these changes. Frankel (1997: 307) also reports insignificant adjacency coefficients until 1975.

Figure 23 — The Evolution of the Language Coefficients

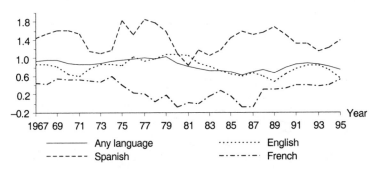

France as the only language.[88] In 1995, speaking English increases export volumes 1.73 fold (= exp 0.55); Spanish increases them 4.04 fold (= exp 1.40), and French 1.68 fold (= exp 0.52). No language coefficient shows a clearly declining or rising trend. This means that in the 1990s, English is no more dominant as *the* language for international trade than in the 1960s, and Spanish is no less so.

The dummy for the joint membership in a free trade area (FTA) is positive at the one percent level of statistical significance for all years. Its coefficient declines from around 1.05 in the end of the 1960s to 0.7 in 1995, meaning that membership in an FTA increases trade volumes by around 2.8 to 2 fold (Figure 24). This is surprising, because economic integration within FTAs is supposed to have become deeper in that period, and most FTAs have not been in place in the beginning of the sample period. At least, it shows that on average these countries that recently formed FTAs are natural trading partners.

In the second regression, I distinguish between the six FTAs and use dummies for each of them. The EFTA dummy is significantly negative or insignificant. The EC12 dummy is significantly negative until 1982 and insignificant for all years but one since then. Although surprising, since the intra-EC12 trade share was 58 percent in 1970 and 62 percent in 1994, these results confirm previous trade bloc estimates as, for instance, by Frankel (1997). Instead, Mercosur, which encompasses only Brazil and Argentina, is significant at the one percent level for almost all years, although Mercosur agreements have only recently been made. Similarly, the Andean Pact dummy is positive but not significant for all years, reflecting a changing success of the FTA. Following a revision of the agreement in 1989, the coefficients are significant at the one percent level since 1990. Finally, the East Asian Caucus — five of its members also take part in ASEAN —, although only formed in 1990, is significant at the one percent level

---

[88] The French-speaking countries in this sample are Canada, Belgium/Luxembourg, Switzerland, France, Algeria, Tunisia, and Morocco.

Figure 24 — The Evolution of the FTA Coefficients

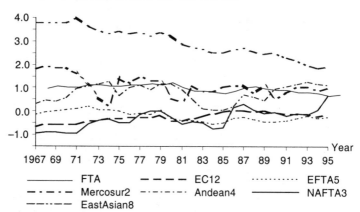

for all years. Although even higher in the 1970s, it still increases trade volumes 7-fold. This shows that it is a natural trading bloc. In 1995, all FTAs besides the EC12 and EFTA5 (Figure 24) are positive and significant at the five percent level, at least.

Freight Costs, Search Costs, and Sectoral Market Structure

The gravity regressions show that distance matters. Still, it remains unclear in what way distance costs reduce trade volumes. The trade-reducing effect of distance can reflect freight costs or search costs, i.e., information and communication costs.[89] These costs may differ between sectors.

In order to examine the relative importance of search and freight costs, Rauch (1999) divides production into homogeneous, near-homogeneous, and differentiated goods. He shows that insurance and freight costs as percentage of customs values are about twice as high for homogeneous and near-homogeneous goods than for differentiated goods. From that, one would expect lower distance coefficients for differentiated than for homogeneous goods.

Another reason for distance to be less important for differentiated goods is the better ability to price to market. New trade theory models assume that sectors with internal EOS produce differentiated goods. Sectors with constant returns to scale produce homogeneous goods, because the high elasticity of substitution between goods means that consumers are not willing to pay a high markup for a specific variety, and product differentiation does not pay. With low markups, it

---

[89] Unfortunately, distance is a very crude measure for several influences. Peschel (1981) argues that distance, for instance, also reflects influences that result from past political and economic developments.

may not pay to ship goods to distant foreign markets. In differentiated-goods industries, markups are high and firms are more flexible in their price setting and can price to market. Thus, in differentiated-goods industries, with low elasticities of substitution between goods and, consequently, high EOS and high markups, one would expect a low distance coefficient, because trade volumes react less sensitive to trade costs.

The alternative hypothesis is that differentiated goods have higher distance coefficients because of search costs.[90] The previous regressions have already shown that communication, as facilitated by speaking a common language, is an important determinant of trade flows. Trade in differentiated goods is subject to higher search costs, because product characteristics can vary along more dimensions than for homogeneous goods.[91] Hence, taking into account search costs, one would expect a higher distance coefficient for differentiated goods. One would also expect a higher common language coefficient, since speaking the same language makes information and search easier.[92]

In order to investigate further the effects of search costs versus freight costs and the sectoral market structure, I draw on the sectoral markup estimates by Oliveira–Martins et al. (1996) which were reported in Chapter C.I.2 (Figure 17). They divide industries into four groups concerning their market structure and product differentiation. The indicator for the sectoral market structure is the relative firm size. It reflects entry conditions through, for instance, internal economies of scale. A sector with the average size of its firms being small is called fragmented, one with the average size of its firms being large is called segmented. In the former, the number of firms increases with an enlargement of the market, in the latter, firm concentration in the sector is relatively stable. One may expect that competition is fiercer in fragmented than in segmented markets due to a larger number of competitors. This leads to lower margins and, hence, to higher distance elasticities.

---

[90] For instance, Cyrus (1997) finds higher border effects for goods in which Canada and the United States have a high portion of intraindustry trade rather than interindustry trade.

[91] For homogeneous goods, the price is the only characteristic which can vary between different producers. Hence, trade can take place in organized commodity exchanges. Otherwise, at least some reference prices exist. For differentiated goods, the importer also has to get information about the quality and the exact type of the product, the terms of delivery, etc. This makes a more detailed communication between importer and exporter necessary. Thus, finding the product that exactly suits the importer's needs is the more difficult, the more goods are differentiated.

[92] Rauch (1999) estimates a gravity model and adjusts his estimates for the different transportability of goods in order to single out the effects of search costs. He finds that distance and a common language or colonial ties are more important for differentiated goods than for homogeneous goods, but the difference is too small in absolute magnitudes to give much support for the importance of search costs.

The indicator for sectoral product differentiation is R&D intensity. Low R&D intensity is associated with low product differentiation. A combination of R&D intensity and relative firm size gives four sectoral groups.

Group 1 consists of sectors with low product differentiation and fragmented markets.[93] Group 2 consists of sectors with low product differentiation and segmented markets.[94] Group 3 consists of sectors with high product differentiation and fragmented markets.[95] Group 4 consists of sectors with high product differentiation and segmented markets.[96]

I reestimate the first gravity regression for the four groups. Table 17 shows detailed results for 1995. For a given market structure, distance is less important if product differentiation is high. This means that lower transport costs outweigh higher search costs for differentiated goods. Still search costs seem to matter, since language coefficients are higher for both groups with high product differentiation. Language coefficients are lower for segmented than for fragmented industries. This is in line with search costs, since search is easier in markets with a few firms only, part of which might be multinational enterprises with intrafirm trade and similar products on all markets. However, given the product differentiation, distance is more important in segmented than in fragmented markets. This result is puzzling, as search costs should be lower in these markets and markups should be higher, since competition between a small number of firms is expected to be less fierce than in markets with a high number of firms. One possible explanation for these findings is that the fragmentation of a sector might also reflect a higher degree of specialization and, hence, product differentiation for which search costs are higher.

Thus, I conclude from this section that search costs are an important determinant of international trade. However, they are outweighed by lower transport costs for differentiated goods. The division between segmented and fragmented markets does not turn out to be a useful proxy for the market structure to explain sectoral differences of distance coefficients.

---

93   These are textiles, articles in wood, furniture, printing and publications, plastic articles, cereal products, fats, meat and fish, preserved food and vegetable products, sugar products, and animal foodstuffs (i.e., sectors D, EA, EB, ED, GH, KA, KB, KC, KE, KF, and KG in the CHELEM data base).

94   These are ceramics, glass, iron and steel, nonferrous metals, ships, rubber articles, refined petroleum products, beverages, and manufactured tobaccos (i.e., sectors BB, BC, CA, CC, FV, GI, IH, KH, and KI in the CHELEM data base).

95   These are watch- and clockmaking, optics and photographic and cinematographic equipment, precision instruments, precious stones, and jewelry and works of art (i.e., sectors FJ, FK, FI, and NA in the CHELEM data base).

96   These are consumer electronics, telecommunications equipment, computer equipment, electrical apparatus, vehicle components, cars, commercial vehicles and transport equipment, aeronautics, basic inorganic chemicals, fertilizers, basic organic chemicals, pharmaceuticals, plastics, and fibers and synthetic resins (i.e., sectors FM, FN, FO, FR, FS, FT, FU, FW, GA, GB, GC, GF, and GG in the CHELEM data base).

Table 17 — Regression Results for Different Sectors in 1995

	Low-differentiated, fragmented	Low-differentiated, segmented	High-differentiated, fragmented	High-differentiated, segmented
Constant	−19.35***	−24.16***	−34.55***	−26.58***
	(1.00)	(1.02)	(0.90)	(0.98)
lngdp	1.00***	1.23***	1.22***	1.14***
	(0.03)	(0.03)	(0.03)	(0.03)
lngdpc	0.24***	0.27***	0.59***	0.47***
	(0.03)	(0.04)	(0.03)	(0.04)
lndis	−0.81***	−1.10***	−0.68***	−0.89***
	(0.06)	(0.07)	(0.07)	(0.07)
Adjacency	0.22	0.39	−0.14	0.25
	(0.19)	(0.28)	(0.24)	(0.26)
Language	0.97***	0.72***	1.27***	0.96***
	(0.15)	(0.17)	(0.15)	(0.17)
FTA	1.13***	0.85***	0.96***	1.07***
	(0.13)	(0.17)	(0.16)	(0.17)
$\overline{R}^2$	0.55	0.60	0.66	0.59
SEE	2.25	2.43	2.33	2.55
F-Test	408	499	641	473

**Significant at 5 percent level, ***significant at 1 percent level. — Number of observations: 1,980; White-heteroskedasticity-consistent standard deviations in parentheses.

Source: Own calculations.

Therefore, I analyze the effects of market structure and distance elasticities with a different, more direct approach. I use the sectoral markup estimates of Oliveira–Martins et al. (1996) and sort sectors accordingly. The sectoral markup is used as an indicator for the degree of product differentiation and the ability to price to market. Since markup estimates were made for 14 OECD countries only, I constrain my estimates to these 14 countries, too.[97] Results for 20 sectors are presented in Table 18.[98] The sectors are sorted according to their markups, such that sector 1 has the highest and sector 20 has the lowest markup. They are presented such that sectors with the highest distance elasticities are at the top of the table.

---

[97]   The fourteen countries are: United States, Japan, Germany, France, Italy, United Kingdom, Canada, Australia, Belgium, Denmark, Finland, Netherlands, Norway, and Sweden. The results turn out not to be very sensitive to the sample of countries. For other samples, the fit of the regressions, however, decrease mildly.

[98]   The sectors are (CHELEM Sector Code in brackets): 1) Drugs and medicine (GF), 2) Office and computing machinery (FO), 3) Beverages (KH), 4) Pottery, china, and glass products (BB, BC), 5) Telecommunications, radio, and TV (FM, FN), 6) Aircraft (FW), 7) Iron and steel (CA), 8) Shipbuilding (FV), 9) Petroleum and coal products (IA, IH), 10) Wood products (EA), 11) Electrical apparatus (FR), 12) Non-ferrous metals (CC), 13) Paper products and pulp, furniture (EB, EC), 14) Metal products (F), 15) Plastic products (GG, GH), 16) Printing and publishing (ED), 17) Food products (KA, KB, KC, KD, KE, KF, KG), 18) Petroleum refineries (IH), 19) Motor vehicles (FF, FU), 20) Textiles (DA, DB, DC, DD).

Table 18 — Regression Results, Sectoral Data 1995

Sector	Constant	lngdp	lngdpc	lndis	Adja-cency	Common language	FTA	$\bar{R}^2$	SEE	F-Test
18	25.93**	0.98***	−1.54***	−2.40***	1.17***	0.05	−2.30***	0.68	1.74	64
	(10.52)	(0.08)	(0.50)	(0.16)	(0.43)	(0.46)	(0.40)			
7	26.46**	0.84***	−1.55**	−1.80***	1.14***	0.17	−1.59***	0.56	1.79	39
	(13.00)	(0.10)	(0.63)	(0.19)	(0.35)	(0.39)	(0.38)			
9	43.94***	0.79***	−2.43***	−1.62***	1.65***	0.01	−1.83***	0.49	1.87	30
	(11.34)	(0.09)	(0.54)	(0.19)	(0.36)	(0.39)	(0.42)			
14	8.20	0.69***	−0.65	−1.57***	0.98***	0.36	−0.42	0.71	1.29	75
	(8.52)	(0.07)	(0.41)	(0.15)	(0.29)	(0.31)	(0.30)			
13	23.54***	0.76***	−1.36***	−1.56***	1.04***	0.10	−1.47***	0.56	1.53	40
	(8.39)	(0.08)	(0.40)	(0.18)	(0.31)	(0.41)	(0.32)			
10	11.51	0.70***	−0.86*	−1.44***	1.32***	0.13	−0.92**	0.57	1.55	41
	(10.13)	(0.08)	(0.49)	(0.16)	(0.36)	(0.33)	(0.40)			
6	32.09***	1.41***	−2.78***	−1.38***	0.19	1.13***	−1.56***	0.62	1.80	51
	(11.61)	(0.10)	(0.56)	(0.18)	(0.42)	(0.37)	(0.46)			
15	3.22	0.88***	−0.61**	−1.35***	0.48**	0.18	−0.18	0.74	1.12	89
	(6.15)	(0.06)	(0.30)	(0.13)	(0.23)	(0.30)	(0.26)			
12	26.51***	0.80***	−1.70***	−1.25***	1.14***	0.41*	−1.13***	0.61	1.30	48
	(8.88)	(0.07)	(0.43)	(0.14)	(0.23)	(0.24)	(0.28)			
8	−8.51	0.79***	−0.12	−1.21***	1.08*	0.43	−1.51***	0.30	2.23	14
	(14.00)	(0.12)	(0.68)	(0.23)	(0.61)	(0.57)	(0.54)			
20	11.33*	0.90***	−1.11***	−1.19***	0.40*	0.33	0.19	0.76	1.05	99
	(6.59)	(0.05)	(0.33)	(0.11)	(0.24)	(0.24)	(0.28)			
16	5.89	0.86***	−0.89**	−1.15***	0.58*	1.44***	−0.09	0.69	1.25	68
	(7.05)	(0.06)	(0.35)	(0.13)	(0.30)	(0.32)	(0.30)			
4	2.90	0.95***	−0.85**	−1.08***	1.06***	0.06	−0.27	0.73	1.11	82
	(6.90)	(0.05)	(0.35)	(0.11)	(0.24)	(0.28)	(0.27)			
19	−3.69	0.79***	−0.26	−1.07***	0.85***	0.46	−0.37	0.64	1.22	54
	(6.89)	(0.07)	(0.33)	(0.13)	(0.27)	(0.32)	(0.29)			
2	−6.32	1.04***	−0.50	−0.93***	−0.20	0.45	0.01	0.74	1.05	88
	(6.66)	(0.05)	(0.32)	(0.10)	(0.28)	(0.30)	(0.29)			
11	−7.98	0.88***	−0.22	−0.92***	0.74***	0.11	−0.27	0.72	1.01	77
	(6.39)	(0.05)	(0.30)	(0.10)	(0.21)	(0.27)	(0.20)			
5	−4.67	0.71***	−0.17	−0.87***	0.35	0.17	−0.25	0.51	1.31	32
	(8.10)	(0.07)	(0.38)	(0.13)	(0.26)	(0.37)	(0.27)			
1	−2.79	0.80***	−0.42	−0.85***	−0.13	0.47	0.26	0.58	1.27	43
	(8.40)	(0.06)	(0.41)	(0.13)	(0.22)	(0.31)	(0.30)			
3	28.77**	0.98***	−2.31***	−0.83***	0.11	0.83**	1.07**	0.58	1.70	43
	(11.07)	(0.08)	(0.53)	(0.16)	(0.30)	(0.37)	(0.43)			
17	−3.47	0.58***	−0.10	−0.79***	0.05	1.02***	1.18***	0.63	1.21	52
	(9.68)	(0.06)	(0.46)	(0.11)	(0.24)	(0.23)	(0.28)			

*Significant at 10 percent level, **significant at 5 percent level, ***significant at 1 percent level. — Number of observations: 182; White-heteroskedasticity-consistent standard deviations in parentheses.

Source: Own calculations.

Distance and absolute GDP are significant at the one percent level in all sectors. Border effects and language effects vary starkly between sectors and should be interpreted with care due to the small sample size and the low number of countries that speak a common language or are adjacent in this sample. Idiosyncratic influences are likely to dominate their results. The coefficient of per capita income is insignificant in several sectors, indicating that differences in factor endowments play a small role only in this relatively homogeneous sample. Sectors in which distance has the most trade-restricting impact are petroleum refineries, iron and steel, petroleum and coal products, and metal products. These industries produce relatively heavy goods with a high ratio of transport costs to value added such that distance between exporters and importers can have an important role for the volume of trade. Distance has the least trade-restricting impact in food products, beverages, drugs and medicine, and telecommunications, radio, and TV. It is striking that these sectors have above-average markups. The positive and significant FTA dummy for food products and beverages is likely to indicate the protection of the agricultural sector of several FTAs against outside competition.

The sectoral market structure was also used as an indicator of the product differentiation within a sector. Lower distance coefficients for differentiated goods could be expected if lower freight costs and the ability to price to market outweigh higher search costs. This is indeed the case. Figure 25 displays sectoral markups and distance coefficients. Distance coefficients are lower (in absolute terms), the higher the average markup in a sector. I run a naive regression with the distance elasticity as dependent variable on the sectoral markup and a constant. The coefficient of the markup equals 1.961 with a t-value of 2.04, and a R^2 of 0.19. This means that a 10 percent markup is associated with a lower distance elasticity (in absolute values) of 0.196. This translates into higher trade flows in the order of 22 percent. This means that there is no evidence that search costs are a major obstacle to trade in this 20 sector sample. "Traditional" freight costs and the market structure are more decisive determinants of trade flows.

Figure 25 — Sectoral Markups and Distance

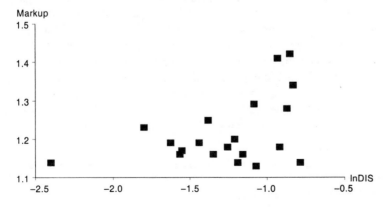

Concluding this chapter, I have shown that distance elasticities did decline in the last three decades. However, the impact of distance on trade flows is still far from negligible. In 1995, doubling the distance between trading partners decreased trade flows by 83 percent (regression two). This shows the empirical relevance of trade costs and, hence, confirms the second main assumption of economic geography models.

III.   The Empirical Relevance of the Economic Geography Model

In the theoretical part, testable hypotheses concerning the working of economic geography models have been derived. It has been shown that several variables are expected to influence spatial concentration. In this section, I test the power of these variables to explain the degree of spatial concentration within countries. I use the country level for data reasons, without implying that economic geography effects work on that level only.[99] This has the advantage that the study can draw on concepts used in the literature of urban and regional economics. As frequently done in this literature, I use the share of the largest city in the total urban population — the so-called primacy ratio — as the measure of spatial concentration within a country.[100]

The main point of the prototype economic geography model is the ambiguous influence of trade costs. High trade costs work in favor of spatial dispersion. Low and intermediate trade costs work in favor of spatial concentration. The sign of the coefficient of the trade cost proxy will tell which effects prevail. The augmented model suggests that congestion effects are an important centrifugal force that pushes industries and workers out of core into peripheral regions. If so, then population density and the possibility to escape from congestion, as indicated by a large land area, decrease spatial concentration. The main point of the development model is the explanation of different spatial structures across regions and throughout the economic development of single countries. Hence, the main focus of this section is to test the prediction that the relationship of economic development and industrial concentration can indeed be described by an inverted U-curve. Since this is a long-studied hypothesis, I am going to refer to the literature and try to embed my analysis therein.

---

[99]   So far, there are still no clear-cut results on which level economic geography phenomena work. See also Section C.I.2.c on this point.

[100] This chapter draws on Junius (1997b).

An alternative hypothesis to the inverted U-curve is that cities grow in a parallel way, which means that spatial concentration is unaffected by urbanization and economic development (Black and Henderson 1997, Eaton and Eckstein 1997, and Krugman 1996). Then, the distribution of the urban population may simply reflect geography or historic shocks, which created a functional system of cities and cemented a size distribution such that further urbanization only increased the population of cities in a parallel way.[101]

This alternative is far less appealing, because it does not promise any relief from the problems that several developing countries have at present with congestion, regional disparities, and the excessive growth of their primate cities. To understand which one of the two development possibilities actually prevails, several papers have tried to reveal an inverted U-curve pattern of primacy and economic development in time-series and cross-country analyses. These empirical papers are surveyed in the next section. While time-series analyses often support the existence of an inverted U-curve, cross-country evidence is mixed.

This chapter makes a new attempt to show the existence of an inverted U-curve in a cross-country setting, using different country samples than previous studies and additional conditional variables for which the economic geography framework has shown an influence on the likelihood that a country develops a dispersed or a concentrated system of urban settlement. I test the impact of the historical spatial concentration in addition to and against these variables. Hence, Section 2 reviews the theoretical arguments for the existence of an inverted U-curve and other determinants of spatial concentration. Section 3 discusses the empirical procedure and presents the results.

1.   Previous Empirical Evidence for the Inverted U-Curve

Time-series studies find ample evidence for the inverted U-curve in single countries. El-Shakhs (1972) shows the existence of an inverted U-curve for the United Kingdom, and Alperovich (1992) shows the existence of such a curve for Israel. Parr (1985) estimates Pareto coefficients for 12 countries and several years between 1850 and 1981.[102] He finds strong evidence for the inverted U-

---

[101] For instance, the fact that Vienna dominates the urban system of Austria so much is more likely to be traced back to its century-long role as a capital of a huge empire than to current GDPC levels. Similarly, France is more concentrated than Germany, because it has no federal political history but has been centrally governed from Paris for the longest part of the recent history.

[102] The estimation of Pareto coefficients is widely used in this literature. It goes back to Singer (1936) who postulated that similar to Pareto's law of income distribution, the size distribution of cities within a country can be described by a "Pareto-function":

curve in the high-income countries, Austria, France, Sweden, and the United States. Concentration peaks around 1910 in Austria, 1930 in the United States and Sweden, and 1954 in France. The evidence for the curve is weaker for Brazil, Japan, Spain, and the USSR, while in the low-income countries, Egypt, India, Nigeria, and Turkey, no clear reversal of the trend toward increasing concentration can be observed yet. Eaton and Eckstein (1997) calculate Lorenz curves for city size distributions for France since 1876 and for Japan since 1925. In contrast to Parr's evidence, these authors argue that relative city sizes in France and Japan did not vary enough to exclude the possibility of parallel growth in the course of economic development.[103]

$R = KP^{-\phi}$, where P is a particular population size of a city, R indicates the rank of a city which equals the number of cities with a population of more than P, and K and ϕ are parameters to be estimated. The higher ϕ, the smaller the concentration of the urban population in the largest cities is. Thus, the existence of an inverted U-curve is shown by a first decreasing and then increasing value of ϕ in the course of economic development.

For a "Pareto coefficient" $\phi = 1$, one gets the so-called rank-size rule, which states that the rank times the population of a city equals a constant, which is the size of the largest city. Most authors test a log-linear form of the relationship, which implies a constant Pareto coefficient. Hsing (1990) argues that the degree of concentration may vary in different stages of development and growth, such that a log-linear form is inappropriate. He uses a general functional form, which includes the log-linear form as a special case. The general functional form turns out to be a much better method for the estimation of Pareto coefficients. The log-linear form is rejected at the 5 percent level. Furthermore, he finds that Pareto coefficients decline with urban size, such that small cities have more population than indicated by the rank-size rule. Alperovich and Deutsch (1995) develop this approach further and also reject the Pareto distribution.

[103] See Carroll (1982) and Kasarda and Crenshaw (1991) for a survey of further early time-series and cross-section studies on the distribution of city sizes. For an overview of determinants of urban concentration, see Mutlu (1989) and Sheppard (1982). Sheppard also provides a thorough discussion of rank-size estimates. Using deviations from the rank-size rule as a primacy measure and Coles' economic development index, he does not find evidence for an inverted U-curve, but also concludes that this might be so because his measure for primacy is of little empirical value (Sheppard 1982: 140). Mutlu (1989) presents a number of variables used in previous studies but finds only weak evidence for an impact of economic variables on concentration measures. GNP per capita reduces concentration in his sample of up to 90 countries. The size of the absolute urban population and absolute total population, as well as the size of the arable land, reduce concentration as well, while greater income inequality increases concentration measures. Mera (1973) uses a sample of 46 developing countries and finds a positive relationship between concentration and development. He argues that urban concentration is a precondition of economic development in early stages. He shows that growth of primacy explains overall GDPC growth rates over a 7-year-period. This relationship is stronger if the analysis is restricted to larger countries, indicating that in small countries, other than economic variables may determine the distribution of the urban population. However, as primacy measures, he uses the share of the largest cities as percentage of total population instead of the share of the largest cities as percentage of the urban population. These

Cross-country studies find mixed evidence for the inverted U-curve. William-son (1965), Kamerschen (1969), El-Shakhs (1972), Wheaton and Shishido (1981), and DeCola (1984) find evidence for the inverted U-curve between ur-ban concentration and economic development. Kamerschen (1969) uses data for 80 countries and the share of the largest city in percent of the four largest cities as a measure of concentration. He finds a negative relationship between urban concentration on the one hand and GDPC and industrialization on the other hand for developing countries, and a positive relationship for developed countries. Wheaton and Shishido (1981) use the *Inverse-H index* for measuring urban con-centration and test the inverted U-curve relationship against a linear relation-ship.[104] Using a sample of 38 countries, that have at least three metropolises, they find that the inverted U-curve explains the data much better.

Rosen and Resnick (1980), Mutlu (1989), Lemelin and Polèse (1995), and Moomaw and Shatter (1996) find a negative relationship between spatial con-centration and economic development. Rosen and Resnick (1980) use a sample of 44 developing and developed countries. They test for the significance of sev-eral variables on calculated Pareto coefficients. Higher GNP per capita and total population lead to a more evenly distributed population. The density of the rail network, the export-to-GNP ratio, the percentage of the nonagricultural labor force, and a dummy for former colonies are not found to be significant in the overall sample. In a sample of 61 countries, Lemelin and Polèse (1995) find that primacy is indirectly linked to the level of economic development. Primacy falls monotonically with the degree of development. They mention, albeit do not prove, that their results are robust to alternative measures of primacy and devel-opment, and to alternative country subsets. Moomaw and Shatter (1996) use panel data for 90 countries and find that primacy ratios increase if the largest city is also the capital of a country. They also find that GDPC, literacy, population, and export orientation reduce primacy. In a prominent recent study, Ades and Glaeser (1995) show the impact of political factors on primacy ratios for 85 countries. Openness and high government expenditures for transportation de-crease primacy ratios, while dictatorships and political instability increase them. As above, primacy is also higher for countries, in which the largest city is also the capital.

---

increase with urbanization and do not solely indicate the concentration of the urban population.

[104] The *Inverse-H index* is: $1/H = \sum_{k=1}^{s} (P_k/P)^2$,

where P_k is population in city k, P is total population, and s is the number of city size categories. This index has been criticized for being correlated with the number of cities in the sample.

Richardson and Schwartz (1988) find no support for the economic development and primacy link at all. For the 116 countries under study, they show that demographic factors are more important and render economic variables insignificant. They also show that 40 percent of the variation of primacy can be explained by national population, urban population, and a Latin America dummy. Their results are criticized by Lemelin and Polèse (1995), partly for not testing for multicollinearity. Urbanization is strongly correlated with economic development and GDPC levels. Hence, insignificant coefficients for GDPC levels in the presence of urbanization or industrialization variables should not come as a surprise. Another problem might be the large sample size, which probably includes a large number of very small countries, where no economic rationale predicts systematic domestic economic forces to be able to unfold and to play a dominant role for the city size distribution.

Arbitrary sample selection is often the reason why the previous empirical results are very sensitive to the group of countries included in the analysis. Therefore, the economic rationale for the selection of countries and explanatory variables is thoroughly discussed in Section 2 and Section 3.2.

2.   Explaining the Inverted U-Curve and Further Determinants of Primacy

The review of the empirical literature of cross-country studies shows that the evidence is mixed as to whether an inverted U-curve exists or not. Thus, the current status and the appropriate attitude toward the inverted U-curve is somewhat similar to what Williamson (1997) writes about the Kuznets Curve: "...now you see it, now you don't. The important inference of that fact, however, is *not* to reject the Kuznets Curve, but to ask why we sometimes see it and sometimes not." Most important for the understanding of changes in the concentration and dispersion of economic activities over time is to understand the interplay between centrifugal and centripetal forces that drives this process. In general, positive economies of scale foster agglomerations and industrial clusters, and negative spillovers and higher factor costs foster population dispersion. From that, some authors have tried to theoretically derive explanations for the inverted U-curve.

Wheaton and Shishido (1981) argue that economic development increases capital intensity in industrial production. As capital intensity increases fixed costs compared to variable costs, scale intensity increases. This favors larger cities. Therefore, efficient city size increases with economic development until some sort of capital saturation sets in as scale economies are not exploitable without bound. This again levels the population concentration in later stages of economic development.

Parr and Jones (1983) suggest a five-stages approach of economic development and primacy. The pre-urban stage is characterized by a low-quality transportation system, which limits the extent of regional markets, intraregional trade, and the exploitation of scale economies. On a later stage, improvements in the transportation system allow for more intraregional trade, which pushes some sites above the critical mass of production. This leads to rapid growth of certain specialized cities. On a third stage, stronger interindustry linkages further allow exploitation of scale economies in larger cities. On the fourth stage, improvements of interurban transportation systems and a high income elasticity of land demand lead to suburbanization and levels economic conditions between cities. This development is extended on the last stage, where several regional markets achieve a sufficient size for the production of a large number of goods. Together with negative externalities from concentration in the core, this leads to a leveling of the population distribution within a country. Thus, falling transport costs have ambiguous effects. They strengthen centripetal forces at low income levels and centrifugal forces at high income levels.

The economic geography prototype model has formalized the impact of transport costs on the pattern of production. High transportation costs between a center and a periphery may lead to the development of two distinct industrial or urban centers. When transport costs are medium high, the possibility of stronger backward and forward linkages makes the center a more attractive place to locate. When transport costs are low, linkage effects can be realized from all possible locations. This leads to a U-curve between the degree of concentration and the level of transport costs.

The model has been augmented by the effects of economic development in Chapter B.IV to derive the inverted U-curve between concentration and economic development. Pecuniary externalities provide forward and backward linkages that strengthen the core of a country in the course of economic development. Core regions benefit from the sectoral change to industrial production that usually accompanies economic development. As a consequence, a higher share of the work force starts working in the footloose industrial sector under increasing returns to scale. The product demand from these workers reinforces centripetal forces that make it even more profitable for firms to cluster. Increasing concentration, however, also leads to negative externalities due to crowding and pollution. These congestion effects decrease the advantages of being in the core. This levels economic conditions between core and peripheral regions. Thus, peripheral regions gain after some level of concentration is reached in the core. Then, the producers of goods that can realize only small EOS or of those that are very costly to transport have few reasons to cluster and are the first to set up business in peripheral sites.[105] The resulting inverted U-curve between urban concentration and economic development is intensified by a fall of transport costs.

Economic factors can only play an important role if they are able to unfold themselves without being dominated by other factors. Neighboring countries and geographic or demographic factors may especially determine the population distribution of small countries, like Luxembourg or Singapore, where two independent metropolises additionally are not distinguishable statistically. Also, internal transport costs do not matter much in small countries, such that any location would have an advantage for just-in-time production. Small countries are unlikely to form a functional system of cities and pattern of industry distribution independent from their neighbors and geographic factors.

In countries with a low absolute (urban) population, the distribution of the population is likely to be determined by endowment factors. Neither positive nor negative external economies of scale are strong enough to determine the population distribution between its different parts. This means that congestion effects are unlikely to push people out of Iceland's Reykjavik with 145,000 inhabitants. Iceland's population distribution is more likely to reflect resource endowments and climatic conditions than scale economies. That is, in order to test for the influence of economic determinants on primacy, only these countries can be used that are not too small in terms of the area or the number of inhabitants.

Concluding from the above models, one would expect a positive coefficient of GDP per capita and a negative coefficient of the squared GDP per capita value on a measure of spatial concentration, provided that countries are equal in all other respects besides GDP per capita. However, countries differ in several respects that influence the likelihood of developing a balanced urban system other than the pure economic forces described by the models. To correct for the different potential to develop several urban agglomerations, the economic geography model suggests to make the degree of concentration conditional on the following variables:

The extent of the transportation system as, for instance, indicated by road kilometers per land area (*ROADLAND*), has an ambiguous effect on the degree of concentration. The economic geography model has shown, that, on the one hand, lower transport costs increase the degree of competition that the few firms in the peripheral region face from the large number of firms in the core region. This reduces the attractiveness of peripheral sites and increases the advantages of the primate city as a location of production and consumption. On the other

---

[105] Hanson (1996) further describes the process of agglomeration and subsequent dispersion of non-external EOS sectors to the periphery, when agglomeration drives up wages, land rents, and congestion costs in the center.

hand, lower transport costs mean that distance is getting less important, such that the need to cluster in order to realize scale economies is less severe. Then, industries are able to escape higher land prices and congestion effects by shifting production away from the core and still benefit from agglomeration and scale economies. The coefficient of the variable measuring the extent of the transportation system may, therefore, be interpreted as an indicator for the prevailing effect.

Densely populated countries (*DENSE*) are likely to be less concentrated for two reasons. First, population concentration comes along with negative externalities like congestion effects and pollution. They constitute an upper bound to city size after which no or only few scale economies can be realized, and, thus, provide strong incentives to disperse. Second, high densities provide the possibility to disperse since a large number of workers will be available in several parts of the country, such that scale economies can be exploited not only in the primate city. They constitute the critical mass of workers and local demand for the production of certain goods that is needed for the formation of a city. Thus, through the existence of a lower and an upper bound to city size, densely populated countries are likely to exhibit several optimal-sized cities. This reduces urban concentration.

A large land area (*LAND*) increases the probability of forming several metropolises and, thus, leads to lower levels of concentration in a country. First, it increases the number of possible sites for potential cities that emerge because of the availability of natural resources or natural advantages like ports or transportation nodes. Second, it implies large distances between different parts of a country. Such differences may have favored the development of different urban systems. This is, because historically, the extent of the market for perishable goods was much more limited than it is today. Additionally, certain services and administrative functions had to be located close to the generally dispersed rural population, such that large countries developed a larger number of medium-size cities.

In addition to these variables indicating the possibilities of a country to disperse, the degree of concentration can be influenced by politics. An open trade regime (*OPEN*) favors export industries and population dispersion, because being close to the center of the home market becomes less important. Instead, being close to the market of the neighboring countries and to transportation nodes and harbors becomes decisive. This disperses industries and population as Krugman and Livas Elizondo (1996) have shown in an extended economic geography model. Openness also means better opportunities for nonindustrial activities like agriculture. Agriculture is often discriminated in less open regimes, which prevents the development of dispersed food processing and other rural industries.

Undemocratic institutions, the deprivation of civil or political rights and of property rights, and domestic unrest (*POLITICS*) are likely to favor urban concentration. In countries with these properties, there often is a strong central and primate bias of government spending. This reflects that in such political systems, spatial politics are often used to assure maximum political control over a country, population, and administration. Government expenditures subsidize services to the advantage of the urban class which is the backbone of political support. Together with a tendency to nepotism in government spending, this increases the size of the primate city.

Finally, a colonial history is likely to favor strong primate cities. For administrative reasons, the capital of a colony had strong links with the colonial power and, consequently, less strong links with the rest of the national urban system. Production and trade was often more oriented toward the demand of the colonial power than toward the demand of the domestic population. Thus, it often took place in export exclaves, which delinked the capital from the rest of the country and prevented the development of a dispersed domestic urban system. That also prevented the establishment of a traffic network with neighboring countries. In addition, innovations and other positive growth shocks diffused more slowly to secondary centers than they did in countries without a colonial history. The result is a persistent dominance of the capital city with few and much smaller rival cities. The dominance is expected to be the stronger, the longer countries have been under colonial rule. Therefore, depending on the date of independence, two colonial dummies are used to approximate their different historic or initial conditions.

3.   Empirical Results

a.   *Estimation Equation*

An inverted U-curve between primacy and economic development exists if primacy depends positively on PPP-adjusted real GDP per capita (*RGDPC*) and negatively on the squared *RGDPC* value. Hence, I estimate variants of the general equation:

[50] $PR = \delta_0 + \delta_1 RGDPC + \delta_2 RGDPC^2 + \delta_3 X + \mu$,

where *PR* is the primacy ratio, *X* is a vector of further explanatory variables, $\delta_0, \delta_1, \delta_2$, and δ_3 are the coefficients to be estimated, and μ is the error term. Since primacy measures are expressed in percentage points and, hence, can only vary between 0 and 1, they are limited dependent variables. Thus, to avoid estimation and interpretation problems, I assume that *PR* is distributed according to the logistic function. That is:

[51] $\quad PR = \dfrac{e^z}{1+e^z}$,

where $z = \delta_1 RGDPC + \delta_2 RGDPC^2 + \delta_3 X$. After transforming equation [51], primacy is not limited to the 0–1 range anymore:

[52] $\quad \dfrac{PR}{1-PR} = e^z$.

Taking logarithms on both sides, one arrives at an estimable equation:

[53] $\quad L = \ln(PR/(1-PR)) = z + \mu \quad$ or

[54] $\quad L = \delta_1 RGDPC + \delta_2 RGDPC^2 + \delta_3 X + \mu$.

b. Data

The sample of countries is selected as follows. I start with all 209 countries listed in World Bank (1996a) and use their 1990 values unless stated otherwise. I first exclude all small countries, i.e., countries with a land area below 30,000 square kilometers, which is slightly below the size of Belgium and slightly above the size of Haiti. I also exclude countries with an urban population below 1,000,000 or a total population below 3,000,000. The reason is that small countries' population patterns are very likely influenced by the spatial structures of their neighbors. They are less likely to have developed an own independent spatial system influenced by systematic economic phenomena only.

From the remaining countries, 16 countries are excluded because no PPP-based GDPC levels are available for either 1989, 1990, or 1991. The Dominican Republic, Myanmar, Saudi-Arabia, Nicaragua, and Sudan are excluded because data is missing for other variables. Observations for Togo, Somalia, Sierra Leone, Senegal, Mozambique, Madagascar, Honduras, Guinea, Chad, and Angola are excluded because the last census from which urban population data for 1990 is estimated or interpolated is older than 15 years. Further excluded are the observations for Costa Rica and Zimbabwe as they show large differences according to different sources, and Malawi for which recent estimates are only available for the capital but not for the primate city of the country. The remaining sample of 70 countries is listed in Table A3 in the Appendix.[106]

---

[106] The former CSFR takes the place of the Czech Republic. Data for Czechoslovakia is taken from the World Bank (1996a).

Data for the size of urban agglomerations is available from the *World Urbanization Prospects* of the UN (1995a) and relies on data from national sources. I complete the urban data by data from the UN *Demographic Yearbooks* (1992, 1995b), because the *World Urbanization Prospects* report urban data only for capital cities and cities with a population of more than 750,000 inhabitants. The advantage of the *World Urbanization Prospect* data is that it provides estimates for all countries in a single common year. However, this comes with the drawback that only estimated or interpolated data can be used, which is likely to inhibit measurement errors. Another problem arising from these data is that estimates for urban agglomerations may differ between the two sources. The statistical concept of measuring city size is different in different countries. Some of them report city proper data, others metropolitan area or urban agglomeration data. I use urban agglomeration data where possible, because it is a better measure of the true concentration of a country. On the basis of equation [53], I construct four dependent variables (*PRIMA1, PRIMA2, PRIMA3, PRIMA4*) indicating the share of the one, two, three, and four largest cities in the total urban population. *PRIMA2–PRIMA4* are frequently used in addition to *PRIMA1* in order to consider the size distribution of cities below the largest city. The different levels of *PRIMA1* are shown in Table A3.

The following variables are taken or calculated from the World Bank (1996a): Population density per square kilometers (*DENSE*), land in square kilometers (*LAND*), density of the transportation system measured as the ratio of road length to land area (*ROADLAND*), total population (*POPTOT*), and urban population (*POPURB*). For Russia, the surface instead of the land area has to be taken. This includes also the surface of interior seas or lakes. Data on road length for Bulgaria, Poland, Romania is from 1989, for Hungary from 1988, and for Iran from 1985.

Data for PPP-adjusted real GDPC (*RGDPC*) is taken from the Penn World Tables (Mark 5.6). See Summers and Heston (1991) for a description. For Niger, Romania, and Russia, *RGDPC* data is from 1989. Data for openness (*OPEN*) and the political regime (*POLITICS*) is taken from Sachs and Warner (1995: 10 f.).[107] According to their definitions, *OPEN* is a dummy variable that takes the value one if "(1) a very high proportion of imports [is] covered by quota restrictions...", "(2) for Sub-Saharan Africa, [if] a high proportion of exports [is] covered by state export monopolies and state-set prices...", the country has "(3) a socialist economic structure...", or if "(4) a black market premium over the official exchange rate of 20 percent or more, on average, [prevailed] either for the

---

[107] Sachs and Warner (1995) as well as Sala-i-Martin (1997) have found this measure of openness to be a statistically robust determinant of growth. It was also found to be superior to tariffs, the black market foreign exchange premium, and the trade to GDP ratio as a measure of openness. Therefore, it was also chosen for this study.

decade of the 1970s or the decade of the 1980s...". POLITICS is a dummy variable that takes the value one if the country has "(1) a socialist economic structure...", "(2) extreme domestic unrest, caused by revolutions, coups, chronic civil
unrest, or a prolonged war with a foreign country that is fought on domestic
territory...", or "(3) extreme deprivation of civil or political rights..." (Sachs and
Warner 1995: 9).

Data on the colonial history and the date of independence is taken from *Der
Fischer Weltalmanach 1998* (1997). I use two dummy variables to distinguish different lengths of colonial rule over a country (*COLONY*1815 and *COLONY*1950).
*COLONY*1815 takes the value 1 if the country was a colony in the year 1815.
Colonial powers, independent countries, and countries with a long urban history,
like China, Germany, Iran, and Thailand, take the value 0 also if they did not exist
as a political entity at that time. *COLONY*1950 indicates countries with a very short
history of independence. It takes the value 1 if a country was still a colony in 1950,
and 0 otherwise. In case the date of the proclaimed independence differs from the
final or recognized one, I use the year of the proclaimed independence.[108]

Data on historic variables is available from Banks (1971) for 45 countries. I
use 1919 data for railroad mileage per square mile (*RAIL*1919), telegraph mileage per square mile (*TEL*1919), and population density (*DENSE*1919). Density
data for China is from 1911, for Ireland from 1922, and for Korea from 1904.
GDPC data from 1913 (*GDPC*1913) is available from Maddison (1995) for 44
countries. For 26 countries, the share of industry in total industrial and agricultural employment in 1870 is taken from Mitchell (1992, 1993, 1995). The agricultural sector encompasses agriculture, forestry, and fishing. The industrial
sector encompasses extractive industry, manufacturing industry, construction,
and services.

Data on historic urban concentration is taken from two sources. For 41 countries, data for the size of the relatively largest of the three largest cities is available from Jefferson (1939). Concentration is measured around the year 1935 according to availability. For European countries, data for the size of cities in the
years 1800 and 1850 is available from Bairoch et al. (1988). From this data, I
calculate primacy ratios for 1800 and 1850 (*HISTO*1800 and *HISTO*1850). It
should be noted that the data used for the construction of today's primacy ratios
is based on the population of urban agglomerations, which are likely to encom-
pass cities and districts that are not included in the population of Bairoch et al.
(1988) city proper data for the 19th century.[109]

---

[108] I use the years 1815 and 1950, because they are two landmarks in world history.
1815 was the end of the Napoleonic Wars and the Congress of Vienna. 1950 roughly
marks the end of World War II and its postwar turmoil.

[109] Therefore, I also use the percentage of the largest city in 1800 and 1850 instead of
the percentage of today's largest city as the share of total urban population in 1800
and 1850.

I also standardize *LAND* by dividing it by the size of the smallest country, which is Belgium with 30,260 square kilometers. The resulting variable *NLAND* varies between 1 and 564. I standardize *RGDPC* by dividing it by the value of the poorest country, namely Zaire. The resulting new variables *NRGDPC* and *NRGDPC2* now range from 1 to 46.3 and from 1 to 2,147. I standardize *TEL*1919 by dividing it by the smallest value of the sample, such that the new variable *NTEL*1919 varies between 1 and 339.

c.   *Results*

As indicated in the last section, data for the size of the largest cities is not collected in a standardized way, but with different statistical concepts and from different sources. Additionally, not all explanatory variables are available for the full sample of 70 countries. Hence, I use different country samples to estimate the likely determinants of urban concentration. The results are reported in Table 19. The reported standard errors are corrected by White's heteroskedasticity-consistent variances and covariances.[110]

I start with the most reliable sample of countries. This sample includes 23 countries for which the *World Urbanization Prospects* reports at least four cities with a population of more than 750,000 inhabitants each.[111] For these countries, all four primacy ratios can be calculated from the same data source without relying on additional data from the UN *Demographic Yearbooks*. This sample is not only most reliable in terms of the data. In these countries, economic forces have the highest potential to unfold and not to be suppressed by idiosyncratic or genuine influences. This is because this sample only consists of large countries with a large urban population and a system of several cities.

In regression 1, the full set of current independent variables is used, with the exception of *COLONY*1950 because the sample does not contain countries that were a colony in 1950. Except for *OPEN*, all variables have the expected sign, but the equation only explains 20 percent of the observed cross-country variation of urban concentration as measured by *PRIMA*1. The coefficients of *NRGDPC* and *NRGDPC2* are statistically significant at the 5 percent level. The coefficient of *NLAND* is significant at the 1 percent level. The coefficients of *OPEN* and *POLITICS* have large standard deviations. The t-tests and a redundant variable F-test do not support the hypothesis that trade policy and "bad" politics influence the degree of urban concentration. The standard deviations of *ROADLAND* and

---

[110]   I also report the White test without cross terms. It shows the probability of no heteroskedasticity in the data, which is, for instance, 12.6 percent in the first regression. In the presence of heteroskedasticity, the coefficients are still unbiased, but not efficient, such that t-test and F-test are not interpretable.

[111]   These countries are marked with a # in Table A3 in the Appendix.

Table 19 — Regression Results for the Determinants of Primacy (PRIMA 1–4)

	Basic results		Different samples		
	1	2	3	4	5
NRGDPC	0.1120**	0.1139***	0.0829**	0.0833**	0.0676**
	(0.0387)	(0.0388)	(0.0346)	(0.0289)	(0.0287)
NRGDPC2	−0.0021**	−0.0021***	−0.0015**	−0.0015**	−0.0013**
	(0.0008)	(0.0007)	(0.0007)	(0.0006)	(0.0006)
NLAND	−0.0027***	−0.0023***	−0.0028***	−0.0027***	−0.0035***
	(0.0008)	(0.0006)	(0.0005)	(0.0005)	(0.0005)
DENSE	−0.0006	—	−0.0032	−0.0030	−0.0037***
	(0.0020)		(0.0019)	(0.0017)	(0.0010)
ROADLAND	−0.1996	−0.2229	—	—	—
	(0.3997)	(0.2854)			
COLONY1815	0.4624	0.4224*	0.3644	0.4097*	0.3641**
	(0.2746)	(0.2365)	(0.2186)	(0.1944)	(0.1767)
COLONY1950	—	—	—	—	0.4645*
					(0.2533)
POLITICS	0.2877	—	—	—	—
	(0.2937)				
OPEN	−0.1809	—	—	—	—
	(0.3649)				
$\bar{R}^2$	0.20	0.30	0.38	0.42	0.53
SEE	0.56	0.53	0.49	0.46	0.53
No. of observations	23	23	19	22	44
Jarque-Bera test for normality of residuals[a]	1.08	1.35	0.38	0.25	0.40
	(0.58)	(0.51)	(0.82)	(0.88)	(0.50)
White test for heteroskedasticity[a]	2.09	1.06	2.32	3.21	0.76
	(0.13)	(0.44)	(0.11)	(0.03)	(0.65)
Ramsey reset test (3)[a]	1.86	0.52	2.48	1.93	0.40
	(0.20)	(0.68)	(0.12)	(0.17)	(0.76)
F-test for omitted variables[a]	—	0.27	0.88	0.91	0.45
		(0.84)	(0.48)	(0.46)	(0.72)

	Different samples		Different measures of urban concentration		
	6	7	8	9	10
NRGDPC	0.0658**	0.0488	0.1039***	0.0985***	0.1008***
	(0.0312)	(0.0340)	(0.0351)	(0.0319)	(0.0331)
NRGDPC2	−0.0012*	−0.0009	−0.0018**	−0.0017**	−0.0017**
	(0.0006)	(0.0007)	(0.0006)	(0.0006)	(0.0006)
NLAND	−0.0033***	−0.0035***	−0.0019***	−0.0022***	−0.0023***
	(0.0006)	(0.0006)	(0.0006)	(0.0006)	(0.0006)
DENSE	−0.0011	−0.0008	—	—	—
	(0.0010)	(0.0008)			
ROADLAND	−0.2003	−0.2245*	−0.2077	−0.2723	−0.3071
	(0.1323)	(0.1168)	(0.2859)	(0.2687)	(0.2651)
COLONY1815	0.4888***	0.3802**	0.5410**	0.5326***	0.5617***
	(0.1662)	(0.1658)	(0.1985)	(0.1805)	(0.1841)
COLONY1950	0.4885*	0.2242	—	—	—
	(0.2614)	(0.2625)			
$\bar{R}^2$	0.41	0.31	0.30	0.37	0.41
SEE	0.57	0.60	0.49	0.45	0.45
No. of observations	54	70	23	23	23
Jarque-Bera test for normality of residuals[a]	0.79	0.06	1.02	0.84	0.96
	(0.67)	(0.97)	(0.60)	(0.66)	(0.62)
White test for heteroskedasticity[a]	1.13	1.27	2.08	1.91	1.64
	(0.36)	(0.26)	(0.11)	(0.14)	(0.20)
Ramsey reset test (3)[a]	0.49	1.45	1.30	1.45	1.60
	(0.69)	(0.24)	(0.31)	(0.27)	(0.23)
F-test for omitted variables[a]	0.06	0.77	0.13	0.16	0.20
	(0.94)	(0.47)	(0.94)	(0.92)	(0.90)

Table 19 continued

	Historic indicators		Historic infrastructure		Historic urban concentration		
	11	12	13	14	15	16	17
NRGDPC	0.0897*	0.0905**	0.0835**	0.0711**	0.0229	0.0225	0.0847**
	(0.0452)	(0.0336)	(0.0320)	(0.0337)	(0.0624)	(0.0650)	(0.0381)
NRGDPC2	−0.0017*	−0.0016**	−0.0017**	−0.0014**	−0.0008	−0.0007	−0.0017**
	(0.0008)	(0.0006)	(0.0006)	(0.0007)	(0.0013)	(0.0014)	(0.0008)
NLAND	−0.0032***	−0.0033***	−0.0035***	−0.0034***	—	—	—
	(0.0005)	(0.0005)	(0.0005)	(0.0006)			
DENSE	−0.0041***	—	—	—	—	—	—
	(0.0012)						
ROADLAND	—	−0.3021***	—	—	—	—	—
	—	(0.1025)					
COLONY1815	0.2539	0.5266**	0.4162**	0.5116***	0.7835**	0.6693*	0.6213***
	(0.2012)	(0.2182)	(0.1758)	(0.1861)	(0.3617)	(0.3532)	(0.2248)
Historic variables							
INDUSTRY1900	−0.8028	—	—	—	—	—	—
	(0.8303)						
GDPC1913	—	−0.0001	—	—	—	—	—
		(0.0001)					
DENSE1919	—	—	−0.0002***	—	—	—	—
			(0.0001)				
NTEL1919	—	—	−0.0018	−0.0022*	—	—	—
			(0.0013)	(0.0013)			
RAIL1919	—	—	—	−0.0003**	—	—	—
				(0.0001)			
JEFFRATIO	—	—	—	—	—	—	3.0756***
							(0.7086)
HISTO1850	—	—	—	—	—	2.7574***	—
						(0.6449)	
HISTO1800	—	—	—	—	2.3547***	—	—
					(0.6391)		
$\bar{R}^2$	0.41	0.30	0.44	0.38	0.32	0.40	0.38
SEE	0.61	0.67	0.58	0.61	0.66	0.62	0.60
No. of observations	27	44	45	45	22	22	41
Jarque-Bera test for normality of residuals[a]	0.76	0.35	0.73	0.48	1.00	0.87	1.29
	(0.68)	(0.84)	(0.70)	(0.79)	(0.61)	(0.65)	(0.52)
White test for heteroskedasticity[a]	1.36	0.50	0.44	0.50	0.46	1.04	0.39
	(0.28)	(0.88)	(0.91)	(0.88)	(0.82)	(0.44)	(0.88)
Ramsey reset test (3)[a]	0.50	0.21	0.35	0.33	2.17	1.18	0.39
	(0.68)	(0.89)	(0.79)	(0.80)	(0.14)	(0.35)	(0.76)
F-test for omitted variables[a]	0.78	1.50	3.65	2.41	3.40	2.84	3.15
	(0.52)	(0.23)	(0.04)	(0.10)	(0.05)	(0.08)	(0.03)

[a]Standard deviations in parenthesis: *Significant at 10 percent level; **significant at 5 percent level; ***significant at 1 percent level. — SEE = Standard error of estimates. — [a]Marginal probability values in parenthesis. — Constants are not reported.

DENSE are large. Together with a high correlation coefficient between the variables, this points to the plausible multicollinearity between population density and density of the road system.

Multicollinearity means that it is impossible to isolate the individual impact of the variables statistically. OLS estimates remain unbiased and consistent, but have larger standard errors. Thus, confidence intervals get larger, so that the sample data does not provide the information required. Therefore, in the following regressions, I exclude one of the variables if collinearity between them is high in that sample and report preferred estimates only. Omitting a variable that should be included on theoretical grounds leads to a specification bias, because the remaining variable then measures the combined effect of the correlated variables. Since I am mainly interested in the coefficients of *NRGDPC* and *NRGDPC2*, I accept this possible bias and focus on the identification of the inverted U-curve.

Regression 2 reports my preferred estimates for the sample of 23 countries, excluding *DENSE, POLITICS*, and *OPEN*. An F-test shows a probability of 84 percent that the omitted variables can indeed be excluded from the regression. I also use the regression specification error test (RESET) to check whether the structural specification is subject to the problem of omitted variables. It tests the null hypothesis, i.e., that the expected value of the disturbance term, conditional on the regressors, equals zero.[112] The probability that this is the case in this regression is 67.7 percent. Additionally, I test the normality assumption of the classical normal linear regression model. I report the Jarque–Bera statistic and the corresponding probability that the residuals are normally distributed, which is 51 percent in this regression. As before, I find that the coefficients of *NRGDPC* and *NRGDPC2* have the expected sign. They are statistically significant at the 1 percent level. The adjusted R^2 rises to 0.30.

In regressions 3–7, I test whether the results are sensitive to the sample of countries included in the regression. I construct the samples according to the national statistical concept that has been used to measure the size of the primate cities. In regression 3, I restrict the previous sample of 23 large countries with 4 cities above 750,000 inhabitants to those 19 countries that use urban agglomeration as the statistical concept. In regression 4, I also use countries that use metropolitan area as the statistical concept. In regression 5, I use all 44 countries that use urban agglomeration as the statistical concept, and in regression 6, I add those 10 countries that report data for metropolitan areas.[113] In regression 7, I use the full set of 70 countries, including those that report city proper data only.

---

[112] The test augments the original regression by a matrix of test variables and tests the null hypothesis H_0, i.e., that the elements of the coefficient vector of these variables are jointly zero. The additional variables can be the original independent variables raised to the 2nd, 3rd, 4th, ... power, depending on the degrees of freedom remaining in the regression. This makes the test also powerful in detecting nonlinearities and a wrong functional form. The drawback of the test is that it cannot discriminate between omitted variables and wrong functional form. See Zietz (1988) for a discussion of several adequacy and misspecification tests.

[113] The 44 and 54 country samples are marked in Table A3 in the Appendix.

Due to the different statistical concepts, the true degree of urban concentration is measured with an error that is increasing with the sample size. OLS estimates remain unbiased and consistent for measurement errors in the dependent variable, but they are not efficient. Therefore, lower levels of statistical significance are to be expected for the larger samples that use primacy measures on the basis of different statistical concepts.

Nevertheless, I find empirical evidence for an inverted U-curve relationship between urban concentration and GDP in all five regressions. The coefficients of *NRGDPC* vary between 0.1139 and 0.0488. The coefficients of *NRGDPC2* vary between –0.0021 and –0.0009. Both decrease in absolute values if the sample gets larger. The coefficients indicate that a maximum level of urban concentration is reached at RGDPC levels between US$11,371 and 13,062. The inverted U-curve is shown in Figure 26 and Figure 27.

Figure 26 is based on Regression 2 with 23 observations from large countries, Figure 27 is based on Regression 5 with all 44 observations that use urban agglomeration as the statistical concept. The horizontal axis shows PPP-based GDP per capita. The vertical axis shows primacy net of the conditional variables. The figures display the individual data points and the estimated regression line. It can be seen that conditional primacy is first increasing and then decreasing with GDP per capita.

Figure 26 — The Inverted U-Curve of the 23 Largest Countries

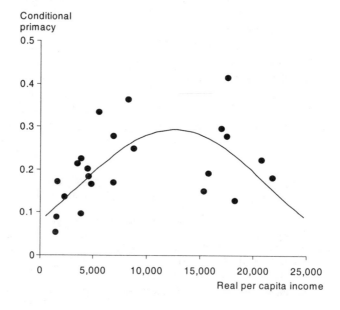

Figure 27 — The Inverted U-Curve of 44 Countries

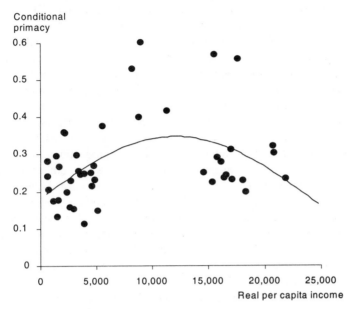

As expected, the dummy variables for colonies in 1815 and colonies in 1950 increase urban concentration. It is remarkable that the coefficient of *NLAND* is significant at the 1 percent level in all regressions 2–7. *ROADLAND* enters all equations in that it is included with a negative coefficient. This indicates that a better transportation infrastructure, which means lower transport costs, mainly benefits non-core regions. Thus, the negative effect of a higher degree of competition is more than offset by the positive effect of a better access of the periphery to the core market.

In regressions 8–10, I use the original sample of 23 countries to test whether the results are sensitive to the measurement of urban concentration, using *PRIMA2*, *PRIMA3*, and *PRIMA4* as dependent variables. The coefficients and the statistical fit of regressions with different dependent variables cannot be compared. However, it can be seen that the existence of the inverted U-curve is robust for different primacy measures, because for all three regressions, I find that the coefficients of *NRGDPC* and *NRGDPC2* have the expected sign and are statistically significant.[114]

---

[114] These results are, for example, confirmed by Rosen and Resnick (1980), who find a high correlation between different primacy measures. In my sample of 70 countries, the correlation between *PRIMA1* and *PRIMA2*, *PRIMA3*, and *PRIMA4* is 97 percent, 93 percent, and 89 percent, respectively. In my sample of 23 countries, that is used in

In regressions 11 and 12, I test the hypothesis that countries that industrialized and, thus, urbanized relatively early are less concentrated today. This would reflect that industrial location decisions in the last century were dictated by natural endowments to a larger degree than nowadays. High costs of internal transportation led to the development of, for instance, steel production close to natural resources and transportation nodes in the "Ruhr area" in Germany and in the "Great Lake region" in the United States. Consequently, early developers did not necessarily set up resource-intensive industrial production close to existing centers.[115] If so, industrialization might have led to population dispersion. Countries that industrialized relatively late could rely on more advanced transportation technologies. Therefore, they could set up industrial production close to the existing centers and benefit from the availability of a larger number of workers, intermediate goods suppliers, and final demand. In this case, industrialization would increase urban concentration. I test this hypothesis, adding *INDUSTRY*1900 in regression 11 and *GDPC*1913 in regression 12 as measures of early development. As expected, both the share of the industrial sector and the per capita GDP level in 1913 have negative coefficients. However, they have large standard errors. The presence of the inverted U-curve is not destroyed by the inclusion of these variables.

Regressions 13 and 14 further investigate the role of ancient conditions on current urban concentration. I exclude *DENSE* and *ROADLAND* from these regressions and include *DENSE*1919, *NTEL*1919, and *RAIL*1919. The density of the telegraph system and the railroad system indicate the costs of overcoming distance. Population density is used as before. Due to a correlation coefficient of 85 percent between *DENSE*1919 and *RAIL*1919, individual effects of these variables cannot be distinguished, and, hence, they are not included together in the equations. The results show that all variables enter the equation with a negative coefficient. Thus, early conditions seem to matter, again leaving intact the previously established U-curve.[116]

Regressions 15–17 explore whether historic patterns of urban concentration can add to the explanation of different degrees of urban concentration nowadays. This might correct for some idiosyncratic or genuine differences between coun-

---

regressions 1, 2, 8, 9, and 10, the correlation is 95 percent, 91 percent, and 88 percent, respectively.

[115] For instance, Mokyr (1995) points out that it is striking that "...neither Brussels nor Paris nor Berlin nor Amsterdam, nor any other major capital city in Europe, became a center of modern industry".

[116] Note that the high probability of having omitted relevant variables in regressions 13 and 14, as indicated by the F-statistic, is most likely due to a 85 percent correlation between *OPEN* and *NRGDPC*. Therefore, *OPEN* would indicate some of the effects that actually should be assigned to *NRGDPC* .

tries resulting from a historic accident[117] or geographic, climatic, or endowment differences. In turn, this might improve the significance of the other economic and conditional variables. However, it is also possible that adding historic degrees of concentration might render all other variables insignificant. In this case, current patterns would be entirely determined by historic patterns. Population growth and further urbanization would then only have resulted in a proportional growth of all cities. Degrees of concentration would then be determined by early historic accidents or climatic, geographic, or endowment differences. It seems reasonable that much of today's concentration can be explained by degrees of concentration in the 1980s and 1970s and maybe even in the 1960s and 1950s, but it is unclear how long the effects take to peter out, if at all.

Therefore, I include, as further independent variables, measures of urban concentration at three points in time. In regression 15, I use the primacy ratio in 1800 (*HISTO*1800). The same ratio is calculated for 1850 (*HISTO*1850) and used in regression 16. In regression 17, I use the percentage of the largest in the three largest cities (*JEFFRATIO*), which is available for 41 countries in the 1930s from Jefferson (1939). As geographic and demographic differences of countries are reflected in the historic measures of urban concentration, only the political and economic explanatory variables are included in the regressions.

The coefficients of the primacy ratios of 1800 and 1850 in regressions 15 and 16 are significant at the 1 percent level. However, the *NRGDPC* and *NRGDPC*2 coefficients are losing its significance if the historic variables are included in this sample. Whether this is due to the small sample size of 22 countries, the different statistical concepts of measuring city size in this sample and the evolving measurement errors in the dependent variable, or the nonexistence of an inverted U-curve in this sample, remains unclear. Also, the F-test and the RESET test point to a misspecification if *HISTO*1850 or *HISTO*1800 are included and the previous explanatory variables are excluded in the sample. Using a sample of 41 countries in regression 17, the *JEFFRATIO* turns out to be significant at the 1 percent level. The inclusion of this ratio does not touch the existence of the inverted U-curve and the coefficient of *COLONY*1815. Apparently, it reduces standard errors, as indicated by the exceptionally high significance levels in this regression. Therefore, future research should continue in this line of identifying the role of path dependencies and the impact that historic patterns of urban concentration have on current patterns of urban concentration.

To sum up, this section shows that several variables have the influence proposed by the economic geography model. Understanding the determinants of

---

[117] An example for such a historic accident is the dissolution of the Austrian–Hungarian empire which left a huge capital with a relatively small hinterland. This results in a very high primacy ratio for Austria.

spatial concentration and transition is necessary for projections of urban growth and regional inequalities. These, in turn, are essential to formulate proper regional, social, and economic policies. The strong appeal of the inverted U-curve is also rooted in the hope that some problems, especially those that developing countries have with regional disparities and the excessive growth of their primate cities, will vanish in the course of further development. This chapter yields some evidence from cross-country regressions that supports this hope.

D.   Summary and Conclusions

This study tries to explain the economic geography of production and trade and the changing pattern of spatial concentration in the course of economic development. For the explanation of these patterns, I begin with the presentation of a general economic geography model. This "prototype" model has two regions, two sectors, and two factors of production. It includes a core and a peripheral region, a mobile increasing returns sector and an immobile constant returns sector, and industrial workers and farmers. Consumer preferences for variety and producer preferences for the availability of a large number of specialized inputs favor a cumulative process toward industrial agglomeration. In favor of industry dispersion works the market access to the demand of a peripheral and immobile part of the population.

Using this prototype model, I show how economic integration influences the spatial distribution of industries between the two regions. The distribution of industries results from the interplay of the realization of economies of scale in the core region and the costs of transporting goods to the peripheral regions. For zero trade costs, space has no restricting role, such that production costs are the same in the core and the periphery, and consumers can be served without costs from both locations. Then, any industrial structure can emerge. For high trade costs, cost savings from concentrated production are outweighed by the high costs of transporting goods to the peripheral market. Hence, an industrial structure emerges, in which both regions produce industrial goods in proportion to their population. For intermediate trade costs, cost savings from concentrated production outweigh the costs of transporting goods to the other market. An industrial structure emerges, in which all production takes place in the core region.

Thus, reducing trade costs from a high to an intermediate level benefits industrial production located in the core, while reducing trade costs from an intermediate to a low level benefits industrial production located in the periphery. Comparing real income levels for different trade costs leads to the following conclusions. Further economic integration and lower trade costs always increase real incomes of industrial workers in the core region and farmers in both regions. For industrial workers in the periphery, partial economic integration can lead to lower real incomes if the integration reduces trade costs from a high to an intermediate level only. Their real incomes rise if integration reduces trade costs to a sufficiently low level. Therefore, both peripheral and core regions that form regional trading blocs have an interest to integrate as closely as possible by reducing all policy-induced trade costs.

Hence, my prototype economic geography model comes to the same conclusions as other approaches. This means that it also shares with them one implication. Except for the extreme cases of zero trade costs or very high trade costs, centripetal forces always outweigh centrifugal forces. Thus, the model predicts a tendency toward complete concentration of all industries in one region for low trade costs. Equilibria exist for some parameter combinations that describe a center-subcenter distribution of industries, but in general, they are unstable. For the United States and the European regions, trade costs are neither zero nor very high, such that the models would predict a tendency toward complete concentration of industrial production. The contrary is the case. Industrial structures do not seem to diverge in Europe and the United States, and fairly stable center-subcenter distributions of industry and population can be observed. I conclude that further centrifugal forces are to be included in the model. Thus, I discuss a number of further centrifugal forces and their theoretically expected impact on the economic geography of industry location. Out of these, the so-called congestion effects seem to be the most relevant in an international and interregional context. I include congestion effects in the prototype model and show that this can lead to the emergence of stable center-subcenter patterns of industry location.

Another striking fact is that economies do not converge to a common spatial structure. Nor are spatial structures within economies fixed over time. That is, the stable equilibria shift over time. For instance, it can be seen that the concentration of economic activities varies considerably in the course of economic development and across countries. One long-discussed hypothesis in development economics as well as in urban and regional economics says that the relationship between economic development, and spatial concentration takes the form of an inverted U-curve. That is, spatial concentration first increases and then decreases with the level of per capita GDP (GDPC).

Due to the lack of an existing rigorous theoretical model to explain the inverted U-curve, I further extend my economic geography model. I consider that in the course of economic development, technologies and the structure of consumer demand change. Hence, I include nonhomothetic demand and exogenous technological change in the model. The resulting model is able to explain the hypothesized inverted U-curve between economic development and industrial concentration.

In the empirical part of this study, I first analyze the empirical evidence for the importance of the two main assumptions of the economic geography model — economies of scale and trade costs. After having established that these two main ingredients of the model are reasonable, I test the ability of the final model to explain real world location patterns.

I start with a classification of different scale effects. For their different theoretical implications, I stress the distinction between different types of EOS. These are internal and external, and static and dynamic EOS. Internal scale economies arise at the level of a single firm. In the economic geography framework, they lead to imperfect competition. External scale economies are externalities which arise at the level of an industry or a region. In the economic geography framework, they may lead to agglomeration. Static scale economies raise productivity levels. Dynamic scale economies raise productivity growth rates.

Engineering estimates as well as econometric estimates provide support for the overall existence of static internal EOS. However, data and methodological reasons complicate the approaches used to estimate internal EOS and invite criticism concerning their results. Dynamic internal EOS or learning effects are found to be significant as well. These effects are most important in skill-intensive industries. Despite the robust evidence for the existence of internal economies of scale, it is less clear how they actually matter for explaining economic phenomena like patterns of production and trade between countries.

Evidence for the existence of static external EOS is found within industries (localization EOS) as well as within regions (urbanization EOS). Both forms of external EOS are able to explain higher productivity levels in densely populated areas. As a general result, localization economies seem to be more important than urbanization economies. However, they peter out beyond a certain city size. Hence, static external EOS can be said to add to the explanation of the existence and structure of urban agglomerations.

R&D and technological spillovers are found to be an important source of dynamic external EOS. These seem to be more important across (Jacobs EOS) than within industries (Marshall–Arrow–Romer EOS), in contrast to the findings on static external EOS. While dynamic external EOS are found to contribute to the explanation of different growth rates of cities and counties, their impact is less clear for larger spatial aggregates. They can be said to be more likely a local or regional phenomenon than a national phenomenon.

In the second part of the empirical chapter, I proceed by analyzing the empirical importance of the costs of overcoming economic distance. These so-called trade costs go far beyond tariffs and transport costs, and also include search costs, for instance. Unfortunately, not many "hard facts" about the overall magnitude of trade costs are reported in the literature. Also, their composition and what really impedes trade between regions is not precisely documented. Therefore, I discuss several types of trade costs and present their evolution in the past years. I find, in general, declining trade costs over time. This is consistent with the common view of an increasingly "globalized" world. However, if trade costs really are at a negligible level, then space and location barely matter. Spatial structures would become largely indeterminate as distance would lose its restricting role. Therefore, I estimated a gravity model for the years 1967–1995 to test for the effects of declining trade costs, and to test whether distance still plays an important role to explain patterns in international trade. I find that the elasticity of geographic distance on the volume of trade has declined by around 25 percent between 1967 and 1995, but distance still constitutes an important determinant of trade patterns. In 1995, a one percent larger distance between trading partners is associated with a 0.83 percent lower trade volume.

The regressions further show that a common border, a common FTA, and a common language enhance trade. In 1995, neighboring countries traded 62 percent more than nonneighboring countries with the same distance. Joint membership in an FTA enhances trade volumes by 101 percent. Countries speaking a common language traded 183 percent more. Common language effects vary across sectors according to product differentiation. Sectors with a high degree of product differentiation show a higher coefficient of speaking a common language. This points to the importance of communication and information, hence, of search costs in the trade of differentiated goods. Distance elasticities are lower (in absolute values) for differentiated goods than for homogeneous goods, indicating that lower freight costs and the ability to price to market outweigh higher search costs for differentiated goods. The size and the statistical significance of the distance coefficients in all regressions show that trade costs still matter for international trade, which substantiates the second main feature of economic geography models.

In the third section of the empirical part, I test the impact of the variables on the spatial distribution of countries according to the economic geography approaches. In the theoretical part, I have argued that it is necessary to augment the prototype model in order to explain real world phenomena like different spatial structures across countries. In order to test whether the augmentations make sense, I estimate the development model's prediction that the relationship of economic growth and spatial concentration can be described by an inverted U-curve. For this prediction to be correct, spatial concentration should depend positively on GDPC and negatively on GDPC squared. The model also suggests to consider conditional variables to take account of different historical developments and different geographic and demographic conditions that influence a country's likelihood to display a concentrated or dispersed pattern of spatial concentration.

Focusing on different country samples and on different conditional variables than previous studies, I find empirical support that the economic geography model can explain differences in the spatial concentration in samples of up to 70 countries. The regressions show the existence of the inverted U-curve. As conditional variables, population density, the size of the country, and the density of the transportation infrastructure all decrease spatial concentration, while a colonial heritage furthers spatial concentration. The empirical analysis confirms the theoretically derived inverted U-curve between economic development and spatial concentration. While the theoretical model shows an ambiguous impact of declining trade costs, the empirical study shows that they more likely reduce regional inequalities than enhance them. From these results, some preliminary policy conclusions can be drawn:[117]

1) Economic integration has an ambiguous effect on equilibrium wage levels, such that small countries may lose through tighter integration if trade costs are reduced from a very high level. They may benefit if trade costs are reduced from an intermediate level.

2) Large countries always benefit from trade liberalization in terms of absolute real wages. At low levels of trade costs, they may benefit less than small countries do, such that real wage levels of the two regions converge.

3) Lowering trade barriers may lead to sudden changes of the industrial structure if these measures are not accompanied by adjustments of the wage levels. The nonergodicity of the models implies that the underlying structure is self-perpetuating. This means that an adverse shock can have long-run consequences for an economy. After a shock, the economy would not necessarily return to its initial state. Therefore, economic policy best provides a stable framework that prevents sudden shocks to the economy.

4) There are multiple equilibria for an economy. Depending on the initial distribution of industries, a region may remain heavily industrialized or underindustrialized. The effect of regional policy cannot be known ex ante. There is the possibility that a large increase in demand from the public sector acts as a "big push" that leads the economy from a lowly-industrialized to a heavily-industrialized economy. However, it may be totally ineffective if such a push is not strong enough. Then, the economy may revert to its initial equilibrium and remain there. There is nothing in the theory up to now that lets policy makers know whether regional or trade policy induce a shift to a new and "better" equilibrium or whether they are totally ineffective.

5) For the same reasons that economic integration may lead to agglomeration of industrial activities in one region and concentration of agricultural activities in the other region, it may lead to increased specialization within the industrial sector. Thereby, scale-intensive industries are most likely to concentrate in the larger or core region of an integrated market, like Germany or Belgium would be in the case of the European Union. This structural change may be accompanied by the appropriate economic and social policies.

---

[117] See also Bröcker (1996) for policy conclusions of the new location theory.

6) The empirical analysis shows that regional inequalities can be reduced in two ways. First, congestion effects seem to be an important centrifugal force. Polluting emissions may have different effects in different regions and cause more harm in densely populated areas than in rural areas. Hence, economic policy that internalizes these effects and considers the different effects polluting emissions may have, balances economic conditions in core and peripheral regions. Environmental instead of regional policies will then reduce some of the problems that especially developing countries have with the excessive growth of their primate cities, and will balance the regional conditions of production. Second, though reducing transport costs has ambiguous theoretical effects, the empirical analysis shows that this will more likely balance economic conditions between core and peripheral regions within a country. Improving the transportation infrastructure, therefore, is an adequate tool to reduce regional inequalities.

Since economic geography is a relatively young field, there are open questions for future research that have to be analyzed to answer policy questions. On the theoretical side, the sensitivity of the models toward their assumptions should be further analyzed. One important recent paper is Davis (1998). He shows that for adequate empirical parameters, the models are sensitive to the assumption of zero trade costs for agricultural goods. He also shows that introducing trade costs for agricultural products significantly weakens centripetal forces. Though his paper tries to assume adequate parameters, he does not consider trade in intermediate inputs, which has a large part in total trade and is an important centripetal force. Therefore, his results should be evaluated within a model that also considers trade in intermediate inputs.

Furthermore, it is not clear in how far the models are sensitive to the specific modeling of imperfect competition. Combes (1997) goes in this direction. As the theoretical discussion of strategic trade policy models shows, the results may rely crucially on the type of competition that is assumed in the models (Siebert 1988).

Bröcker (1998) points into another direction in which future research should go. He calibrates and simulates a spatial computable general equilibrium model based on economic geography elements to show how an EU membership of Visegrad countries would affect Europe's economic geography. Combining theoretical and empirical elements in one analysis clearly strengthens the substance of the political conclusions and enables the analysis of concrete rather than abstract questions.

On the empirical side, it should be analyzed at what level home market effects work. Davis and Weinstein (1996, 1999) offer excellent starting points.[118] They

---

[118]   See also Chapter C.I.2.c of this study for a presentation of their findings.

suggest that home market effects work at the country level rather than the international level. These results are surprising, since trade costs are higher internationally than nationally. Their results for Japanese prefectures can be checked via price level data for a large array of products. Home market effects also imply that larger prefectures have lower price levels on average, since goods have to be transported over shorter distances. Only if distance has an impact on regional price levels and, hence, also plays a role within countries, the results of Davis and Weinstein do make sense. Davis and Weinstein (1998) partly reverse their results of the 1996 paper by using a broader concept of the home market. Further evidence is clearly needed to come to more stable results.

My analysis so far did not find that openness decreases spatial concentration within a country as suggested by the model of Krugman and Livas Elizondo (1996). Other openness proxies should be used to check the sensitivity of my results. It also remains unclear whether regional or economic policies did influence the spatial distribution of industries. Again, my proxy did not find a significant effect. Further evidence is needed on that point. It also remains unclear what role path dependencies play. In how far does spatial concentration depend on past concentration, and how do the dynamics work?

It is therefore necessary to find more empirical evidence for the nature of trade costs, their composition, and the relative importance of search costs, as for example in Rauch (1999) and Trindade and Rauch (1998). That would make projections on the spatial effects of a further decline of freight costs, information-, and communication costs more reliable.

Further evidence is also needed for the effects of economic integration on the specialization and concentration of industries. Amiti (1998) provides a useful start in an economic geography framework. The question is whether we already find a tendency that scale-intensive production is centered in the hub of the European Union. Studies for the United States (Kim 1997) find that there are only small effects.

Answering these questions will give further insights into the theory and empirics of the economic geography of production, trade, and development. My study shows that economic geography models provide an adequate tool for such an analysis. Despite many open research questions, I show how different spatial structures across countries and in the course of economic development can be explained theoretically and empirically by an economic geography model.

Appendix

I. Derivation of Equations in Chapter B

1. Derivation of Equation [10], the Marginal Costs

Solving [8] for L_{cj} yields:

[A.1] $$L_{cj} = \frac{1-\mu}{\mu} \frac{M_j T_c}{w_c}.$$

Inserting [A.1] and [4] into [3] yields:

[A.2] $$\left(\frac{1-\mu}{\mu} \frac{T_c}{w_c}\right)^{1-\mu} M_j = \alpha + \beta Q_{cj}.$$

After rearranging equation [A.2], one gets:

[A.3] $$M_j = \left(\alpha + \beta Q_{cj}\right) T_c^{\mu-1} w_c^{1-\mu} \left(\frac{1-\mu}{\mu}\right)^{\mu-1}.$$

The total costs of production of a firm equal the sum of cash outlays for labor and industrial goods:

[A.4] $$K_{cj} = w_c L_{cj} + T_c M_j.$$

Inserting [A.1] into the above cost function gives:

[A.5] $$K_{cj} = M_j T_c (1-\mu)/\mu + M_j T_c \text{ , which equals:}$$

[A.6] $$K_{cj} = M_j T_c /\mu.$$

Substituting [A.3] for M_j in [A.6] gives:

[A.7] $$K_{cj} = \mu^{-1} T_c T_c^{\mu-1} (1-\mu)^{\mu-1} \mu^{1-\mu} w_c^{1-\mu} \left(\alpha + \beta Q_{cj}\right).$$

After rearranging equation [A.7], one gets the costs of production as a function of output and factor prices:

[A.8] $K_{cj}(Q_{cj}, T_c, w_c) = T_c^\mu w_c^{1-\mu}(1-\mu)^{\mu-1}\mu^{-\mu}(\alpha + \beta Q_{cj})$.

From this, one can derive the marginal costs:

[A.9] $MC_c = \dfrac{dK_{cj}}{dQ_{cj}} = T_c^\mu w_c^{1-\mu}(1-\mu)^{\mu-1}\mu^{-\mu}\beta$.

2. Derivation of Equation [11], the Number of Firms in a Region

Since all firms employ the same number of workers, the number of firms in a region can be expressed by:

[A.10] $N_c = L_c / L_{cj}$.

Inserting [6] and [4] into [3] gives:

[A.11] $L_{cj}^{1-\mu}M_j^\mu = \sigma\alpha$.

Substituting [8] for M_j in [A.11] yields:

[A.12] $L_{cj}^{1-\mu}\left(\dfrac{\mu}{1-\mu}\dfrac{w_c}{T_c}L_{cj}\right)^\mu = \sigma\alpha$.

After substituting [A.10] for L_{cj}, one gets:

[A.13] $\sigma\alpha = \left(\dfrac{\mu}{1-\mu}\dfrac{w_c}{T_c}\right)^\mu \dfrac{L_c}{N_c}$.

After rearranging, the number of firms in a region results as:

[A.14] $N_c = \dfrac{L_c}{\sigma\alpha}\left(\dfrac{\mu}{1-\mu}\dfrac{w_c}{T_c}\right)^\mu$.

3. Derivation of Equation [14], the Wage Rate

The expenditure of residents of region c on industrial goods from both regions is:

[A.15] $X_c = \sum\limits_{j=1}^{N_c+N_p} c_{jc}P_{jc}$.

Any good c_c produced and sold in region c will be bought according to:

[A.16] $\quad \dfrac{c_{jc}}{c_c} = \left(\dfrac{p_c}{p_{jc}}\right)^{\sigma}$,

where c_{jc} is any other good from any region sold in region c for the price p_{jc}. Multiplying by c_c and $p_c^{1-\sigma}$, one gets:

[A.17] $\quad p_c^{1-\sigma} c_{jc} = p_c c_c p_{jc}^{-\sigma}$.

Multiplying by p_{jc} and taking the sum over j yields:

[A.18] $\quad p_c^{1-\sigma} \displaystyle\sum_{j=1}^{N_c+N_p} c_{jc} p_{jc} = p_c c_c \sum_{j=1}^{N_c+N_p} p_{jc}^{1-\sigma}$.

Dividing by $\sum p_{jc}^{1-\sigma}$ gives the expenditure of c residents on good c_c:

[A.19] $\quad \dfrac{p_c^{1-\sigma} \sum c_{jc} p_{jc}}{\sum p_{jc}^{1-\sigma}} = p_c c_c$.

Inserting [A.15] for $\sum c_{jc} p_{jc}$ gives:

[A.20] $\quad p_c c_c = \dfrac{p_c^{1-\sigma} X_c}{\sum p_{jc}^{1-\sigma}}$.

In region c there are N_c such goods competing with $N_c + N_p$ goods from both regions. Therefore, multiplying [A.20] by N_c gives total sales of region c's goods in its home market:

[A.21] $\quad S_{cc} = \dfrac{N_c p_c^{1-\sigma} X_c}{\sum_{j=1}^{N_c+N_p} p_{jc}^{1-\sigma}}$.

Because prices equal marginal costs plus markup and trade costs, the price of a good produced and sold in c is $MC_c\, \sigma/(\sigma-1)$. The price of a good produced in p and sold in c is $\tau MC_p\, \sigma/(\sigma-1)$. Substituting for prices in [A.21], one gets:

[A.22] $\quad S_{cc} = \dfrac{N_c MC_c^{1-\sigma} X_c}{N_c MC_c^{1-\sigma} + N_p \left(\tau MC_p\right)^{1-\sigma}}$.

Sales of goods of region c in region p are equivalently:

$$[A.23] \quad S_{cp} = \frac{N_c \left(\tau MC_c \right)^{1-\sigma} X_p}{N_c \left(\tau MC_c \right)^{1-\sigma} + N_p \left(MC_p \right)^{1-\sigma}} \; .$$

Because the denominator of [A.22] equals $T_c^{1-\sigma} \left(N_c + N_p \right) (\sigma/\sigma - 1)^{\sigma-1}$, one can use the definition of the price index from [9] and transform [A.22] and [A.23] to:

$$[A.24] \quad S_{cc} = \frac{N_c}{N_c + N_p} \left(\frac{\sigma}{\sigma - 1} \right)^{1-\sigma} X_c \frac{MC_c^{1-\sigma}}{T_c^{1-\sigma}} \; ,$$

$$[A.25] \quad S_{cp} = \frac{N_c}{N_c + N_p} \left(\frac{\sigma}{\sigma - 1} \right)^{1-\sigma} X_p \frac{\tau MC_c^{1-\sigma}}{T_p^{1-\sigma}} \; .$$

Adding S_{cc} and S_{cp} yields the total sales of region c:

$$[A.26] \quad S_c = \frac{N_c}{N_c + N_p} \left(\frac{\sigma}{\sigma - 1} \right)^{1-\sigma} \left(X_c \left[\frac{T_c}{MC_c} \right]^{\sigma-1} + X_p \left[\frac{T_p}{\tau MC_c} \right]^{\sigma-1} \right).$$

Total revenue times the share of labor in production equals the sum of wages:

$$[A.27] \quad (1 - \mu) S_c = w_c L_c \; .$$

[A.26] and [A.27] give the wage rate in region c.

$$[A.28] \quad w_c = \frac{(1 - \mu) N_c}{\left(N_c + N_p \right) L_c} \left(\frac{\sigma}{\sigma - 1} \right)^{1-\sigma} \left[X_c \left(\frac{T_c}{MC_c} \right)^{\sigma-1} + X_p \left(\frac{T_p}{\tau MC_c} \right)^{\sigma-1} \right].$$

II.   Analytical Solutions to the Theoretical Model

Two types of approaches have been used to derive analytical solutions for economic geography models, in addition to the commonly used numerical solutions. Krugman and Venables (1995) and Venables (1995) use the "algebra of symmetry breaking", i.e., they derive conditions for which equal dispersion of industries between two regions becomes unstable. They use these conditions to analyze the effects of parameter changes.

Krugman (1991b) uses the "algebra of corner solutions", i.e., he derives conditions for which complete concentration becomes unstable. In the following, I apply this method to my model in order to show the effects of marginal parameter changes. I derive a condition for which it is profitable for a single firm to leave the complete concentration of industries in a region c and to start producing in a region p. In order to evaluate whether a firm wants to produce in region c or p, one has to compare the value of sales and the production costs in the two respective regions.

I assume that all industrial production takes place in region c, total income in both regions is normalized to one, consumers spend a share ε of total income on industrial goods, producers spend a share μ of total sales on industrial goods for intermediate input use, and the total number of firms is expressed by N. Then the value of sales of a single firm producing in region c is:[119]

$$[A.29] \quad S_{cj} = \frac{\varepsilon}{(1-\mu)N} .$$

The value of sales of a defecting firm that starts producing in region p depends on the consumers' income in region c and p, demand from the industrial sector in region c, the relative prices of goods produced in c and p, and the elasticity of substitution. Total income in region c equals $1 + \varepsilon / 2$. Total income in region p equals $1 - \varepsilon/2$. The demand from the industrial sector in region c equals $\varepsilon\mu / 1 - \mu$.

In order to attract workers from region c to region p, a defecting firm has to offer real wages that equal at least those of region c. Workers have to pay trade costs on all industrial goods, apart from the goods produced by the defecting firm, which has a marginal contribution to the price level. Prices for agricultural goods equal 1 in both regions. A share ε of total income is spent on industrial goods. Hence, the real price index is τ^{ε} higher in region p than in region c. To ensure equal real wages in both regions, wages in region p are higher by the factor τ^{ε}, too.

For the same reason, the price level for intermediate inputs is τ times higher in region p. Using equation [A.9], the ratio of peripheral to core marginal costs can be expressed as:

$$[A.30] \quad \frac{MC_p}{MC_c} = \frac{(\tau \, p_c)^{\mu} \, (\tau^{\varepsilon}\omega_c)^{1-\mu} \, \beta_p}{p_c^{\mu} \, \omega_c^{1-\mu} \, \beta_c} = \tau^{\varepsilon+\mu-\varepsilon\mu} .$$

---

[119]   From equations [12] and [13] and $\pi = \varepsilon$ for $Y = 1$, it follows that $w_c L_c + w_p L_p + (1-\varepsilon) = Y_p + Y_c = 1$, and that total expenditure on industrial goods in both regions equals $X_p + X_c = \varepsilon/1 - \mu$. Divided by the number of firms, this yields the value of sales of a representative firm in region c.

I define $h = \varepsilon + \mu - \varepsilon\mu$. Since prices are set with a constant markup on marginal costs, producer prices in the two regions differ by the factor τ^h, too:

[A.31] $\dfrac{p_p}{p_c} = \tau^h$.

The prices that consumers face for the goods from the other region additionally incur trade costs. For consumers in region c, the relative price for a good imported from region p is $\tau p_p / p_c$. For consumers in region p, the relative price for a good from region p is $p_p / \tau p_c$. Given the elasticity of substitution, σ, the value of sales of the defecting firm in region c is $(\tau p_p / p_c)^{1-\sigma}$ of the value of sales of a nondefecting firm. Its value of sales in region p is $(p_p / p_c \tau)^{1-\sigma}$ of the value of sales of a nondefecting firm. The defecting firm faces demand from the industrial sector of region c for its intermediate inputs, which increases its sales to that region by $\mu / (1 - \mu)$. No such demand exists in region p. Given the income in the two regions as determined above, its total value of sales is:

[A.32] $S_{pj} = \dfrac{\varepsilon}{N}\left[\left(\dfrac{\tau p_p}{p_c}\right)^{1-\sigma}\dfrac{1+\varepsilon}{2} + \left(\dfrac{p_p}{p_c\,\tau}\right)^{1-\sigma}\dfrac{1-\varepsilon}{2}\right] + \dfrac{\varepsilon}{N}\dfrac{\mu}{1-\mu}\left(\dfrac{\tau p_p}{p_c}\right)^{1-\sigma}$.

The first term presents consumer demand, the second term presents demand from the industrial sector. Demand from the industrial sector comes from region c only, because all other firms are located there, and demand from the defecting firm for its own products is negligible. [A.32] can be rearranged to:

[A.33] $S_{pj} = \dfrac{\varepsilon}{N}\left[\left(\dfrac{\tau p_p}{p_c}\right)^{1-\sigma}\left(\dfrac{1+\varepsilon}{2} + \dfrac{\mu}{1-\mu}\right) + \left(\dfrac{p_p}{p_c\tau}\right)^{1-\sigma}\dfrac{1-\varepsilon}{2}\right]$ and

[A.34] $S_{pj} = \dfrac{\varepsilon}{N}\left[\left(\dfrac{\tau p_p}{p_c}\right)^{1-\sigma}\dfrac{(1+\varepsilon)(1-\mu)+2\mu}{2(1-\mu)} + \left(\dfrac{p_p}{p_c\tau}\right)^{1-\sigma}\dfrac{1-\varepsilon}{2}\dfrac{1-\mu}{1-\mu}\right]$.

Equation [A.34] shows that trade costs work to the defecting firm's disadvantage in its sales to region c (the first term in brackets) and to its advantage in its sales to region p (the second term in brackets).

Dividing [A.34] by [A.29], the relative sales of a firm producing in region p and c can be expressed as:

[A.35] $\dfrac{S_{pj}}{S_{cj}} = \left(\dfrac{\tau p_p}{p_c}\right)^{1-\sigma} \dfrac{1+\varepsilon(1-\mu)+2\mu}{2} + \left(\dfrac{p_p}{p_c\tau}\right)^{(1-\sigma)} \dfrac{1-\varepsilon}{2}(1-\mu).$

Using equation [A.31], the relative sales can be expressed as:

[A.36] $\dfrac{S_{pj}}{S_{cj}} = \left(\tau\,\tau^h\right)^{1-\sigma} \dfrac{1+\varepsilon(1-\mu)+2\mu}{2} + \left(\tau^{-1}\tau^h\right)^{1-\sigma} \dfrac{1-\varepsilon}{2}(1-\mu).$

Besides the value of sales, the costs of production also differ for firms producing in region c and p. Using equation [A.8], the average production costs in region p compared to those in region c can be expressed as:

[A.37] $\dfrac{AC_p}{AC_c} = \dfrac{T_p^\mu\, w_p^{1-\mu}(1-\mu)^{\mu-1}\,\mu^{-\mu}(\alpha+\beta\,Q_{pj})/Q_{pj}}{T_c^\mu\, w_c^{1-\mu}(1-\mu)^{\mu-1}\,\mu^{-\mu}(\alpha+\beta\,Q_{cj})/Q_{cj}}.$

α, β, and Q are the same in both regions. The ratio of region p's and region c's price levels for intermediate inputs is τ, and the wage ratio was shown to be τ^ε. It follows that:

[A.38] $\dfrac{AC_p}{AC_c} = \tau^{\varepsilon+\mu-\varepsilon\mu} = \tau^h.$

I define a variable $V = S_p\,AC_c/S_c\,AC_p$. It is equally profitable for a firm to remain in region c or to defect and to start production in region p if the ratio of sales in region p to region c equals the ratio of average costs in region p to region c:

[A.39] $\dfrac{S_p}{S_c} = \dfrac{AC_p}{AC_c}$ or $V = 1.$

Moving from region c to region p is profitable if $V > 1$. Inserting equations [A.36] and [A.38] in [A.39] gives:

[A.40] $V = \left[\left(\tau\tau^h\right)^{1-\sigma} \dfrac{(1+\varepsilon)(1-\mu)+2\mu}{2} + \left(\tau^{-1}\tau^h\right)^{1-\sigma} \dfrac{(1-\varepsilon)}{2}(1-\mu)\right]\tau^{-h}.$

After rearranging, this is:

[A.41] $V = \tau^{1-\sigma}\,\tau^{-\sigma h}\, \dfrac{(1+\varepsilon)(1-\mu)+2\mu}{2} + \tau^{-(1-\sigma)}\,\tau^{-\sigma h}\, \dfrac{(1-\varepsilon)}{2}(1-\mu)$

and

[A.42] $V = \dfrac{\tau^{1-\sigma-\sigma h}}{2}\left((1+\varepsilon)(1-\mu)+2\mu+\tau^{2\sigma-2}(1-\varepsilon)(1-\mu)\right).$

Now, V can be evaluated for marginal changes of the exogenous parameters. A positive derivative of V with respect to a change in an exogenous parameter indicates a strengthening of centrifugal forces. However, first I have to exclude cases for which agglomeration always occurs, no matter how high trade costs are. Otherwise, the model would be meaningless, because it could never explain industrial location in a peripheral region. This means, I have to exclude parameter combinations for which $V < 1$ for all τ. This is:

$$\tau^{1-\sigma-\sigma h}\left[(1+\varepsilon)(1-\mu)+2\mu+\tau^{2\sigma-2}(1-\mu)(1-\varepsilon)\right] < 2\,.$$

This condition only holds if σ, ε, and μ are close to 1, that is, economies of scale are extremely large, the share of consumers' expenditure on industrial goods is very large, or intraindustry linkages are very important. In those cases, agglomeration would always occur, which is why they will be excluded in the following.

1.   Marginal Changes of Trade Costs

From inspection of equation [A.42], it can be seen that $V = 1$ for $\tau = 1$. This means that no region has an advantage, if trade costs are zero. For infinite trade costs, equation [A.42] approaches zero, since $2\sigma - 2 > 1 - \sigma - \sigma h$. This means that for large trade costs, moving from region c to region p is profitable.

The first derivative of V with respect to τ shows the effect of marginal changes of the level of trade costs between these two extreme cases:

[A.43] $\dfrac{dV}{d\tau} = \dfrac{(1-\sigma-\sigma h)V}{\tau} + \left((2\sigma-2)(1-\varepsilon)(1-\mu)\tau^{2\sigma-3}\right).$

Now, a condition can be derived for which an increase of trade costs works in favor of region p. This is $dV/d\tau > 0$, or:

[A.44] $\left((2\sigma-2)(1-\varepsilon)(1-\mu)\tau^{2\sigma-3}\right) > \dfrac{-(1-\sigma-\sigma h)V}{\tau}\,.$

It follows:

[A.45] $\left[(2\sigma-2)(1-\varepsilon)(1-\mu)\right] > \dfrac{(\sigma+\sigma h-1)V}{\tau^{2\sigma-2}}$ and

[A.46] $(2\sigma-2)(1-\varepsilon)(1-\mu)\dfrac{1}{(\sigma+\sigma h-1)V} > \dfrac{1}{\tau^{2\sigma-2}}$.

The condition is evaluated in the vicinity of $V = 1$. The left hand side is always positive and below one, while the right hand side approaches 1 for $\tau \to 1$, and it approaches 0 for $\tau \to \infty$. Consequently, $dV/d\tau < 0$ for small τ, and $dV/d\tau > 0$ for large τ. It was also shown that $V_{\tau=1} = 1$ and $V_{\tau\to\infty} = \infty$. This means that increasing trade costs from a low level benefit the core region c in terms of relative real wages, while increasing trade costs from a high level benefit the peripheral region p. This relationship is reflected in the U-curve shape of Figure 4.

2.   Marginal Changes of Other Parameters

The first derivative of V with respect to the share of income that is spent on industrial goods (ε) is:

[A.47] $\dfrac{dV}{d\varepsilon} = -\sigma(1-\mu)\ln \tau V + \dfrac{\tau^{1-\sigma-\sigma h}}{2}\left[(1-\mu)-\tau^{2\sigma-2}(1-\mu)\right]$.

The first term of equation [A.47] and the term in parenthesis are always negative such that it always holds that:

[A.48] $\dfrac{dV}{d\varepsilon} < 0$.

This means that the advantage of being in the core region c is the higher, the higher the share of income that is spent on industrial goods. This relationship was shown in Figure 3c.

The first derivative of V with respect to the share of industrial goods in total inputs (μ) is:

[A.49] $\dfrac{dV}{d\mu} = -\sigma(1-\varepsilon)\ln \tau V + \dfrac{\tau^{1-\sigma-\sigma h}}{2}\left[-(1+\varepsilon)+2-(1-\varepsilon)\tau^{2\sigma-2}\right]$ or

[A.50] $\dfrac{dV}{d\mu} = -\sigma(1-\varepsilon)\ln \tau V + (1-\varepsilon)\dfrac{\tau^{1-\sigma-\sigma h}}{2}\left[1-\tau^{2\sigma-2}\right] < 0$.

Again, the first term of equation [A.50] and the term in the last parenthesis are always negative. Hence, the derivative is always negative, and being in the core region c is the more advantageous, the stronger intraindustry linkages are. This relationship was shown in Figure 3b.

The first derivation of V with respect to the elasticity of substitution (σ) is:

[A.51] $\dfrac{dV}{d\sigma} = (-1-h)\ln\tau\, V + \dfrac{\tau^{1-\sigma-\sigma h}}{2}\left[2(1-\varepsilon)(1-\mu)\tau^{2\sigma-2}\ln\tau\right],$

which equals:

[A.52] $\dfrac{dV}{d\sigma} = \ln\tau\left[-(1+h)V + \left[(1-\varepsilon)(1-\mu)\tau^{\sigma-1-\sigma h}\right]\right].$

The derivative is positive if the term in brackets is sufficiently larger than 1, which is the case for low to intermediate economies of scale, interindustry linkages, and consumer demand for industrial goods. Figure 3 has shown numerical solutions for this relationship.

Equation [A.42] can be evaluated for different parameters to show the critical values of τ for which $V = 1$, i.e., both regions are equally attractive as a location of production. The following table shows such critical values.

$\varepsilon = 0.4$ $\mu = 0.2$		$\varepsilon = 0.4$ $\sigma = 6$		$\sigma = 6$ $\mu = 0.2$	
σ	τ	μ	τ	ε	τ
3	25.62	0.4	4.38	0.5	3.16
5	2.77	0.3	2.79	0.4	2.14
7	1.83	0.2	2.14	0.3	1.17
9	1.54	0.1	1.79	0.2	1.47

In order to analyze marginal changes of the sensitivity toward congestion (ξ), two cases have to be distinguished. For fixed-cost-congestion effects, equation [A.42] remains valid. For variable-cost-congestion effects, variable costs differ between the two regions. Instead of equation [A.30] and [A.37], the ratios of marginal costs and average costs in the two regions are:

[A.53] $\dfrac{MC_p}{MC_c} = \tau^h e^{-\xi N}$ and

[A.54] $\dfrac{AC_p}{AC_c} = \dfrac{T_p^{\mu}\, w_p^{1-\mu}(1-\mu)^{\mu-1}\,\mu^{-\mu}\left(\alpha+\beta\,Q_{pj}\right)/Q_{pj}}{T_c^{\mu}\, w_c^{1-\mu}(1-\mu)^{\mu-1}\,\mu^{-\mu}\left(\alpha+\beta e^{\xi N}\,Q_{cj}\right)/Q_{cj}}$,

since N_p is close to zero. It follows that V now reads:

[A.55] $V = \dfrac{\tau^{1-\sigma-\sigma(\varepsilon+\mu-\varepsilon\mu)}}{2}\left((1+\varepsilon)(1-\mu)+2\mu+\tau^{2\sigma-2}(1-\varepsilon)(1-\mu)\right)$

$\times \dfrac{\left(\alpha+\beta e^{\xi N} Q_c\right)Q_p}{\left(\alpha+\beta Q_p\right)Q_c}$.

The derivation of V with respect to the sensitivity toward congestion (ξ) is:

[A.56] $\dfrac{dV}{d\xi} = V > 0$.

Higher congestion effects work in favor of region p as a location of production.

3.   The Effects of Economic Development

The model has been augmented in Chapter B.III for the effects of economic development and technological change. To evaluate marginal technological changes, V can still be expressed as in [A.55], because in this chapter, congestion effects only influence variable costs. The difference to the previous case is that ε and N are endogenous in the sense that they increase in the course of economic development. This also means that no specific solutions can be given. To determine V, the whole system of equations would have to be determined simultaneously. However, the problem of determining how V changes in the course of economic development, that is, the sign of dV/dt, can be reduced to determining dN/dt and $d\varepsilon/dt$, which can be solved indirectly. Similarly to equation [11], the number of firms can be shown to be:

[A.57] $N = \dfrac{L}{\alpha\sigma(1-\rho)^t}\left[\dfrac{\mu}{1-\mu}\dfrac{w}{T}\right]^{\mu}$.

It can be seen that $dN/dt > 0$. Per capita GDP is increasing in the course of economic development, such that $dRGDPC/dt > 0$. From equation [44], it can be seen that $d\varepsilon/dRGDPC > 0$. Hence, $d\varepsilon/dt > 0$, which means nonhomothetic demand. It also holds that $\varepsilon_{t=0}$ and $\lim \varepsilon_{t\to\infty} = 1$.

With the knowledge that $d\varepsilon/dt > 0$ and $dN/dt > 0$, a qualitative solution can be given for dV/dt. The term $e^{\xi N}$ increases exponentially in the course of economic development, i.e.:

[A.58] $\lim_{t\to\infty} e^{\xi N} \to \infty$, and $\lim_{N\to 0} e^{\xi N} \to 1$.

In equation [A.55], the terms $\tau^{1-\sigma-\sigma(\varepsilon+\mu-\varepsilon\mu)}$ and $\tau^{2\sigma-2}(1-\varepsilon)(1-\mu)$ decrease with a larger ε, while $(1+\varepsilon)(1-\mu)$ increases with a larger ε. Hence, there are two opposing forces; one increases V, the other decreases V in the course of economic development.

The nonhomothetic utility function means that $\varepsilon_{RGDPC<A_x} = 0$ and $\varepsilon_{t\to\infty} = 1$. If no income is spent on industrial goods, there are no firms producing industrial goods, and $\mu = 0$ holds as well. Hence, $N_{\varepsilon=0} = 0$ and it follows that:

[A.59] $\underset{\varepsilon=0}{V} = \tau^{1-\sigma}\left(2+\tau^{2\sigma-2}\right)$,

[A.60] $\underset{\varepsilon\to 1}{\lim V} \to \tau^{1-2\sigma}\dfrac{\left(\alpha + \beta e^{\xi N}Q_c\right)Q_p}{\left(\alpha + \beta Q_p\right)Q_c}$.

The shape of the function $V(t)$ can now be concluded from $dN/dt > 0$, $d\varepsilon/dt > 0$ and equations [A.58], [A.59], and [A.60]. It follows that V is first decreasing and then increasing with the level of economic development, which leads to the curve shown in Figure 17.

III. Modeling Economies of Scale

In the following, I lay out the modeling of EOS in the production function and cost function framework and show how to arrive at equations to test for the existence of EOS on the different levels of aggregation as outlined in Chapter C.I.1 and surveyed in Chapter C.I.2 and C.I.3. See also Berndt (1991: 66–81) and Backus et al. (1992) for a technical description and derivation of different types of EOS. For simplicity, I use the following Cobb–Douglas production function:

[A.61] $Y = A x_1^{\alpha_1} x_2^{\alpha_2}$,

where Y denotes firm output, A denotes a general productivity parameter, and x_1 and x_2 are inputs with α_1 and α_2 as their elasticities. Returns to scale can be expressed as $r = \alpha_1 + \alpha_2$, because output increases by the factor r of input expansion. There are increasing returns to scale for $r > 1$, constant returns to scale for $r = 1$, and decreasing returns to scale for $r < 1$. The notion economies of scale describes $r - 1$. They are positive for $r > 1$, zero for $r = 1$, and negative for $r < 1$.

The general cost function is:

[A.62] $C = p_1 x_1 + p_2 x_2$,

where p_1, p_2 are the prices of inputs 1 and 2.

In order to transform [A.61] into a cost function that can be estimated, first cost minimization subject to [A.61] is assumed:

[A.63] $\min L_{x_1, x_2} = p_1 x_1 + p_2 x_2 + \lambda \left(Y - A x_1^{\alpha_1} x_2^{\alpha_2} \right)$.

Solving the Lagrangian for x_1 and x_2 yields:

[A.64] $x_1 = \dfrac{\alpha_1}{\alpha_2} \dfrac{p_2}{p_1} x_2$,

$x_2 = \dfrac{\alpha_2}{\alpha_1} \dfrac{p_1}{p_2} x_1$.

Plugging expression [A.64] into the production function and rearranging terms yields:

[A.65] $x_1 = \left[\dfrac{Y}{A} \left(\dfrac{\alpha_2}{\alpha_1} \dfrac{p_1}{p_2} \right)^{-\alpha_2} \right]^{1/r}$,

$x_2 = \left[\dfrac{Y}{A} \left(\dfrac{\alpha_1}{\alpha_2} \dfrac{p_2}{p_1} \right)^{-\alpha_1} \right]^{1/r}$.

Plugging these expressions into the cost function [A.62] and rearranging terms yields:

[A.66] $C = r \left(A \alpha_1^{\alpha_1} \alpha_2^{\alpha_2} \right)^{-1/r} \left(Y p_1^{\alpha_1} p_2^{\alpha_2} \right)^{1/r}$.

This function is dependent on prices and output only. Defining $k = r(A \alpha_1^{\alpha_1} \alpha_2^{\alpha_2})^{-1/r}$, taking logarithms, and including a stochastic disturbance term (μ), it can be transformed into a loglinear function, which can be used to estimate static lnEOS:

[A.67] $\ln C = \ln k + \dfrac{1}{r} \ln Y + \dfrac{\alpha_1}{r} \ln p_1 + \dfrac{\alpha_2}{r} \ln p_2 + \mu$.

Estimating dynamic InEOS aims at describing cost reductions due to learning effects through cumulative production. These effects can be included in the production function by specifying the productivity term as $A_t = A' n_t^{\alpha_c}$, where n_t is the amount of cumulative output produced up to but not including time t, α_c is the elasticity of unit costs with respect to cumulative output, and A' is the general productivity parameter net of learning effects. The loglinear cost function is now described by:

[A.68] $\ln C = \ln k' + \dfrac{\alpha_c}{r} \ln n_t + \dfrac{1}{r} \ln Y_t + \dfrac{\alpha_1}{r} \ln p_1 + \dfrac{\alpha_2}{r} \ln p_2 + \mu$,

where $k' = r \left(A \alpha_1^{\alpha_1} \alpha_2^{\alpha_2} \right)^{-1/r}$.

Making the assumption that the change in the two price terms of equation [A.68] can be measured by the GNP deflator and subtracting the price terms on both sides yields an expression for real costs. By further subtracting $\ln Y_t$ from both sides, real unit costs can be expressed as:

[A.69] $\ln c = \ln k' + \dfrac{\alpha_c}{r} \ln n_t + \left(\dfrac{1-r}{r} \right) \ln Y_t + \mu$.

Equation [A.69] is the cost function that can be estimated including static and dynamic InEOS, where $\ln k' = \ln c_1$ can be regarded as the costs of the first unit produced. If the restriction of constant returns to scale, i.e., $r = 1$, cannot be rejected, one arrives at the learning curve function as usually estimated in the literature:

[A.70] $\ln c_t = \ln c_1 + \alpha_c \ln n_t + \mu$.

The equation implies that if cumulative output increases by a factor n, costs decrease to n^{α_c} percent of their previous level. To standardize a measure for cost reductions, the learning curve is commonly said to have a d percent slope if cumulative output doubles, i.e., $n = 2$, such that $d = 2^{\alpha_c}$.

The estimation of static ExEOS works in a similar way as the estimation of dynamic InEOS. With static ExEOS, productivity increases, i.e., unit costs decrease with the amount of total production of all firms at a point in time. In the case of LocEOS, productivity is dependent on the number of firms of the same industry. In the case of UrbEOS, firm productivity depends on the output of all industries. The productivity term can be specified to be:

$$[A.71] \quad A = A' \left(\sum_{i=1}^{N} Y_{ij} \right)^{\rho} \left(\sum_{j=1}^{M} \sum_{i=1}^{N} Y_{ij} \right)^{\gamma},$$

where Y_{ij} denotes output of firm i in industry j, ρ is the elasticity of productivity toward own industry output, γ is the elasticity of productivity toward output of all industries, and A' is again a general productivity term net of these effects.

Specifying the cost function [A.66] by expression [A.71], the log-linear form can be used to test for the existence of LocEOS and UrbEOS by:

$$[A.72] \quad \ln C = \ln k' + \frac{\rho}{r}\left(\sum_{i=1}^{N} Y_{ij} \right) + \frac{\gamma}{r}\left(\sum_{j=1}^{M} \sum_{i=1}^{N} Y_{ij} \right) + \frac{1}{r}\ln Y + \frac{\alpha_1}{r}\ln p_1 + \frac{\alpha_2}{r}\ln p_2 + \mu$$

$$\text{and } k' = r\left(A' \alpha_1^{\alpha_1} \alpha_2^{\alpha_2} \right)^{-1/r}.$$

For $\rho \neq 0$ and $\gamma \neq 0$, the existence of localization and urbanization EOS is confirmed.

Dynamic ExEOS influence the growth rate of the productivity parameter. In the presence of MAREOS, productivity growth depends positively on the output of all firms of the own industry in the region. In the presence of JaEOS, productivity growth depends positively on the output of all industries in the region. Productivity growth can be expressed as:

$$[A.73] \quad \Delta A = \Delta A' \left(\sum_{i=1}^{N} Y_{ij} \right)^{\beta} \left(\sum_{j=1}^{M} \sum_{i=1}^{N} Y_{ij} \right)^{\sigma},$$

where β is the elasticity of productivity growth toward own industry output, σ is the elasticity of productivity growth toward all industry output, and $\Delta A'$ is the productivity growth net of these effects.

Using production function [A.61], output growth can be decomposed into productivity growth and input growth. Taking [A.73] as a description of productivity growth and including a stochastic disturbance term, one arrives at:

$$[A.74] \quad \ln \Delta Y = \ln \Delta A' + \beta \ln\left(\sum_{i=1}^{N} Y_{ij} \right) + \sigma \ln\left(\sum_{j=1}^{M} \sum_{i=1}^{N} Y_{ij} \right)$$

$$+ \alpha_1 \Delta \ln x_1 + \alpha_2 \Delta \ln x_2 + \mu.$$

For $\beta \neq 0$ and $\sigma \neq 0$, the existence of MAREOS and JaEOS is confirmed.

Hence, static internal EOS can be estimated by equation [A.67], dynamic internal EOS by equation [A.70], static external EOS by equation [A.72], and dynamic external EOS by equation [A.74]. Some of the studies surveyed in Chapter C.I.2 and C.I.3 may use different production functions, include further regressors, or adjust to specific data sets. Then, they may also use different equations to estimate the existence of EOS than the above ones. The underlying principles of modeling the various forms of EOS, however, remain the same.

IV.   Tables and Figures

Table A1 —Countries Used in the Regressions of Chapter C.II

Algeria	Greece[a]	Pakistan
Argentina[c]	Hong Kong[f]	Peru[d]
Australia	India	Philippines[f,g]
Austria[b]	Indonesia[f,g]	Portugal[a]
Belgium/Luxembourg[a]	Ireland[a]	Singapore[f,g]
Brazil[c]	Israel	South Korea[f]
Canada[e]	Italy[a]	Spain[a]
Chile	Japan[f]	Sweden[b]
Colombia[d]	Malaysia[f,g]	Switzerland[b]
Denmark[a]	Mexico[e]	Thailand[f,g]
Ecuador[d]	Morocco	Tunisia
Egypt	Netherlands[a]	Turkey
Finland[b]	New Zealand	United Kingdom[a]
France[a]	Nigeria	United States[e]
Germany[a]	Norway[b]	Venezuela[d]

[a]Country takes part in EC12. — [b]Country takes part in EFTA. — [c]Country takes part in Mercosur. — [d]Country takes part in Andean. —[e]Country takes part in NAFTA. — [f]Country takes part in the East Asian Economic Caucus. — [g]Country takes part in ASEAN.

Table A2 — Classification Scheme for Different Forms of Nontariff Trade Measures on Imports

Type I measures (Trade-distorting intent for imports)	Type II measures (Secondary trade-restrictive intent)	Type III measures (Spillover effects on trade)
A. Quantitatively-operating 1. Global import quotas 2. Bilateral import quotas 3. Restrictive licensing 4. Liberal licensing 5. Voluntary export restraints 6. Embargoes 7. Government procurement 8. State-trading practices 9. Domestic-content regulations B. Operating on prices/costs 1. Variable import levies 2. Advance deposit requirements 3. Antidumping duties 4. Countervailing charges 5. Subsidies to import competitors 6. Credit restrictions on importers 7. Tax benefits for import competitors 8. Discriminatory internal freight costs 9. International commodity agreements 10. Orderly-marketing arrangements	A. Quantitatively-operating 1. Communications media restrictions 2. Quantitative advertising restrictions B. Operating on prices/costs 1. Packaging & labeling regulation measures 2. Health and sanitary regulations 3. Safety and industrial standards 4. Border tax adjustments 5. User taxes and excises 6. Customs clearance procedures 7. Customs classification procedures 8. Customs valuation procedures 9. Exchange restrictions 10. Disclosure regulations 11. Government-provided entrepreneurship R&D financing and related aids for import-competing industries	A. Quantitatively-operating 1. Government manufacturing and distribution monopolies covering products like armaments 2. Government structural and regional development policies 3. Ad hoc government balance of payments measures 4. Variations in national tax schemes 5. Variations in national social insurance systems 6. Variations in allowable capital-depreciation methods 7. Spillovers from government-financed defense, aerospace, and nonmilitary projects 8. Scale effects induced by government procurement 9. Variation in national standards regulations and practices 10. External transport charges and government-sanctioned international transport agreements 11. Port transfer costs

Source: Laird and Yeats (1990a: 303).

Table A3 —Countries Used in the Regressions of Chapter C.III

		RGDPC	Primacy			RGDPC	Primacy
Algeria	*	2,957	0.2353	Kenya		1,080	0.2756
Argentina	*#	5,532	0.3793	Korea	#	8,271	0.3337
Australia	#+	17,517	0.2452	Malaysia		5,997	0.1275
Austria	*	15,560	0.4814	Mali	*	714	0.3366
Bangladesh	+	1,641	0.3462	Mexico	#+	6,896	0.2459
Belgium	*	16,533	0.1195	Morocco	*	2,554	0.2509
Benin		1,128	0.3989	Netherlands	*	16,096	0.0794
Bolivia		1,890	0.2815	New Zealand	*	14,591	0.3078
Brazil	*#	4,792	0.1340	Niger	*	563	0.3804
Bulgaria		7,529	0.2157	Nigeria	*	1,117	0.2287
Burkina Faso		608	0.3941	Norway	*	16,345	0.2221
Cameroon		1,249	0.2155	Pakistan	*#	1,661	0.2205
Canada	*#	20,752	0.1771	Paraguay	+	2,496	0.2984
Chile	+	5,279	0.4160	Peru	+	2,603	0.4297
China	*#	1,536	0.0452	Philippines	*	2,112	0.2686
Colombia	*#	3,902	0.2080	Poland	*#	4,564	0.1448
Côte d'Ivoire	*	1,372	0.4482	Portugal	*	9,005	0.5015
Czech Republic	*	5,066	0.0990	Romania	*	2,656	0.1697
Denmark	+	17,217	0.3086	Russian Federation	*#	8,780	0.0836
Ecuador	*	3,163	0.2653	South Africa	*#	3,886	0.1258
Egypt, Arab Rep. of	*	2,153	0.3696	Spain	+	11,765	0.1409
Finland	*	17,080	0.2848	Sri Lanka		2,468	0.1671
France	*#	16,956	0.2264	Sweden	*	18,024	0.2095
Germany	*#	18,235	0.0938	Switzerland	*	20,729	0.2031
Ghana	+	1,101	0.2751	Syrian, Arab Rep. of	*	4,714	0.2888
Greece	*	8,203	0.5449	Thailand		4,270	0.5708
Guatemala		2,535	0.2324	Tunisia	*	3,392	0.3930
Hungary		6,430	0.3134	Turkey	*#	4,489	0.1905
India	*#	1,505	0.0567	Uganda	*	625	0.4019
Indonesia	*#	2,323	0.1697	United Kingdom	*#	15,741	0.1434
Iran, Islamic Rep. of	*#	3,577	0.1914	United States	*#	21,827	0.0854
Ireland	*	11,273	0.4596	Uruguay		5,336	0.4679
Italy	*#	15,309	0.1210	Venezuela	#+	6,859	0.1573
Japan	*#	17,625	0.2623	Zaire		471	0.3284
Jordan		3,774	0.4284	Zambia		799	0.2860

Note: RGDPC denotes PPP-adjusted GDP per capita levels. Primacy denotes the share of the largest city in total urban population. Both values are for 1990. — #Country has at least 4 cities with more than 750,000 inhabitants (23 countries). — *Country reports urban agglomeration data (44 countries). — +Country reports metropolitan area data (10 countries).

Source: United Nations (1995a); World Bank (1996a).

Figure A1 — Trade Costs in International Trade

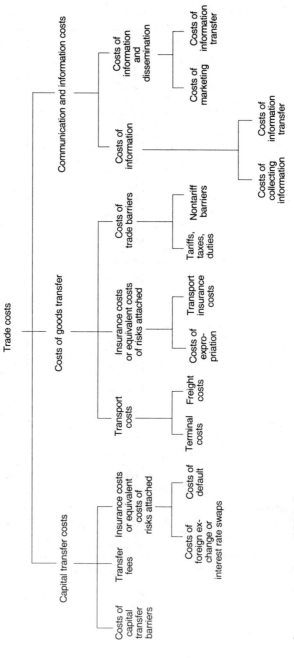

Source: Amelung (1990: 6).

References

Abdel-Rahman, H.M. (1988). Product Differentiation, Monopolistic Competition and City Size. *Regional Science and Urban Economics* 18 (1): 69–86.

Abdel-Rahman, H.M., and M. Fujita (1990). Product Variety, Marshallian Externalities, and City Sizes. *Journal of Regional Science* 30 (2): 165–183.

Ács, Z.J., and D.B. Audretsch (1990). *Innovation and Small Firms*. Cambridge, Mass.: Massachusetts Institute of Technology Press.

Ács, Z.J., D.B. Audretsch, and M.P. Feldman (1992). Real Effects of Academic Research: Comment. *American Economic Review* 82 (1): 363–367.

— (1994). R&D Spillovers and Recipient Firm Size. *Review of Economics and Statistics* 76 (2): 336–345.

Ades, A.F., and E.L. Glaeser (1995). Trade and Circuses: Explaining Urban Giants. *Quarterly Journal of Economics* 440 (1): 195–227.

Alonso, W. (1960). A Theory of the Urban Land Market. *Regional Science Association* 6 (Papers and Proceedings): 149–157.

— (1964). *Location and Land Use*. Cambridge, Mass.: Harvard University Press.

— (1980). Five Bell Shapes in Development. *Papers of the Regional Science Association* 45: 5–16.

Alperovich, G. (1992). Economic Development and Population Concentration. *Economic Development and Cultural Change* 41 (1): 63–74.

Alperovich, G., and J. Deutsch (1995). The Size Distribution of Urban Areas: Testing for the Appropriateness of the Pareto Distribution Using a Generalized Box-Cox Transformation Function. *Journal of Regional Science* 35 (2): 267–276.

Amelung, T. (1990). Explaining Regionalization of Trade in Asia Pacific: A Transaction Cost Approach. Kiel Working Papers 423. Institute of World Economics, Kiel.

Amiti, M. (1998). Inter-Industry Trade in Manufactures: Does Country Size Matter? *Journal of International Economics* 44 (2): 231–255.

Amjadi, A., and A.J. Yeats (1995). Non-Tariff Barriers Facing Africa. The Uruguay Round. *South African Journal of Economics* 63 (3): 384–404.

Amjadi, A., U. Reincke, and A.J. Yeats (1996). Did External Barriers Cause the Marginalization of Sub-Saharan Africa in World Trade? World Bank Discussion Papers 348. The World Bank, Washington, D.C.

Anderson, J.E. (1979). A Theoretical Foundation for the Gravity Equation. *American Economic Review* 69 (1): 106–116.

Anselin, L., A. Varga, and Z.J. Ács (1997). Local Geographical Spillovers Between University Research and High Technology Innovations. *Journal of Urban Economics* 42 (3): 422–448.

Argote, L., and D.N. Epple (1990). Learning Curves in Manufacturing. *Science* 247 (4945): 920–924.

Arrow, K.J. (1962). The Economic Implications of Learning by Doing. *Review of Economic Studies* 29 (3): 155–173.

Arthur, W.B. (1987). Self-Reinforcing Mechanisms in Economics. CEPR Discussion Paper 111. Center for Economic Policy Research, Stanford, Calif.

— (1989). Competing Technologies, Increasing Returns, and Lock-in by Historical Events. *Economic Journal* 99 (March): 116–131.

— (1990). Positive Feedbacks in the Economy. *Scientific American* 2: 92–99.

— (1996). Increasing Returns and the New World of Business. *Harvard Business Review* (July–August): 100–108.

Asilis, C.M., and L.A. Rivera-Batiz (1994). Geography, Trade Patterns and Economic Policy. In Centre for Economic Policy Research (ed.). *The Location of Economic Activity*. London: CEPR.

Audretsch, D.B., and M.P. Feldman (1996). R&D Spillovers and the Geography of Innovation and Production. *American Economic Review* 86 (3): 630–640.

Audretsch, D.B., and P.E. Stephan (1996). Company-Scientist Locational Links: The Case of Biotechnology. *American Economic Review* 86 (3): 641–652.

Backus, D.K., P.J. Kehoe, and T.J. Kehoe (1992). In Search of Scale Effects in Trade and Growth. *Journal of Economic Theory* 58 (2): 377–409.

Bain, J.S. (1956). *Barriers to New Competition: Their Characters and Consequences in Manufacturing Industries*. Cambridge, Mass.: Harvard University Press.

Bairoch, P. (1988). *Cities and Economic Development: From the Dawn of History to the Present*. Chicago: University of Chicago Press.

Bairoch, P., J. Batou, and P. Chèvre (1988). *The Population of European Cities: Data Bank and Short Summary Results*. Publications du Centre d' Histoire Economique Internationale de l'Université de Genève 2. Geneva: Droz.

Balassa, B.A., and L. Bauwens (1988). *Changing Trade Patterns in Manufactured Goods. An Econometric Investigation*. Contributions to Economic Analysis 176. Amsterdam: North-Holland.

Baldwin, J.R., and P.K. Gorecki (1986). The Role of Scale in Canada-U.S. Productivity Differences in the Manufacturing Sector, 1970–1979. The Collected Research Studies 6. Royal Commission on the Economic Union and Development Prospects for Canada, Toronto: University of Toronto Press.

Banks, A. (1971). *Cross-Polity Time-Series Data*. Cambridge, Mass.: Massachusetts Institute of Technology Press.

Barro, R.J., and X. Sala-i-Martin (1995). *Economic Growth*. New York: McGraw-Hill.

Bartelsman, E.J., R.J. Caballero, and R.K. Lyons (1994). Customer- and Supplier-Driven Externalities. *American Economic Review* 84 (4): 1075–1084.

Basu, S., and J.G. Fernald (1997). Returns to Scale in US Production. Estimates and Implications. *Journal of Political Economy* 105 (2): 249–283.

Bergstrand, J.H. (1985). The Gravity Equation in International Trade: Some Microeconomic Foundations and Empirical Evidence. *Review of Economics and Statistics* 67 (3): 474–481.

— (1989). The Generalized Gravity Equation, Monopolistic Competition, and the Factor-Proportions Theory in International Trade. *Review of Economics and Statistics* 71 (1): 143–153.

— (1990). The Heckscher–Ohlin–Samuelson Model, the Linder Hypothesis and the Determinants of Bilateral Intra-Industry Trade. *Economic Journal* 100 (December): 1216–1229.

Berndt, E.R. (1991). *The Practice of Econometrics: Classic and Contemporary*. Reading, Mass.: Addison–Wesley Publishing Company.

Bernstein, J.I., and M.I. Nadiri (1988). Interindustry R&D Spillovers, Rates of Return, and Production in High-Tech Industries. *American Economic Review, Papers and Proceedings* 78 (2): 429–434.

— (1989). Research and Development and Intraindustry Spillovers. An Empirical Application of Dynamic Duality. *Review of Economic Studies* 56 (2): 249–267.

Berry, R.A. (1992). Firm (or Plant) Size in the Analysis of Trade and Development. In G.K. Helleiner (ed.), *Trade Policy, Industrialization, and Development: New Perspectives*. Oxford: Clarendon Press.

— (1993). Methodological Complexities in Relating Firm or Plant Size to Economic Efficiency. *Industry and Development* 33 (June): 95–107.

Bikker, J.A. (1987). An International Trade Flow Model with Substitution: An Extension of the Gravity Model. *Kyklos* 40 (3): 315–337.

Black, D., and V. Henderson (1997). Urban Growth. NBER Working Paper Series 6008. National Bureau of Economic Research, Cambridge, Mass.

Bode, E. (1998). *Lokale Wissensdiffusion und regionale Divergenz in Deutschland*. Kieler Studien 293. Tübingen: Mohr Siebeck.

Boisso, D., and M. Ferrantino (1997). Economic Distance, Cultural Distance, and Openness in International Trade: Empirical Puzzles. *Journal of Economic Integration* 12 (4): 456–484.

Bostic, R.W., J.S. Gans, and S. Stern (1997). Urban Productivity and Factor Growth in the Late Nineteenth Century. *Journal of Urban Economics* 41 (1): 38–55.

Bottazzi, L., and G.I.P. Ottaviano (1996). Modelling Transport Costs in International Trade: A Comparison among Alternative Approaches. Working Paper Series 105. Innocenzo Gasparini Institute for Economic Research, Milano.

Brada, J.C., and J.A. Méndez (1985). Economic Integration Among Developed, Developing and Centrally Planned Economies. A Comparative Analysis. *Review of Economics and Statistics* 67 (4): 549–556.

Brakman, S., H. Garretsen, R. Gigengack, C.v. Marrewijk, and R. Wagenvoort (1996). Negative Feedbacks in the Economy and Industrial Location. *Journal of Regional Science* 36 (4): 631–652.

Branstetter, L. (1997). Are Knowledge Spillovers International or Intranational in Scope? Microeconometric Evidence from the US and Japan. NBER Working Paper Series 5800. National Bureau of Economic Research, Cambridge, Mass.

Brezis, E.S., and P.R. Krugman (1993). Technology and the Life Cycle of Cities. NBER Working Paper Series 4561. National Bureau of Economic Research, Cambridge, Mass.

Bröcker, J. (1987). Ökonometrische Handelsmodelle, Modellspezifikationen und Schätzverfahren. Seminarberichte 24. Gesellschaft für Regionalforschung, Deutschsprachige Gruppe der Regional Science Association, Heidelberg.

— (1996). Economic Integration and the Space Economy: Lessons from New Theory. In K. Peschel (ed.), *Regional Growth and Regional Policy Within the Framework of European Integration*. Heidelberg: Physica.

— (1998). How Would an EU-Membership of the Visegrad-Countries Affect Europe's Economic Geography? *Annals of Regional Science* 32 (1): 91–114.

Bröcker, J., and H.C. Rohweder (1990). Barriers to International Trade: Methods of Measurement and Empirical Evidence. *Annals of Regional Science* 24 (4): 289–305.

Brülhart, M., and J. Torstensson (1996). Regional Integration, Scale Economies and Industry Location in the European Union. CEPR Discussion Paper Series 1435. Centre for Economic Policy Research, London.

Burnside, A.C. (1996). Production Function Regressions, Returns to Scale, and Externalities. *Journal of Monetary Economics* 37 (2): 177–201.

Burnside, A.C., M.S. Eichenbaum, and S.T. Rebelo (1995). Capital Utilization and Returns to Scale. CEPR Discussion Paper Series 1221. Centre for Economic Policy Research, London.

Caballero, R.J., and R.K. Lyons (1989). The Role of External Economies in US Manufacturing. NBER Working Paper Series 3033. National Bureau of Economic Research, Cambridge, Mass.

— (1992). External Effects in US Procyclical Productivity. *Journal of Monetary Economics* 29 (2): 209–225.

Caballero, R.J., R.K. Lyons, D. Cohen, and H. König (1990). Internal Versus External Economies in European Industry. *European Economic Review* 34 (4): 803–826.

Cairncross, F. (1995). The Death of Distance: A Survey of Telecommunications. *The Economist* 335 (October): S1–S40.

— (1997). A Connected World: A Survey of Telecommunications. *The Economist* 344 (September): S1–S42.

Carlino, G.L. (1979). Increasing Returns to Scale in Metropolitan Manufacturing. *Journal of Regional Science* 9: 1–18.

Carlton, D.W. (1983). The Location and Employment Choices of New Firms: An Econometric Model with Discrete and Continuous Endogenous Variables. *Review of Economics and Statistics* 65: 440–449.

Carroll, G.R. (1982). National City-Size Distributions: What Do We Know after 67 Years of Research? *Progress in Human Geography* 6 (1): 1–43.

Chatterjee, S., and G. Carlino (1997). On the Evolution of the Spatial Distribution of Aggregate Employment in Postwar United States. Working Paper 97.26. Federal Reserve Bank of Philadelphia, Philadelphia, Pa.

CHELEM (Comptes harmonisés sur les échanges et l'économie mondiale) (1995). *CD-ROM.* Paris: Centre d'Etudes Prospectives et d'Informations Internationales (CEPII).

Chenery, H.B. (1949). Engineering Production Functions. *Quarterly Journal of Economics* 63 (4): 507–531.

Cheshire, P. (1995). A New Phase of Urban Development in Western Europe? The Evidence for the 1980's. *Urban Studies* 32 (7): 1045–1063.

Chiang, A.C. (1984). *Fundamental Methods of Mathematical Economics.* New York: McGraw-Hill.

Christaller, W. (1933). *Zentrale Orte in Süddeutschland.* Darmstadt: New Edition 1980. Wissenschaftliche Buchgesellschaft.

Christensen, L., and W. Green (1976). Economies of Scale in US Electric Power Generation. *Journal of Political Economy* 84 (4): 655–676.

Ciccone, A., and R.E. Hall (1996). Productivity and the Density of Economic Activity. *American Economic Review* 86 (1): 54–70.

Coe, D.T., and E. Helpman (1995). International R&D Spillovers. *European Economic Review* 39 (5): 859–887.

Coe, D.T., E. Helpman, and A.W. Hoffmaister (1997). North-South R&D Spillovers. *Economic Journal* 107 (January): 134–149.

Combes, P.-P. (1997). Industrial Agglomeration under Cournot Competition. *(Economie publique locale et économie géographique). Annales d'économie et de statistique* 45 (janvier/mars): 161–182.

Commission of the European Communities (1992). Urbanisation and the Functions of Cities in the European Community. In Office for Official Publications of the European Communities (ed.), *Regional Development Studies*, Vol. 4. Brussels: European Institute of Urban Affairs, John Moores University, Liverpool.

Connor, J.M., R.T. Rogers, B.W. Marion, and W.F. Müller (1984). *The Food Manufacturing Industry*. Aldershot, Hamphire: Gower Publishing.

Cowing, T., and V.K. Smith (1978). The Estimation of a Production Technology: A Survey of Econometric Analyses of Steam-Electric Generation. *Land Economics* 54 (2): 156–186.

Cullen, J.B., and S.D. Levitt (1997). Crime, Urban Flight, and the Consequences for Cities. NBER Working Paper Series 5737. National Bureau of Economic Research, Cambridge, Mass.

Cyrus, T.L. (1997). Why Do National Borders Matter? University of California, Berkeley. Mimeo.

D'Aspremont, C., R. dos Santos Ferreira, and L.-A. Gérard-Varet (1996). On the Dixit–Stiglitz Model of Monopolistic Competition. *American Economic Review* 86 (3): 623–629.

Davis, D.R. (1998). The Home Market, Trade, and Industrial Structure. *American Economic Review* 88 (5): 1264–1276.

Davis, D.R., and D.E. Weinstein (1996). Does Economic Geography Matter for International Specialization? NBER Working Paper Series 5706. National Bureau of Economic Research, Cambridge, Mass.

— (1998). Market Access, Economic Geography and Comparative Advantage: An Empirical Assessment. NBER Working Paper Series 6787. National Bureau of Economic Research, Cambridge, Mass.

— (1999). Economic Geography and Regional Production Structure: An Empirical Investigation. *European Economic Review* 43 (2) 379–407.

Deardorff, A.V. (1995). Determinants of Bilateral Trade: Does Gravity Work in a Neoclassical World? NBER Working Paper Series 5377. National Bureau of Economic Research, Cambridge, Mass.

DeCola, L. (1984). Statistical Determinants of the Population of a Nation's Largest City. *Economic Development and Cultural Change* 33 (1): 71–98.

Dendrinos, D. (1982). On the Dynamic Stability of Interurban Regional Labor and Capital Movements. *Journal of Regional Science* 22 (4): 529–540.

Der Fischer Weltalmanach 1998. Zahlen Daten Fakten (1997). Frankfurt am Main: Fischer.

Dixit, A., and J. Stiglitz (1977). Monopolistic Competition and Optimum Product Diversity. *American Economic Review* 67 (3): 297–308.

— (1993). Monopolistic Competition and Optimum Product Diversity: Reply. *American Economic Review* 83 (1): 302–304.

Domowitz, I., R.G. Hubbard, and B.C. Petersen (1988). Market Structure and Cyclical Fluctuations in US Manufacturing. *Review of Economics and Statistics* 70 (1): 55–66.

Dornbusch, R., S. Fischer, and P.A. Samuelson (1977). Comparative Advantage, Trade and Payments in a Ricardian Model with a Continuum of Goods. *American Economic Review* 67 (5): 823–839.

Eaton, J., and Z. Eckstein (1997). Cities and Growth: Theory and Evidence from France and Japan. *Regional Science & Urban Economics* 27 (4/5): 443–474.

Eaton, J., and A. Tamura (1994). Bilateralism and Regionalism in Japanese and US Trade and Direct Foreign Investment Patterns. *Journal of the Japanese and International Economies* 8 (4): 478–510.

The Economist (1995). Turn up the Lights: A Survey of Cities. 336 (7925), July 29–August 4: 45–60.

Eichengreen, B.J., and D.A. Irwin (1995). Trade Blocs, Currency Blocs and the Reorientation of World Trade in the 1930s. *Journal of International Economics* 38 (1/2): 1–24.

— (1998). The Role of History in Bilateral Trade Flows. In J.A. Frankel (ed.), *The Regionalization of the World Economy*. Chicago: University of Chicago Press.

Eisen, R. (1994). Größenvorteile in der deutschen Lebensversicherung: Eine empirische Untersuchung mit Hilfe der "Survivor-Technik". In R. Schwebler (ed.), *Dieter Farny und die Versicherungswissenschaft*. Karlsruhe: Versicherungswirtschaft e.V.

El-Shakhs, S. (1972). Development, Primacy, and the System of Cities. *Journal of Developing Areas* 7: 11–36.

Emerson, M. (1988). *The Economics of 1992: The EC Commission's Assessment of the Economic Effects of Completing the Internal Market*. Oxford: Oxford University Press.

Engelbrecht, H.-J. (1997). International R&D Spillovers, Human Capital and Productivity in OECD Economies: An Empirical Investigation. *European Economic Review* 41 (8): 1479–1488.

Engländer, O. (1926). Kritisches und Positives zu einer allgemeinen reinen Lehre vom Standort. *Zeitschrift für Volkswirtschaft und Sozialpolitik*. Neue Folge 5: 435–505.

Enright, M.J. (1990). *Geographic Concentration and Industrial Organization*. Cambridge, Mass.: Harvard University Press.

Ethier, W.J. (1982). National and International Returns to Scale in Modern Theory of International Trade. *American Economic Review* 72 (3): 810–822.

Evenett, S.J., and W. Keller (1998). On Theories Explaining the Success of the Gravity Equation. NBER Working Paper Series 6529. National Bureau of Economic Research, Cambridge, Mass.

Feldman, M.P. (1994). *The Geography of Innovation*. Dordrecht: Kluwer Academic Publishers.

Finger, J.M., M.D. Ingco, and U. Reincke (1996). *The Uruguay Round: Statistics on Tariff Concessions Given and Received*. Washington, D.C.: International Bank for Reconstruction and Development. World Bank.

Frankel, J.A. (1993). Is Japan Creating a Yen Bloc in East Asia and the Pacific? Working Paper 93.007. Center for International and Development Economics Research, University of California, Berkeley, Calif.

Frankel, J.A. (1997). *Regional Trading Blocs in the World Economic System*. Washington, D.C.: Institute for International Economics.

Frankel, J.A., and S.-J. Wei (1993). Trade Blocs and Currency Blocs. NBER Working Paper Series 4335. National Bureau of Economic Research, Cambridge, Mass.

Frankel, J.A., E.H. Stein, and S.-J. Wei (1995). Trading Blocs and the Americas: The Natural, the Unnatural, and the Super-Natural. *Journal of Development Economics* 47 (1): 61–95.

Fujita, M. (1988). A Monopolistic Competition Model of Spatial Agglomeration: A Differentiated Product Approach. *Regional Science and Urban Economics* 18 (1): 87–124.

Fujita, M., and P.R. Krugman (1995). When Is the Economy Monocentric? Von Thünen and Chamberlin Unified. *Regional Science & Urban Economics* 25 (4): 505–528.

Fujita, M., and J.-F. Thisse (1996). Economics of Agglomeration. *Journal of the Japanese and International Economies* 10 (4): 339–378.

Fujita, M., P.R. Krugman, and T. Mori (1999). On the Evolution of Hierarchical Urban Systems. *European Economic Review* 43 (2): 209–251.

Fukao, K., and R.J.-M. Bénabou (1993). History Versus Expectations: A Comment. *Quarterly Journal of Economics* 108 (2): 535–542.

GATT (General Agreement on Tariffs and Trade) (1994). News of the Uruguay Round of Multilateral Trade Negotiations. Uruguay Round of Multilateral Trade Negotiations GATT/1994-4. General Agreement on Tariffs and Trade Secretariat, Geneva.

Ghemawat, P. (1985). Building Strategy on the Experience Curve. *Harvard Business Review* 64 (2): 143–149.

Glaeser, E.L. (1998). Are Cities Dying? *Journal of Economic Perspectives* 12 (2): 139–160.

Glaeser, E.L., H.D. Kallal, J.A. Scheinkman, and A. Shleifer (1992). Growth in Cities. *Journal of Political Economy* 100 (6): 1126–1152.

Greene, W.H. (1981). On the Asymptotic Bias of the Ordinary Least Squares Estimator of the Tobit Model. *Econometrica* 49 (2): 505–513.

Greytak, D., and P. Blackley (1985). Labor Productivity and Local Industry Size: Further Issues in Assessing Agglomeration Economies. *Southern Economic Journal* 51 (4): 1121–1129.

Griliches, Z. (1979). Issues in Assessing the Contribution of Research and Development to Productivity Growth. *Bell Journal of Economics* 10 (1): 92–116.

— (1992). The Search for R&D Spillovers (Proceedings of a Symposium on Productivity Concepts and Measurement Problems). *The Scandinavian Journal of Economics* 94: S29–S47.

Griliches, Z., and V. Ringstad (1971). *Economies of Scale and the Form of the Production Function: An Econometric Study of Norwegian Manufacturing Establishment Data*. Amsterdam: North-Holland.

Grossman, G.M. (1995). Pollution and Growth: What Do We Know? In I. Goldin (ed.), *The Economics of Sustainable Development.* Cambridge: Cambridge University Press.

Grossman, G.M., and A.B. Krueger (1995). Economic Growth and the Environment. *Quarterly Journal of Economics* 110 (2): 353–377.

Grossman, G.M., A.B. Krueger, and J. Laity (1994). Determinants of Air Pollution in US Counties. Discussion Papers in Economics 169. Woodrow Wilson School of Public and International Affairs, Princeton University, Princeton, N.J.

Hall, R.E. (1988). The Relation between Price and Marginal Cost in U.S. Industry. *Journal of Political Economy* 96 (5): 921–947.

— (1990). *Invariance Properties of Solow's Productivity Residual.* Growth, Productivity, Unemployment. Cambridge, Mass.: Massachusetts Institute of Technology Press.

Hamilton, C., and L.A. Winters (1992). Opening Up Trade with Eastern Europe. *Economic Policy* 7 (14): 77–116.

Hansen, E.R. (1990). Agglomeration Economies and Industrial Decentralization: The Wage-Productivity Trade-Offs. *Journal of Urban Economics* 28 (2): 140–159.

Hanson, G.H. (1996). Localization Economies, Vertical Organization, and Trade. *American Economic Review* 86 (5): 1266–1278.

Harrigan, J.E. (1993). OECD Imports and Trade Barriers in 1983. *Journal of International Economics* 35 (1/2): 91–111.

— (1994). Scale Economies and the Volume of Trade. *Review of Economics and Statistics* 76 (2): 321–328.

Havrylyshyn, O., and L.H. Pritchett (1991). European Trade Patterns After the Transition. Policy, Research, and External Affairs Working Papers 748. World Bank, Washington, D.C.

Hay, D.A. (1979). The Location of Industry in a Developing Country: The Case of Brazil. *Oxford Economic Papers* 31 (1): 93–120.

Head, C.K., J.C. Ries, and D.L. Swenson (1995). Agglomeration Benefits and Location Choice: Evidence from Japanese Manufacturing Investments in the United States. *Journal of International Economics* 8 (3/4): 223–247.

Helliwell, J.F. (1996). Do National Borders Matter for Quebec's Trade? *Canadian Journal of Economics* 29 (3): 507–522.

Helpman, E. (1987). Imperfect Competition and International Trade: Evidence from 14 Industrial Countries. *Journal of the Japanese and International Economies* 1 (1): 62–81.

— (1995). The Size of Regions. Working Paper 95,14. The Eitan Berglas School of Economics, Tel Aviv University, Foerder Institute for Economic Research, Tel Aviv.

Helpman, E., and P.R. Krugman (1985). *Market Structure and Foreign Trade.* Cambridge, Mass.: Massachusetts Institute of Technology Press.

Helsley, R.W., and W.C. Strange (1990). Matching and Agglomeration Economies in a System of Cities. *Regional Science & Urban Economics* 20 (2): 189–212.

Henderson, J.V. (1974). The Sizes and Types of Cities. *American Economic Review* 64 (4): 640–656.

— (1975). Congestion and Optimal City Size. *Journal of Urban Economics* 2: 48–62.

— (1986). Efficiency of Resource Usage and City Size. *Journal of Urban Economics* 19 (1): 47–70.

— (1988). *Urban Development: Theory, Fact, and Illusion.* New York: Oxford University Press.

— (1994). Where Does an Industry Locate? *Journal of Urban Economics* 35 (1): 83–104.

— (1997). Externalities and Industrial Development. *Journal of Urban Economics* 42 (3): 449–470.

Henderson, J.V., A. Kuncoro, and M.A. Turner (1995). Industrial Development in Cities. *Journal of Political Economy* 103 (5): 1067–1090.

Herrmann, H., W.-D. Smidtke, J. Bröcker, and K. Peschel (1982). *Kommunikationskosten und internationaler Handel.* München: Florentz.

Hibdon, J.E., and M.J. Mueller (1990). Economies of Scale in Petroleum Refining, 1947-1984: A Survivor Principle Time Series Analysis. *Review of Industrial Organization* 5 (3): 25–43.

Hirschman, A.O. (1958). *The Strategy of Development.* New Haven, Conn.: Yale University Press.

Hohmeyer, O.H., R.L. Ottinger, and K. Rennings (eds.) (1996). *Social Costs and Sustainability: Valuation and Implementation in the Energy and Transport Sector.* Berlin: Springer.

Hoover, E.M. (1937). *Location Theory and the Shoe and Leather Industries.* Cambridge, Mass.: Harvard University Press.

— (1948). *The Location of Economic Activity.* New York: McGraw-Hill.

Hsing, Y. (1990). A Note on Functional Forms and the Urban Size Distribution. *Journal of Urban Economics* 27 (1): 73–79.

Hummels, D.L., and J.A. Levinsohn (1995). Monopolistic Competition and International Trade: Reconsidering the Evidence. *Quarterly Journal of Economics* 110 (3): 799–836.

Irwin, D.A., and P.J. Klenow (1994). Learning-By-Doing Spillovers in the Semiconductor Industry. *Journal of Political Economy* 102 (6): 1200–1227.

Isard, W. (1956). *Location and Space Economy.* Cambridge, Mass.: Massachusetts Institute of Technology Press.

ITU (International Telecommunication Union) (1997). *World Telecommunication Development Report 1996/97.* Geneva: ITU.

Jacobs, J. (1969). *The Economy of Cities*. New York: Vintage.

— (1984). *Cities and the Wealth of Nations: Principles of Economic Life*. New York: Vintage.

Jaffe, A.B. (1986). Technological Opportunity and Spillovers of R&D: Evidence from Firms' Patents, Profits, and Market Value. *American Economic Review* 76 (5): 984–1001.

— (1989). Real Effects of Academic Research. *American Economic Review* 79 (5): 957–970.

Jaffe, A.B., M. Trajtenberg, and R.M. Henderson (1993). Geographic Localization of Knowledge Spillovers as Evidenced by Patent Citations. *Quarterly Journal of Economics* 108 (3): 577–598.

Jefferson, M. (1939). The Law of the Primate City. *Geographical Review* 29 (2): 226–232.

Jorgenson, D.W. (1986). Econometric Methods for Modeling Producer Behavior. In Z. Griliches and M.D. Intriligator (eds.), *Handbook of Econometrics*, Vol. 3. Amsterdam: North-Holland.

Junius, K. (1996a). Limits to Industrial Agglomeration. Kiel Working Papers 762. Institute of World Economics, Kiel.

— (1996b). Economic Development and Industrial Concentration: An Inverted U-Curve. Kiel Working Papers 770. Institute of World Economics, Kiel.

— (1997a). Economies of Scale: A Survey of the Empirical Literature. Kiel Working Papers 813. Institute of World Economics, Kiel.

— (1997b). The Determinants of Urban Concentration. Kiel Working Papers 835. Institute of World Economics, Kiel.

Junius, K., E. Nijsse, and D. Urban (1995). Congestion and the Location of Vertically Linked Industries. Kiel Advanced Studies Working Papers 280. Institute of World Economics, Kiel.

Kamerschen, D.R. (1969). Further Analysis of Overurbanization. *Economic Development and Cultural Change* 17 (2): 235–253.

Kanemoto, Y. (1975). Congestion and Cost Benefit Analysis in Cities. *Journal of Urban Economics* 2: 246–264.

Kanemoto, Y., T. Ohkawara, and T. Suzuki (1996). Agglomeration Economies and a Test for Optimal City Sizes in Japan. *Journal of the Japanese and International Economies* 10 (4): 379–398.

Kasarda, J.D., and E.M. Crenshaw (1991). Third World Urbanization: Dimensions, Theories, and Determinants. *Annual Review of Sociology* 17: 467–501.

Kim, S. (1995). Expansion of Markets and the Geographic Distribution of Economic Activities: The Trends in US Regional Manufacturing Structure, 1860–1987. *Quarterly Journal of Economics* 110 (4): 881–908.

Kim, S. (1997). Economic Integration and Convergence: US Regions, 1840–1987. NBER Working Paper Series 6335. National Bureau of Economic Research, Cambridge, Mass.

Kirwan, K., M. O'Mahony, and D. O'Sullivan (1995). Speed-Flow Relationships for Use in Urban Transport Policy Assessment Model. Trinity College, Dublin. Mimeo.

Kopp, A. (1994). Price Search, Bargaining and Agglomeration. Kiel Working Papers 618. Institute of World Economics, Kiel.

Krugman, P.R. (1980). Scale Economies, Product Differentiation, and Pattern of Trade. *American Economic Review* 70 (5): 950–959.

— (1991a). *Geography and Trade.* Cambridge, Mass.: Massachusetts Institute of Technology Press.

— (1991b). Increasing Returns and Economic Geography. *Journal of Political Economy* 99 (3): 483–499.

— (1991c). History Versus Expectations. *Quarterly Journal of Economics* 106 (2): 651–667.

— (1993). On the Number and Location of Cities: Economic Geography. *European Economic Review* 37 (1): 293–298.

— (1996). Confronting the Mystery of Urban Hierarchy. *Journal of the Japanese and International Economies* 10 (4): 399–418.

Krugman, P.R., and R.A. Livas Elizondo (1996). Trade Policy and the Third World Metropolis. *Journal of Development Economics* 49 (1): 137–150.

Krugman, P.R., and A.J. Venables (1990). Integration and the Competitiveness of Peripheral Industry. In C. Bliss (ed.), *Unity With Diversity.* Cambridge, Mass.: Cambridge University Press.

— (1995). Globalization and the Inequality of Nations. *Quarterly Journal of Economics* 110 (4): 857–880.

— (1996). Integration, Specialization, and Adjustment. *European Economic Review* 40 (3/5): 959–967.

Laird, S., and A.J. Yeats (1990a). Trends in Nontariff Barriers of Developed Countries: 1966–1986. *Weltwirtschaftliches Archiv* 126 (2): 299–325.

— (1990b). *Quantitative Methods for Trade-Barrier Analysis.* Basingstoke, Hampshire: Macmillan.

Leamer, E.E. (1984). *Sources of International Comparative Advantage: Theory and Evidence.* Cambridge, Mass.: Massachusetts Institute of Technology Press.

— (1992). Testing Trade Theory. Working Paper Series 3957. NBER National Bureau of Economic Research, Cambridge, Mass.

Leamer, E.E., and J.A. Levinsohn (1995). *International Trade Theory: The Evidence.* Handbook of International Economics 3. Amsterdam: North-Holland.

Lemelin, A., and M. Polèse (1995). What About the Bell-Shaped Relationship between Primacy and Development? *International Regional Science Review* 18 (3): 313–330.

Linnemann, H. (1966). *An Econometric Study of International Trade Flows.* Amsterdam: North-Holland.

Little, I.M.D., D. Mazumdar, and J.M. Page (1987). *Small Manufacturing Enterprises: A Comparative Study of India and Other Economies.* A World Bank Research Publication. New York: Oxford University Press.

Lösch, A. (1941). *The Economics of Location.* New Haven, Conn.: Yale University Press.

— (1962). *Die räumliche Ordnung der Wirtschaft.* Stuttgart: Fischer.

Low, P., and A.J. Yeats (1995). Nontariff Measures and Developing Countries: Has the Uruguay Round Leveled the Playing Field? *The World Economy* 18 (1): 51–70.

Lyons, B.R. (1980). A New Measure of Minimum Efficient Plant Size in UK Manufacturing Industry. *Economica* 47 (185): 19–34.

MacPhee, C.R., and R.D. Peterson (1990). The Economies of Scale Revisited: Comparing Census Costs, Engineering Estimates, and the Survivor Technique. *Quarterly Journal of Business and Economics* 29 (2): 43–67.

Maddison, A. (1995). Monitoring the World Economy 1820–1992. OECD Development Centre Studies 48139. Organisation for Economic Co-Operation and Development, Development Centre, Paris.

Maddison, D., D. Pearce, O. Johansson, E. Calthrop, T. Litman, and E. Verhoef (1996). *The True Costs of Road Transport.* London: Earthscan Publications.

Marcus, M. (1969). Profitability and Size of Firm. *Review of Economics and Statistics* 51: 104–107.

Markusen, A.R. (1996). Interaction between Regional and Industrial Policies: Evidence from Four Countries. *International Regional Science Review* 19 (1/2): 49–77.

Markusen, J.R. (1989). Trade in Producer Services and in Other Specialized Intermediate Inputs. *American Economic Review* 79 (1): 85–95.

Marshall, A. (1920). *Principles of Economics.* 8th Edition. London: Macmillan.

Matsuyama, K. (1991). Increasing Returns, Industrialization, and Indeterminacy of Equilibrium. *Quarterly Journal of Economics* 106 (2): 617–650.

— (1995). Complementarities and Cumulative Processes in Models of Monopolistic Competition. *Journal of Economic Literature* 33 (2): 701–729.

Maurer, R. (1998). *Economic Growth and International Trade with Capital Goods: Theories and Empirical Evidence.* Kieler Studie 289. Tübingen: Mohr Siebeck.

Mayeres, I., S. Ochelen, and S. Proost (1996). The Marginal External Costs of Urban Transport. Public Economics Research Paper 51. Centrum voor Economische Studien, Katholieke Universiteit Leuven, Departement Economie, Leuven.

McCallum, J. (1995). National Borders Matter: Canada-US Regional Trade Patterns. *American Economic Review* 85 (3): 615–623.

Mera, K. (1973). On the Urban Agglomeration and Economic Efficiency. *Economic Development and Cultural Change* 21: 309–324.

Miracky, W.F. (1995). *Economic Growth in Cities: The Role of Localization Externalities.* Cambridge, Mass.: Massachusetts Institute of Technology Press.

Mitchell, B.R. (1992). *International Historical Statistics: Europe 1750–1988.* London: Macmillan.

— (1993). *International Historical Statistics: The Americas 1750–1988.* Basingstoke, Hampshire: Macmillan.

— (1995). *International Historical Statistics: Africa, Asia & Oceania; 1750–1988.* New York: Stockton.

Mokyr, J. (1995). Urbanization, Technological Progress, and Economic History. In H. Giersch (ed.), *Urban Agglomeration and Economic Growth.* Berlin: Springer.

Molle, W. (1997). The Regional Economic Structure of the European Union: An Analysis of Long-Term Developments. In K. Peschel (ed.), *Regional Growth and Regional Policy within the Framework of European Integration.* Heidelberg: Physica-Verlag.

Molle, W., and S. Boeckhout (1995). Economic Disparity under Conditions of Integration: A Long-Term View of the European Case. *Papers in Regional Science. The Journal of the RSAI* 74 (2): 105–123.

Moomaw, R.L. (1981). Productive Efficiency and Region. *Southern Economic Journal* 48 (2): 344–357.

— (1983). Spatial Productivity Variations in Manufacturing: A Critical Survey of Cross-Sectional Analysis. *International Regional Science Review* 8 (1): 1–22.

Moomaw, R.L., and A.M. Shatter (1996). Urbanization and Economic Development: A Bias toward Large Cities? *Journal of Urban Economics* 40 (1): 13–37.

Müller, J., and N. Owen (1985). The Effect of Trade on Plant Size. In J. Schwalbach (ed.), *Industry Structure and Performance.* Berlin: Edition Sigma.

Murphy, K.M., A. Shleifer, and R.W. Vishny (1989). Industrialization and the Big Push. *Journal of Political Economy* 97 (5): 1003–1026.

Muth, R. (1969). *Cities and Housing.* Chicago: University of Chicago Press.

Mutlu, S. (1989). Urban Concentration and Primacy Revisited: An Analysis and Some Policy Conclusions. *Economic Development and Cultural Change* 37 (3): 611–639.

Myrdal, G. (1957). *Economic Theory and Under-Developed Regions.* London: Duckworth.

Nakamura, R. (1985). Agglomeration Economies in Urban Manufacturing Industries: A Case of Japanese Cities. *Journal of Urban Economics* 17 (1): 108–124.

Nitsch, V. (1997). National Borders and International Trade: Evidence from the European Union. Mimeo.

Nothdurft, W.E. (1992). *Going Global: How Europe Helps Small Firms Export.* A German Marshall Fund of the United States Book. Washington, D.C.: Brookings Institution.

OECD (Organisation for Economic Co-Operation and Development) (1991). *The State of the Environment.* Paris: OECD.

— (1997). *Communication Outlook 1997.* Paris: OECD.

Oguledo, V.I., and C.R. MacPhee (1994). Gravity Models: A Reformulation and an Application to Discriminatory Trade Arrangements. *Applied Economics* 26 (2): 107–120.

Oliveira-Martins, J., S. Scarpetta, and D.-J. Pilat (1996). Mark-Up Ratios in Manufacturing Industries: Estimates for 14 OECD Countries. OECD Working Papers 4.24. Organisation for Economic Co-Operation and Development, Paris.

Oulton, N. (1996). Increasing Returns and Externalities in UK Manufacturing: Myth or Reality? *Journal of Industrial Economics* 44 (1): 99–113.

Owen, N. (1983). *Economies of Scale, Competitiveness and Trade Patterns within the European Community.* Oxford: Clarendon Press.

Palander, T. (1935). *Beiträge zur Standorttheorie.* Stockholm: Almquist and Wicksell.

Parr, J.B. (1985). A Note on the Size Distribution of Cities over Time. *Journal of Urban Economics* 18 (2): 199–212.

Parr, J.B., and C. Jones (1983). City Size Distributions and Urban Density Functions: Some Interrelationships. *Journal of Regional Science* 23 (3): 283–307.

Peschel, K. (1981). On the Impact of Geographical Distance on the Interregional Patterns of Production and Trade. *Environmental and Planning A* 13 (5): 605–622.

Piazolo, D. (1997). Trade Integration Between Eastern and Western Europe. Policies Follow the Market. *Journal of Economic Integration* 12 (3): 259–297.

— (1998). Überwindung des Protektionismus. Handelsliberalisierung als Motor für Entwicklung. *Zeitschrift für Internationale Politik* 53 (1): 51–57.

Pollard, S. (1981). *Peaceful Conquest: The Industrialization of Europe 1760–1970.* New York: Oxford University Press.

Porter, M.E. (1990). *The Competitive Advantage of Nations.* London: Macmillan.

Pratten, C.F. (1971). Economies of Scale in Manufacturing Industry. Occasional Paper 28. University of Cambridge, Department of Applied Economics, Cambridge.

— (1988). A Survey of the Economies of Scale. Economic Papers 67. Commission of the European Communities, Directorate-General for Economic and Financial Affairs, Brussels.

Predöhl, A. (1925). Das Standortproblem in der Wirtschaftslehre. *Weltwirtschaftliches Archiv* 21 (2): 294–331.

Rauch, J.E. (1999). Networks Versus Markets in International Trade. *Journal of International Economics*: forthcoming.

Rees, R.D. (1973). Optimum Plant Size in the United Kingdom Industries: Some Survivor Estimates. *Economica* 40 (160): 394–401.

Ricci, L.A. (1999). Economic Geography and Comparative Advantage: Agglomeration versus Specialization. *European Economic Review* 43 (2): 357–377.

Richardson, H.W., and G. Schwartz (1988). Economic Development, Population, and Primacy. *Regional Studies* 22: 467–475.

Ringstad, V. (1978). Economies of Scale and the Form of the Production Function. *Scandinavian Journal of Economics* 80 (3): 251–264.

Rivera-Batiz, L.A. (1988). Increasing Returns, Monopolistic Competition, and Agglomeration Economies in Consumption and Production. *Regional Science and Urban Economics* 18 (1): 125–153.

Roehner, B.M. (1996). The Role of Transportation Costs in the Economics of Commodity Markets. *American Journal of Agricultural Economics* 78 (2): 339–353.

Röger, W. (1995). Can Imperfect Competition Explain the Difference between Primal and Dual Productivity Measures? Estimates for US Manufacturing. *Journal of Political Economy* 103 (2): 316–330.

Rogers, R.P. (1993). The Minimum Optimal Steel Plant and the Survivor Technique of Cost Estimation. *Atlantic Economic Journal* 21 (3): 30–37.

Rohweder, H.C. (1988). Ökonometrische Methoden zur Schätzung von Gravitationsmodellen des internationalen Handels — Darstellung, Kritik und Alternativen. *Allgemeines Statistisches Archiv* 72 (2): 150–170.

— (1989). *Wechselkursvariabilität und internationaler Handel. Eine empirische Analyse der räumlichen Handelsverflechtung im Rahmen eines TOBIT-Regressionsansatzes.* München: Florentz.

Romer, P.M. (1986). Increasing Returns and Long-Run Growth. *Journal of Political Economy* 94 (5): 1002–1037.

Rosen, K., and M. Resnick (1980). The Size Distribution of Cities. *Journal of Urban Economics* 8 (2): 165–186.

Rosenstein-Rodan, P. (1943). Problems of Industrialisation of Eastern and South-Eastern Europe. *Economic Journal* 53 (June-September): 202–211.

Sachs, J.D., and A.M. Warner (1995). Economic Convergence and Economic Policies. NBER Working Paper Series 5039. National Bureau of Economic Research, Cambridge, Mass.

Sala-i-Martin, X.X. (1997). I Just Ran Two Million Regressions. *American Economic Review* 87 (2): 178–183.

Samuelson, P.A. (1954). The Transfer Problem and Transport Costs, II: Analysis of Effects of Trade Impediments. *Economic Journal* 64 (June): 264–289.

Sands, S.S. (1961). Changes in Scale of Production in US Manufacturing Industry 1904–1947. *Review of Economics and Statistics* 43 (4): 365–368.

Sapir, A., K. Sekkat, and A.A. Weber (1994). The Impact of Exchange Rate Fluctuations on European Union Trade. CEPR Discussion Paper Series 1041. Centre for Economic Policy Research, London.

Saving, J.R. (1961). Estimates of Optimum Size of Plant by the Survivor Technique. *Quarterly Journal of Economics* 75 (4): 569–607.

Scherer, F.M. (1980). *Industrial Market Structure and Economic Performance*. Chicago: Rand McNally College Publications.

Scherer, F.M., and D.R. Ross (1990). *Industrial Market Structure and Economic Performance*. Boston: Houghton Mifflin.

Scherer, F.M., A. Beckenstein, E. Kaufer, and R. Murphy (1975). *The Economics of Multiplant Operation: An International Comparison Study*. London: Harvard University Press.

Schumacher, D., W.G.Ch. Maennig, and E.E. Meade (1997). Impact on German Trade of Increased Division of Labor with Eastern Europe. In S.W. Black (ed.), *Europe's Economy Looks East: Implications for Germany and the European Union*. Cambridge: Cambridge University Press.

Schwalbach, J. (1988). Economies of Scale and Intra-Community Trade. Studies on the Economics of Integration: Document. Luxembourg: Office for Official Publications of the European Communities.

Scotchmer, S., and J.-F. Thisse (1992). Space and Competition: A Puzzle. *Annals of Regional Science* 26 (3): 269–286.

Segal, D. (1976). Are there Returns to Scale in City Size? *Review of Economics and Statistics* 58 (3): 339–350.

Selden, T.M., and D. Song (1994). Environmental Quality and Development: Is there a Kuznets Curve for Air Pollution Emissions? *Journal of Environmental Economics and Management* 27 (2): 147–162.

Shapiro, M. (1987). Measuring Market Power in US Industry. NBER Working Paper Series 2212. National Bureau of Economic Research, Cambridge, Mass.

Shefer, D. (1973). Localization Economies in SMSAs: A Production Function Analysis. *Journal of Regional Science* 13 (1): 55–64.

Shepherd, W.G. (1967). What Does the Survivor Technique Show About Economies of Scale? *Southern Economic Journal* 34 (2): 113–122.

Sheppard, E. (1982). City Size Distributions and Spatial Change. *International Regional Science Review* 7 (2): 127–151.

Siebert, H. (1969). *Regional Economic Growth: Theory and Policy*. Scranton, Pa: International Textbook Company.

— (1988). Strategische Handelspolitik: Theoretische Ansätze und wirtschaftspolitische Empfehlungen. *Aussenwirtschaft* 43 (4): 549–584.

— (1994). *Außenwirtschaft*. Stuttgart: Fischer.

— (1997). *Weltwirtschaft*. Stuttgart: Lucius & Lucius.

Singer, H.W. (1936). The "Courbe des Populations": A Parallel to Paretos Law. *Economic Journal* 46 (June): 254–263.

Smith, D.F.jr., and R.L. Florida (1994). Agglomeration and Industrial Location: An Econometric Analysis of Japanese-Affiliated Manufacturing Establishments in Automotive-Related Industries. *Journal of Urban Economics* 36 (1): 23–41.

Smith, V.K. (1986). Another View of the State of Engineering Production Functions. *Economica* 53 (212): 529–532.

Spence, A.M. (1976). Product Selection, Fixed Costs, and Monopolistic Competition. *Review of Economic Studies* 43 (2): 217–236.

Spinanger, D. (1997). The WTO After the Singapore Ministerial: Much to Do About What? Kiel Discussion Papers 304. Institute of World Economics, Kiel.

Starret, D.A. (1978). Market Allocations of Location Choice in a Model with Free Mobility. *Journal of Economic Theory* 17 (1): 21–37.

Stern, D.I., M.S. Common, and E.B. Barbier (1996). Economic Growth and Environmental Degradation: The Environmental Kuznets Curve and Sustainable Development. *World Development* 24 (7): 1151–1160.

Stigler, G.J. (1958). The Economies of Scale. *The Journal of Law and Economics* 1 (October): 54–71.

Summers, R., and A.W. Heston (1991). The Penn World Table (Mark 5): An Expanded Set of International Comparisons, 1950–1988. *Quarterly Journal of Economics* 106 (2): 327–368.

Sveikauskas, L. (1975). The Productivity of Cities. *Quarterly Journal of Economics* 89 (3): 393–413.

Sveikauskas, L., J.M. Gowdy, and M. Funk (1988). Urban Productivity: City Size or Industry Size. *Journal of Regional Science* 28 (2): 185–202.

Sveikauskas, L., P.M. Townroe, and E.R. Hansen (1985). Intraregional Productivity Difference in Sao Paulo State Manufacturing Plants. *Weltwirtschaftliches Archiv* 121 (4): 722–740.

Syrquin, M. (1989). Patterns of Structural Change. In H. Chenery and T. Srinivasan (eds.), *Handbook of Development Economics*, Vol. 1. Amsterdam: Elsevier.

Thursby, J.G., and M.C. Thursby (1987). Bilateral Trade Flows, the Linder Hypothesis, and Exchange Risk. *Review of Economics and Statistics* 69 (3): 488–495.

Tolley, G.S. (ed.) (1987). *The Economics of Urbanization and Urban Policies in Developing Countries*. A World Bank Symposium 12. Washington, D.C.: World Bank.

Torstensson, J. (1998). Country Size and Comparative Advantage: An Empirical Study. *Weltwirtschaftliches Archiv* 134 (4): 590-611.

Trindade, V., and J.E. Rauch (1998). Ethnic Chinese Networks in International Trade. University of California, San Diego, La Jolla, Calif. Mimeo.

Tybout, J.R. (1993). Internal Returns to Scale as a Source of Comparative Advantage: The Evidence. *American Economic Review* 83 (2): 440–444.

Tybout, J.R., and M.D. Westbrook (1992). Trade Liberalization and the Structure of Production in Mexican Industries. Working Paper 92.03. Georgetown University, Department of Economics, Washington, D.C.

UN (United Nations) (1992). *Demographic Yearbook 1991*. New York: United Nations.

— (1995a). *World Urbanization Prospects: The 1994 Revision; Estimates and Projections of Urban and Rural Populations and of Urban Agglomerations*. New York: United Nations.

— (1995b). *Demographic Yearbook 1994*. New York: United Nations.

UNCTAD (United Nations Conference on Trade and Development) (1992). *Review of Maritime Transport 1991*. New York: UNCTAD Secretariat.

— (1994). *Review of Maritime Transport 1993*. New York: UNCTAD Secretariat.

— (1996). *Review of Maritime Transport 1995*. New York: UNCTAD Secretariat.

Vance, J.E. (1986). *Capturing the Horizon: The Historical Geography of Transportation since the Transportation Revolution of the Sixteenth Century*. New York: Harper & Row.

Venables, A.J. (1995). Economic Integration and the Location of Firms. *American Economic Review* 85 (2): 296–300.

— (1996). Equilibrium Locations of Vertically Linked Industries. *International Economic Review* 37 (2): 341–359.

Von Hagen, J., and G.W. Hammond (1994). Industrial Localization: An Empirical Test for Marshallian Localization Economies. In CEPR (ed.), *The Location of Economic Activity: New Theories and Evidence*. London: Centre for Economic Policy Research.

Von Thünen, J.H. (1826). *Der isolierte Staat in Beziehung auf Landwirtschaft und Nationalökonomie*. Hamburg: Perthes. English Translation: The Isolated State. Oxford: Pergamon Press 1966.

Wang, Z., and L.A. Winters (1992). The Trading Potential of Eastern Europe. *Journal of International Economic Integration* 7 (2): 113–136.

Weber, A. (1909). *Standort der Industrien*. Tübingen: Mohr Siebeck.

Wei, S.-J. (1996). Intra-national Versus International Trade: How Stubborn Are Nations in Global Integration? NBER Working Paper Series 5531. National Bureau of Economic Research, Cambridge, Mass.

Weiss, L.W. (1964). The Survival Technique and the Extent of Suboptimal Capacity. *Journal of Political Economy* 72 (3): 246–261.

— (1976). Optimal Plant Size and the Extent of Suboptimal Capacity. In R.T. Masson and P.D. Qualls (eds.), *Essays on Industrial Organization in Honour of Joe S. Bain*. Cambridge, Mass.: Ballinger Publishing.

WEPZA (World Export Processing Zone Association) Research Center (1991). Transport Costs to the US Market. *Journal of the Flagstaff Institute* 15 (1): 57–78.

Westbrook, M.D., and J.R. Tybout (1993). Estimating Returns to Scale with Large, Imperfect Panels: An Application to Chilean Manufacturing Industries. *World Bank Economic Review* 7 (1): 85–112.

Wheaton, W.C. (1977). Income and Urban Residence: An Analysis of Consumer Demand for Location. *American Economic Review* 67 (4): 620–631.

Wheaton, W.C., and H. Shishido (1981). Urban Concentration, Agglomeration Economics and the Level of Economic Development. *Economic Development and Cultural Change* 30 (1): 17–30.

Wheeler, D., and A. Mody (1992). International Investment Location Decisions: The Case of US Firms. *Journal of International Economics* 33 (1/2): 57–76.

White, H. (1980). A Heteroskedasticity-Consistent Covariance Matrix Estimator and Direct Test for Heteroskedasticity. *Econometrica* 48 (4): 817–838.

Wibe, S. (1984). Engineering Production Functions: A Survey. *Economica* 51 (210): 401–411.

— (1986). Observable and Non-Observable Data: A Reply. *Economica* 53 (212): 535–536.

Williamson, J.G. (1965). Regional Inequality and the Process of National Development: A Description of Patterns. *Economic Development and Cultural Change* 13 (4): 3–84.

— (1982). Was the Industrial Revolution Worth It? Disamenities and Death in 19th Century British Towns. *Explorations in Economic History* 19 (3): 221–245.

— (1995). Migration and City Growth During Industrial Revolutions. In H. Giersch (ed.), *Urban Agglomeration and Economic Growth*. Berlin: Springer.

— (1997). *Industrialization, Inequality and Economic Growth*. Cheltenham: Elgar.

World Bank (1994). *Infra-Structure and Development*. World Development Report 1994. New York: Oxford University Press.

— (1996a). *CD-ROM, World Development Indicators*.

— (1996b). *From Plan to Market*. World Development Report 1996. New York: Oxford University Press.

Wright, T.P. (1936). Factors Affecting the Cost of Airplanes. *Journal of Aeronautical Science* 3: 122–128.

Yang, X., and B.J. Heijdra (1993). Monopolistic Competition and Optimum Product Diversity: Comment. *American Economic Review* 83 (1): 295–301.

Zietz, J. (1988). Adequacy Tests for Linear Regression Models: A Nontechnical Overview with Applications. *Jahrbücher für Nationalökonomie und Statistik* 204 (3): 255–272.

Index

Institut für Weltwirtschaft an der Universität Kiel

Symposia and Conference Proceedings

Horst Siebert, Editor

Sozialpolitik auf dem Prüfstand
Leitlinien für Reformen
Tübingen 1996. 224 pages. Hard cover. DM 98/Sch 715/SFr 89.

Elemente einer rationalen Umweltpolitik
Expertisen zur umweltpolitischen Neuorientierung
Tübingen 1996. 378 pages. Hard cover. DM 148/Sch 1085/SFr 126.

Monetary Policy in an Integrated World Economy
Tübingen 1996. 280 pages. Hard cover. DM 128/Sch 934/SFr 109.

Towards a New Global Framework for High-Technology Competition
Tübingen 1997. 223 pages. Hard cover. DM 98/Sch 715/SFr 89.

Quo Vadis Europe?
Tübingen 1997. 343 pages. Hard cover. DM 128/Sch 934/SFr 109.

Structural Change and Labor Market Flexibility
Experience in Selected OECD Economies
Tübingen 1997. 292 pages. Hard cover. DM 118/Sch 861/SFr 101.

Redesigning Social Security
Tübingen 1998. 387 pages. Hard cover. DM 148/Sch 1085/SFr 126.

Globalization and Labor
Tübingen 1999. 320 pages. Hard cover. DM 138/Sch 1007/SFr 118.

Mohr Siebeck, Tübingen

KIELER STUDIEN

Institut für Weltwirtschaft an der Universität Kiel

Herausgeber: *Horst Siebert*

Schriftleitung: *Harmen Lehment*

Mehr Informationen über Publikationen des Instituts für Weltwirtschaft unter http://www. uni-kiel.de/ifw/pub/pub.htm, mehr Informationen über das IfW unter http://www.uni-kiel.de/ifw

Mohr Siebeck, D-72010 Tübingen